VIKING SOCIETY FOR NORTHERN RESEARCH
TEXT SERIES

GENERAL EDITORS

Anthony Faulkes and Richard Perkins

VOLUME XII

GUTA SAGA

THE HISTORY OF THE GOTLANDERS

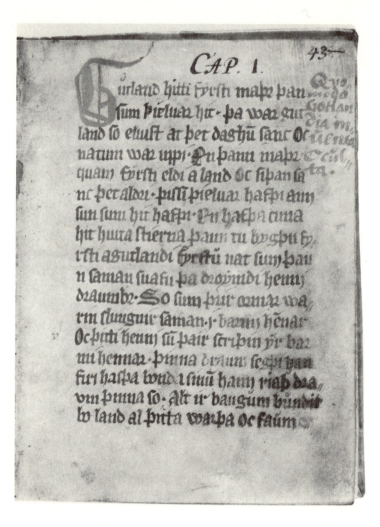

The first page of *Guta saga* in B64 (reduced)
(reproduced by permission of Kungliga Biblioteket, Stockholm)

# GUTA SAGA

## THE HISTORY OF THE GOTLANDERS

Edited by Christine Peel

VIKING SOCIETY FOR NORTHERN RESEARCH
UNIVERSITY COLLEGE LONDON
1999

ISBN: 0 903521 44 X

The cover illustration is from a photograph (by K. Peel) of a miniature replica in silver by Hans Helmer of a pierced disc, about two and a half inches in diameter, which was found in a woman's grave at Ihre in Hellvi parish, in north-eastern Gotland. The disc has been dated to the eighth century; cf. Note to 2/8. The illustration shows the disc rather larger than the actual size of the original, which is held in Statens Historiska Museum, Stockholm.

Printed by Short Run Press Limited, Exeter

# CONTENTS

# PREFACE

This book started life as an MPhil thesis, written under the exacting but always encouraging and enthusiastic supervision of Dr Richard Perkins. He suggested, even before I had completed it, that I approach Professor Anthony Faulkes with a view to its being published by the Viking Society. This volume is the result.

I owe a debt of gratitude to Dr Perkins for his original suggestion, to Professor Faulkes for his clear and sympathetic editing, which sharpened my discipline and perception, and to Dr Alison Finlay and Dr Rory McTurk who encouraged me to pursue the project.

During the writing of the thesis my husband was able to increase his familiarity with and love for London, Stockholm and Visby, and I shall always be grateful for his patience and encouragement, even when every available surface in the house seemed to be covered with my drafts.

Finally, I would like to thank the staff in the libraries in London, Stockholm and Visby who helped me to satisfy the requirements for chapter and verse upon which Dr Perkins so rightly insisted.

C. I. P.

# INTRODUCTION

## (i) *Historical background*

Gotland (*Gottland* prior to 1923) is the largest of Sweden's Baltic islands. It is a chalky plateau, 83 metres above sea level at its highest, with an area of approximately 3,000 square kilometres. There is evidence of habitation on the island from the Stone Age, and of an advanced Iron Age culture. In particular, the picture-stone is an art-form well developed in Gotland from the fifth century. Originally independent, the island was at some uncertain date incorporated into the Swedish kingdom. During the Middle Ages Gotland's main town, Visby, on the island's west coast, became an important trading town in the Hanseatic league, with a Gotlandic, Swedish, Danish and German population. In 1361, however, the island was taken over by the Danish crown, after a violent invasion by Valdemar Atterdag, and remained in Danish hands until 1645. Then, at the Peace of Brömsebro, which concluded the war of Baltic supremacy between Denmark and Sweden, Gotland returned to Swedish rule. The short legendary history of the island, called *Guta saga*, was written in the thirteenth or perhaps the fourteenth century.

It is relevant, perhaps, to consider the events that were taking place during the period of writing and publication of *Guta saga*. As Olrik remarks (1921, 56–57), every re-telling of a story is affected by the circumstances and attitude of the author. If we assume that *Guta saga* was written between 1220 and 1330 the following may help to highlight possible influences. In 1164 the Swedish arch-bishopric was founded in Uppsala. Sweden was from this time officially a Christian country and the ecclesiastical administration therefore in place for the incorporation of Gotland into a Swedish see to become a possibility. During the reign of Sverker (the Younger) Karlsson (r. 1196–1208) the importance of Gotland to Sweden in terms of both trade and defence seems to have in-creased, and in 1203 the name *Wysbu* first appears, in an entry in the chronicle of Henry of Livonia; cf. *Heinrici Chronicon Livoniae*, 1959, 24–26. In 1207 Andreas Suneson, archbishop of Lund, visited Gotland and it is possibly as a result of this visit that the codification of a law for Gotland was encouraged and the ecclesiastical arrange-ments formalised.

In 1208, at the Battle of Lena, Sverker was defeated and Erik Knutsson (who had been driven into exile in 1205) became king.

Sverker himself went into exile after the battle, and it is possible that it is this event that is referred to at the end of *Guta saga*; see below, pp. xlix–l. Sverker died two years later, and in 1216 Erik was succeeded as king by Johan Sverkersson. During Johan's reign, and that of Erik Eriksson who succeeded him in 1222, a number of diplomas and other letters refer to Gotland and the Baltic. In 1217 Pope Honorius III confirmed the tithe law in Gotland, which was more lenient than that for other parts of Sweden, causing tension between the Gotlanders and successive bishops of Linköping, who attempted to claim a portion of the tithe. The arrangement was again confirmed in 1230 by Pope Gregory IX. In 1219 King Valdemar of Denmark and Andreas Suneson instigated a crusade against Estonia, and the *ledung* ('levy') was called out to support this. The name *Visby* appears again in 1225, in a letter from Bishop Bengt of Linköping concerning the foundation of Mariakyrkan in Visby, and at around the same date, records concerning Riga mention *ius Gutorum* as having applied since the town's foundation, which would seem to imply that the Gotlandic law had been codified by that date; see below, pp. l–li. In 1248 Birger Magnusson was appointed *jarl*, the last, in fact, to have the title. The *jarl* was the king's representative, particularly in Götaland, and was responsible, amongst other duties, for calling out the levy. When Erik Eriksson died in 1249, Birger took over the government, and the following year Valdemar Birgersson was crowned, with Birger jarl as regent during his minority. Three years later, a new tithe arrangement was put in place, with the receipts divided between church, priest and the poor.

By 1255 there seems to have been a change in the trading situation in Gotland, and Visby in particular. There is evidence in England of German infiltration in Gotlandic trade and, when Magnus Birgersson became king in 1275, tension was beginning to become apparent. In October 1285 Magnus wrote to the Gotlanders setting out the new arrangements for an annual tax, the *laiþingslami*, knowledge of which does not seem to be incorporated in *Guta saga*. The next major recorded contact between Gotland and the Swedish crown was in 1288 when Magnus intervened in the civil war between Visby and the rest of Gotland, which resulted in Visby receiving an independent law, but which also forced the inhabitants to apologise for their insubordination.

Magnus died in 1290 and in 1310, to resolve civil conflict, Sweden was divided between his three sons, with Gotland being subject to Birger. He increased the tax payable on the island and in 1313 attempted to annexe Gotland. He was defeated at the Battle of Röcklingebacke, in the parish of Lärbro. Despite this, Birger fled to Gotland in 1318, after *Nyköpings gästabud* (the Feast at Nyköping). He was succeeded as king the following year by his nephew Magnus Eriksson. In 1320 Magnus cancelled the increase of tax in Gotland imposed by Birger, and two years later wrote to confirm Visby's privileges. From that time on, however, the influence of Gotland in the Baltic was in decline and, following the Black Death in 1350, it fell to an invasion by Valdemar Atterdag in 1361, a culmination of his seizure of Southern Swedish territory.

### (ii) *Title*

There is no heading over the short text that forms the appendix to the manuscript of *Guta Lag*, designated B64 Holmiensis and held in the Royal Library (Kungliga Biblioteket) in Stockholm; see frontispiece. The title *Guta saga* was given to it by Carl Säve. He mentions it first in an article (1852, 132) in which he describes the text as follows:

> En verklig Gotlands-Saga eller liten Gutnisk Landnamabok i endast 6 kapitel, skrifven på samma Gutniska eller Forngotländska tunga som Guta Lag, och derföre alltid tryckt tillhopa med denna. Likväl är sagans språk ovedersägligen något yngre än lagens äldsta hufvuddel, Kapp. 1–61. Hon kallas i Schlyters nyligen utkomna förträffliga upplaga af Gotlands-Lagen *Historia Gotlandiæ*, och finnes der sidd. 93–104.

Later, in his thesis (*GU*, 31), Säve uses the title *Guta saga*. He was in this translating the title *Gotlændinga saga*, which had been given to the text by Uno von Troil in his list of Icelandic and Norwegian sagas (1777, 147–169), which he acknowledges. C. J. Schlyter (*CIG*, 93) had, as Säve says, given the passage the title *Historia Gotlandiae* and this title is later used by Hugo Yrwing (1940, 21). The text is, however, neither a saga, despite Säve's assumption (*GU*, viii), nor a history in the accepted sense, in comparison for example to the histories of Viking-Age and early medieval Norway. To be regarded as a 'saga', *Guta saga* would need, one feels, to have a more structured narrative and some sort of dénouement and resolution, whereas it ends abruptly in legalistic language and matter. On the other hand it is not, in reality, comparable to *Landnámabók*, although there are certain similarities to *Íslendingabók*; see below, p. xv. It is possible that some such designation as *Gutabok* would have been preferable, but in the current edition the accepted title *Guta saga* is retained. It is worth noting, as does Gustavson (1940–1948, I, vii), that there is nothing in exactly the same genre in any of the other Scandinavian languages; in particular there is no parallel legendary history of Öland.

### (iii) *Preservation*

The only surviving manuscript of the text in Gutnish is the one in B64. It is an octavo manuscript in the same hand as the preceding law text and shows linguistic similarities, as Säve indicated, to the later sections of *Guta lag*, which are not listed in the index at the front of the law text. The manuscript as a whole is dated by Schlyter (*CIG*, i) to the middle of the fourteenth century and later scholars, including Wessén (*LG*, xxvi), are in agreement with this. The text covers eight leaves of vellum from 43 recto to 50 verso of the manuscript. In the blank portion of the final page a sixteenth-century hand has made historical notes. The writer, according to Lundmark (1925, 170) and Wessén (*LG*, xxvi), was probably David Bilefeld († 1596), the Dutch headmaster, later suffragan bishop of Gotland. As well as these notes, there are later additions of chapter numbers and headings, and some marginal notes. The manuscript of *Guta lag* containing this text is designated *A* by Schlyter (*CIG*, iv). *Guta saga* is not present in manuscript *B* of *Guta lag* (AM 54 4to), copied out by David Bilefeld, nor is there any evidence that it was attached to his original, dated by him to 1470 and now lost; cf. *GLGS*, xvii; Ljunggren, 1959, 9.

A German translation of *Guta lag*, which is also preserved in the Royal Library in Stockholm as B65, contains a translation of *Guta saga*. This latter, set in two columns, extends from leaf 28 verso to 32 verso, with additions stretching over to 33 recto, and like the text in B64, is without any heading. This manuscript is dated by Wessén (*LG*, xxix–xxx) to around 1400. Although the translation (which Schlyter describes as being a mixture of Middle High and Middle Low German) is on the whole apparently adequate, Schlyter comments that such mistakes as can be noted in the easily compre-hended passages preclude the use of the translation to elucidate the more obscure ones; cf. *CIG*, xiv–xv. The law section of B65 con-tains two chapters on slaves not found in B64, but is without chapters 62, 63 and 65 of B64. The final chapters are also in a different sequence. Wessén (*LG*, xxxi) concludes that the missing chapters were not present in the Gutnish original from which the German was translated and this seems to point to its representing an earlier version of *Guta lag* than that in B64. It is worth noting in this connection that the chapters listed above as missing from B65 are those that in B64 resemble in language the version of *Guta saga* that appears in the latter.

In addition to these complete versions, there are three incomplete Danish translations (not noted by Schlyter or Pipping), and a partial one in Old Swedish. The oldest of the Danish translations is in a paper manuscript in the Ny kongelig Samling of the Royal Library (Det Kongelige Bibliotek) in Copenhagen, 408 8vo. It contains only *Guta saga* and was first published by Suhm in a collection of these manuscripts, but in fact edited by Rasmus Nyerup (1792–1795, 133–138), and later by Ljunggren (1959, 19–27). Lis Jacobsen (1911, 51) dates this manuscript on linguistic grounds to the sixteenth century, rejecting Nyerup's suggestion (Suhm, 1792–1795, 133) that the handwriting points to the fifteenth century; cf. Ljunggren, 1959, 18. The manuscript itself is described as being in poor condition with the first page worn through, but not to the extent of obscuring the text. It consists of nine leaves, but has earlier had a tenth. The lost leaf is the second, which would have held the start of *Guta saga*. The content and scope are broadly similar to that in B64 but with such differences as point to the one not being a translation of the other; cf. Jacobsen, 1911, 52. The similarities, particularly in detail, indicate, however, that B64 and the original of which 408 is a translation had the same redaction as their starting-point.

The second Danish translation, in the Gammel kongelig Samling of the Royal Library in Copenhagen and designated 2414 4to, is dated, again on linguistic grounds, to the first half of the seventeenth century; cf. Jacobsen, 1911, 53. This translation is bound at the end of a manuscript of Niels Pedersen's *Cimbrorum et Gothorum origines . . .*, headed *de Cimbris et Gothis Libri II*. Two hands have apparently taken part in the main work and a third has written out *Guta saga*. Even the paper is different from that used in the main part of the book. The translation covers nine pages of the last eight leaves, 69 recto onwards. The remaining pages are blank and the end of the text of *Guta saga* is missing. The free nature of the translation makes it difficult to judge the relationship between its original and B64, but it differs substantially from the translation in 408.

Ljunggren (1959, 10) mentions the similarities that Jacobsen (1911, 59) finds between 2414 and the German translation, B65, which he says represent an independent tradition from the other versions. He suggests, however, that these two go back to a common original. Thirdly, there are two small fragments appended to Syv (1663), hereinafter designated *S*. Peder Syv (1631–1702), the priest and philologist, mentions in his book versions of the text in Gutnish and in German. The translation is described by Jacobsen (1911, 53) as a good one and clearly independent of the other two. She concludes from Syv's explanation of his source that he had a copy of Niels Pedersen's *Cimbrorum et Gothorum origines* . . ., his so-called *Gullandskrønike*, to which was appended a translation of *Guta saga* in the same manner as in 2414, but representing a third strain of translation. Syv certainly owned a copy of this work (2415 4to), but this manuscript does not contain *Guta saga*; see Gigas, 1903–1915, III, 26–27.

The Old Swedish translation of the second chapter of *Guta saga* is to be found in D2 Holmiensis in the Royal Library in Stockholm. It is commonly called 'Spegelbergs bok' after Johan Spegelberg, the well-known scribe of Bishop Hans Brask; see Ljunggren, 1959, 10. Schlyter was apparently unaware of this translation, as he does not mention it in his account of the manuscripts, whereas he otherwise includes 'Afskrifters Afskrifter' in his list of versions; cf. Jacobsen, 1911, 51. Klemming (*Svenska medeltidens rim-kröniker* III, 1867–1868, 243) seems to have been the first to have taken account of it and it has since been noted by Geete (1903, 112, no. 316). Cf. also Noreen, 1904, 14; *GLGS*, xx. Wessén (*SL* IV, 296) describes it as a rewriting, but Ljunggren (1959, 11) considers it is more properly a translation and dates this part of the manuscript to between 1425 and 1470.

These four late medieval and reformation translations complete the preserved manuscript tradition of *Guta saga*. It is missing, as stated, from the paper manuscript written in 1587 by Bilefeld, held in the Arnamagnean collection in Copenhagen. Bilefeld states that the manuscript he was copying dated from 1470, but there is a possibility that the original of this latter manuscript was older than that of B64; cf. *LG*, xxviii. Following Jacobsen (1911, 66), it is convenient to designate the original manuscript of the text *\*G*. This text she dates provisionally to circa 1250. Given the paucity of the material, it is to be expected that the stemmas constructed by different scholars would diverge in detail, and the opinions held by Jacobsen (1911, 66) and Ljunggren (1959, 98) are indicated below. Jacobsen proposes that three traditions, which she calls $x$, $y$ and $z$, developed as follows. The first gave rise directly to B64 and indirectly to the Danish translation 408. The second tradition, through a no longer extant German translation $y_1$, gave rise directly to the German translation B65 and indirectly to the Danish translation 2414. Finally, $z$, after several copyings (shown on the stemma as $z_1$ to $z_n$), gave rise to S. Jacobsen's conclusions are based on the wording of individual passages and are fully tabulated (1911, 66–72). Ljunggren (1959, 97) finds her reasoning relating to the status of S as the end result of an independent strain unconvincing, and derives it as shown below directly from B64. He is willing, however, to concede her argument for the existence of $x$, while preferring to regard B64 as itself the original for $x_1$. It seems logical to agree with Jacobsen that B64 lies less close to the original *G than would be indicated by Ljunggren's stemma (dashed lines), and to consider also that S is less likely to be derived directly from B64 than he infers. This may appear to be erring on the side of caution, but the difference to which Jacobsen (1911, 67) refers seems certainly to indicate that Syv was less than likely to be using B64 or a derivative as his model. She notes, for example, that S has *lidet til at see*, which would suggest a Gutnish original with *oliust*, where B64 has *eliust*.

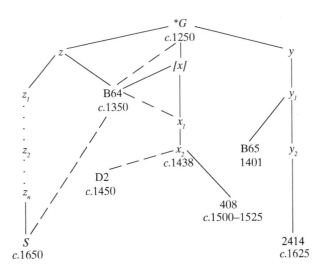

The preceding stemma shows the suggestions of both Jacobsen and Ljunggren. The unbroken lines represent derivations on which both agree, the dotted lines in the *z* branch of the stemma indicate a number of copyings and the dashed lines show derivations that Ljunggren suggests as opposed to Jacobsen, who does not include D2.

## (iv) *Content*

The text of *Guta saga* consists of just over 1,800 words but the content is remarkably wide-ranging. Although there are no original chapter headings, and the ones added to the manuscript later number only four, the text has been divided in most editions into six sections. The first of these opens with the discovery of Gotland by the legendary Þieluar, his removal of the enchantment upon it by the introduction of fire and the settlement of the island by his son, Hafþi, and daughter-in-law, Huitastierna. These two have three sons, their birth having been predicted in a dream, and the island is divided between the three of them and inhabited by their progeny. The population increases to such an extent that a proportion of them is forced to emigrate and continue their flight eastwards. They finally reach Byzantium and by means of a verbal trick persuade the emperor to allow them to stay. It is stated here as an aside that there are still people in that region whose language contains Scandinavian elements. The end of this section gives a number of details relating to heathen practices.

The second section describes conflicts between the Gotlanders and other nations and the entering of the former into a treaty with the king of Sweden, facilitated by Avair Strabain. The terms of the treaty involve an annual tax and, in return, toll concessions and protection.

The third, very short, section describes the visit of St Olaf and the building of the first chapel by Ormika of Hejnum, while the fourth section expands on the description of the conversion to Christianity, led by Botair of Akubek and his father-in-law, Likkair Snielli, followed by the building of churches throughout Gotland.

The fifth section describes the arrangements made regarding visitations by the bishop of Linköping, and the final section details the obligations of providing ships and men for the king of Sweden with a short postscript concerning what action should be taken in the event of the Swedish king being deposed.

The narrative sections of the text are laconic and, as Rolf Pipping (1943, 67) comments, have something in common with the less pretentious Icelandic sagas. The characters of the protagonists are presented through their actions and words, rather than through comment, and the dramatic events are described in few words, which nevertheless result in vivid tableaux. They remind one also of the early sections of Ari Þorgilsson's *Íslendingabók*, as has already been suggested, the opening words having a superficial similarity: *Gutland hitti fyrst*... and *Ísland byggðisk fyrst*... Both tell of the first settlers, the division of the respective islands and the early political machinations, followed by missionary activity, which was finally successful. It might even be argued that the description of the settlement of Greenland in *Íslendingabók* is paralleled by the emigration episode in *Guta saga*. The chief differences between the two are first that the author of the Icelandic work is known, and secondly that there is little in *Íslendingabók* that is obviously legendary as opposed to historical, whereas the story of the discovery of Gotland is clearly fictitious.

After the brief description of the conversion to Christianity and the negotiations with the bishop of Linköping, the style of *Guta saga* changes and the rights and duties of the bishop are set out in language that must be very close to that which appeared in the actual documents laying down those rights and duties; cf. Notes to 10/22–12/20. The levy obligations to the king of Sweden are couched in legal language and must be more or less directly copied from the original statutes.

The style of *Guta saga* reflects the varied content. The four earliest (narrative) sections are not homogeneous in their nature either. The first section is of a legendary character, covering the prehistory of Gotland and including folk-motifs as well as what must have been more specific oral tradition. The second section, covering the negotiations with the king of Sweden, probably records a historical event, although how much of the detail is factual must be open to question, while the third and fourth sections, covering the conversion, possibly have a historical framework, but do not provide a very detailed account.

### (v) *Oral and written sources*

In general, the oral sources behind *Guta saga* relate primarily to the legendary and quasi-historical elements of the text, while written sources may be found both for these and for the historical and legal elements. The two types of source material will be considered together within the framework of the text of *Guta saga*.

Oral traditions sometimes have a tangible kernel to them, such as an object or a place-name, or they may be centred around a verse or a folk-tale, using that term in its widest sense. Frequently, however, the origin of an oral tradition is not identifiable, even in the broadest terms. Whatever that origin might be the tradition needs informants to pass it on. There is, admittedly, little mention in *Guta saga* of possible informants, or sources, of oral tradition. One of the people about whom traditions would be expected to exist, Likkair Snielli, is simply said to have 'carried most authority at the time' and of another, Avair Strabain, it is stated that there are stories about his being *fielkunnugr*, 'skilled in many things', but with no further indication as to what these stories were. It is obvious, though, from the strikingly dramatic presentation of the incidents, that at least some of the legends presented must have had oral traditions as their basis; cf. Säve, 1978–1983, I, 6–9.

Written sources can be broadly divided into works of a similar kind to the text under consideration (i. e. those containing similar literary motifs, although not necessarily of the same scale) and those of a different nature: legal texts, letters and other factual material. The varying prose styles within *Guta saga* and the broad spectrum of material that it covers indicate that there are several disparate sources for its content. In considering the written sources behind *Guta saga*, therefore, it is appropriate to deal separately with the sources that relate to the clearly historical material and those which might have provided inspiration for the legendary and more problematic parts of the text. It is clear from the content of *Guta saga* that the further on in the text one moves, the more the sources become formal in style, and the more likely they are to be factual rather than fictional. There have been suggestions, most recently by Mitchell (1984, 168–169), that *Guta saga* is a loose compilation from other written sources, but it seems more reasonable to assume that it was composed as a whole, with a purpose.

Oral sources in general, as Olrik (1921, 88–89) has pointed out, are most likely to have been changed by the author to suit his taste, current conditions and perhaps other sources, which he knew of but did not incorporate to any great degree. Any postulations about these sources are bound to be merely informed guesses based on the balance of probabilities. The use of literary parallels is similarly uncertain and it is clearly not possible to state categorically that an author used a particular written source, unless he indicates that this is the case.

The following elements in the text, which might have been based on either oral or written sources, will be considered in the sequence in which they occur in *Guta saga*.

## A *The discovery of Gotland*

The story of the discovery of Gotland and the name *Þieluar* pose the first problem: to determine who Þieluar might have been, and what historical or traditional connection, if any, he had with Gotland. A variant of the name is known from a pair of runic inscriptions found on stones in Öster Skam in Östergötland; cf. Note to 2/1. These runestones presumably predate the original text of *Guta saga*, although according to Brate (*ÖR*, 25–27) doubt has been placed on their antiquity, and it was suspected that they were the work of a seventeenth-century antiquarian, although Brate himself considers the inscriptions as recorded to be genuine. P. A. Säve writes (1862, 59) that he was unable to find evidence of the stone or stones and that no one in the parish could offer any information, even the local dean, who was of the opinion that they did not exist and had never existed. There might seem to be no great similarity between the Þieluar of *Guta saga* and Þjálfi, Thor's servant in Snorri Sturluson's *Edda* (1982, 37, 40, 43, 177), although it has been suggested by several scholars, including Läffler (1908–1909, Part 1, 170–171) and Gordon (1962, 255), and has been taken up by Uwe Lemke (1986, 14), who sees Þieluar as the representative of Thor, the thunder, lightning and life god. In that role, he would be an appropriate agent to free the island of its enchantment. Olrik (1905, 136–138) wonders if there is not a mystical aspect to Þieluar/ Þjálfi, despite the fact that he is usually in Thor's shadow, but points out that fire is so commonly called upon to dispel spirits that the world of the gods need not be involved. Olrik notes also that the name is thought to be related to a presumed Icelandic *\*þjálf,* 'work', leading to speculation that he might be a work-god, but dismisses much of this as mere conjecture. No such form occurs in Old Icelandic, but it is worth noting that *Þjálfi* could be a weak form of *Þieluar*; cf. *ÍO,* s. v. *þjálfa*; de Vries, 1956–1957, II, 129.

The existence of oral traditions in connection with Þieluar is perhaps shown by the fact that a later Bronze Age grave (1000–300 BC), near the east coast of Gotland and lying almost directly east of Visby, in the parish of Boge, is called *Tjelvars grav.* This is not, however, the oldest grave in Gotland, which was inhabited prior to the Bronze Age, and even if it were, the name could be secondary to *Guta saga,* so it cannot be regarded as a source.

## B *Sinking islands*

In relation to the legend of the island of Gotland sinking by day and rising up by night, there is geological evidence to support a number of changes in sea level and these could well have been compressed in folk memory into a diurnal change, followed by the final fixing of Gotland above sea level. Gotland was below sea level at the end of the last Ice Age, having been above it previously, and it appears that the sea level then slowly fell, resulting in a series of steps in the coastline; cf. Klintberg, 1909, 33, 35–36. What is certain, geologically, is that the sea was once very much higher than it is today and there could therefore have been a period during which parts of the island at least were sometimes above sea level and sometimes below it. The various levels of sea-wall testify to this and geologists point to the movements in the Baltic basin and the sinking of the land in the Ice Age as a cause; cf. Lemke, 1970, 4. Gotland itself is relatively flat, so if the sea level were near to the top of the present cliffs, it might well seem as if the island were disappearing and re-appearing in a mysterious manner, especially in bad weather. That being the case, it is not surprising that some folk memory remained of this period and that it was included in a legendary history of the island.

There are, however, legends from Iceland and other parts of Scandinavia, Ireland, Finland and England, which can be cited as related to the motif of a floating island. Particularly fertile islands were frequently the subject of legends concerning their magical origins; cf. Gordon, 1962, 255–256. Several islands are deemed to have been disenchanted by fire or steel. Svínoy, the most easterly of the Faeroe Islands, is one of a number mentioned by Strömbäck (1970, 146–148) in this connection. Svínoy is described by Lucas Debes (1673, 21–22) as a *flydøe* bewitched by the devil, which had to be 'fixed' with steel. A similar tale from 1676 is told of the mythical island Utröst, west of Lofoten in Nordland, and from later times of Sandflesa (west of Træna), Utvega (to the west of Vega), Hillerei-øi, Ytter-Sklinna (in Nord-Trøndelag), and other islands in Norway; cf. Storm, 1895, 208; Nansen 1911, 286. Steel would have rendered them visible and thus disenchanted, but they were too far out to sea to have been reached by a domestic animal carrying it, so they remained submerged. The 'lucky' island O'Brasil or Hy Breasail, off the west coast of Ireland, was said only to appear every seven years and would stay in sight if someone could throw fire on it; cf. Nansen 1911, 287. Giraldus Cambrensis (1867, Part 2, 94–95) writes in the twelfth century of an island off the coast of Ireland, which disappeared as a group of young men attempted to disembark, but was 'fixed' by an arrow of red-hot iron being thrown on it as they approached. Another island off the west coast of Ireland, Inishbofin, 'white cow island', was 'fixed' when two sailors landed on it and lit a fire; cf. Palmenfelt, 1979, 128. William of Malmesbury (1981, 44–47, 52–53) tells the story of Glasteing being led by his sow to the island of Avalon at Glastonbury and there are tales of islands, including Svínoy, being disenchanted by tying steel to a sow that was in the habit of visiting the island. Whether any of these tales could have been known to the author of *Guta saga* is difficult to assess, although such stories were clearly common, at least throughout Europe. Spegel (1901, 22) lists several more of them in his account of the history and geography of Gotland. First, the island of Delos in the Aegean, which was said by the Greek poet Callimachus, in his *Hymn to Delos* (*c.*275–262 BC), to have sailed to and fro over the sea, being sometimes visible and sometimes not; see Mineur, 1984, 75–95. In legend, the mysterious Delos was said to have been called from the bottom of the sea by Poseidon and eventually chained to the sea-bed by Zeus. The island was the birthplace of Apollo and Artemis and sacred to the former. Secondly, Spegel cites the island of San Borondon, of which the sixteenth-century Dutchman, van Linschoten, reports that the Spaniards thought it lay about 100 miles west of the Canaries; see Linschoten, 1598, 177. They could see the island, but never find it, and assumed it was either enchanted, or small and covered with clouds. Thirdly, Chemmis, an island on a lake at the mouth of the Nile, which Herodotus (Book 2, §156) was told floated while it was being used as a hiding-place for Apollo. Cf. also Nansen, 1911, 283–285 and references.

## C *Hallowing with fire*

The motif of hallowing or removing a spell with fire is found widely in Scandinavia and there is also evidence for its actual occurrence. Examples are found in Danish, Icelandic and Irish literature, and have been discussed in detail by Strömbäck (1970, 142–159). He supports the theory that as well as, or as an alternative to, any legal implications, the ringing of land with fire in some way placated the land spirits who had bewitched it. To reinforce this he interprets *eluist* as a form of *eluiskt* meaning 'bewitched', and suggests that the account in *Guta saga* represents merely a more pointed version of the belief lying behind land-claiming customs, similar to those mentioned concerning Jǫrundr goði in *Landnámabók* (*ÍF* I, 350, 351) and Þórólfr in *Eyrbyggja saga* (ch. 4; *ÍF* IV, 8) as well as in *Vatnsdœla saga* (ch. 10; *ÍF* VIII, 28) and *Hœnsa-Þóris saga* (ch. 9; *ÍF* III, 25). These are, however, simply parallels and it is probable that there was a similar oral tradition associated with Gotland itself. The idea lying behind the fire legend may be that the island could only be inhabited once it was dry enough to sustain fire, that is, when the water level was low enough.

D *Mythical or mystical ancestors*

Having removed the spell from the island, Þieluar disappears from the scene and is not mentioned as a permanent settler. This puts him in the role of 'mystical ancestor', on a parallel with *Tuisto*, referred to by Tacitus (1914, 32), and the Gothic *Gaut/Gapt*, in Jordanes (1997, 70), discussed, along with other examples, by Schütte (1907, 135–136). There are many parallels for such an ancestor and it is not possible to determine whether one of the accounts extant at the time was the inspiration for the tale incorporated by the writer of *Guta saga*, or whether a separate oral tradition existed.

E *The settlement of the island*

There follows the description of a further two generations of mythical ancestors from whom the inhabitants of Gotland are deemed to have descended. Hafþi, the son of Þieluar, marries Huitastierna ('white star') and they have three sons who are all given names starting with 'G'. Legendary genealogies consisting of sets of alliterating names are common in the early histories of several peoples. According to Tacitus (1914, 32), the Germans worshipped an earth-born god, Tuisto, who had a son Mannus, himself the father of three sons, the founders of the three races of Ingaevones, (H)erminones and Istaevones, who were celebrated in songs. These sons were named Inguo, Ermenus and Istio in sixth-century sources; cf. Tacitus, 1914, 136. Similarly, the Gothic tribes recognised one ancestor by the name of Gapt (or Gaut), who had a son named Hulmul (Humli or Humal), called the father of the Danes, himself the father of Augis (Agis or Avigis), the father of Amal, the father of Hisarna, the father of Ostrogotha, the father of Hunuil, the father of Athal and so on; see Jordanes, 1997, 70; Wolfram, 1988, 31. In medieval Scandinavian literature, several mythical genealogies are mentioned, including those in Snorri's *Gylfaginning* and *Ynglinga saga*. In *Gylfaginning* (Snorri Sturluson, 1982, 11) Snorri writes of Auðhumla, the giant cow, which licks Búri out of a block of salt. This Búri marries Bestla and has a son Borr, in turn the father of Óðinn, Vili and Vé. The earliest extant version of a genealogy of the Norse people is probably represented by *Upphaf allra frásagna* (*ÍF* XXXV, 39–40), which is thought to be the beginning of a lost *Skjǫldunga saga*. In it, Fróði, the great-grandson of Óðinn, is described as a bringer of peace and prosperity and a contemporary of

Christ; cf. Faulkes, 1978–1979, 94–95, 107–108. In *Ynglinga saga* ch. 10–13 (*ÍF* XXVI, 23–29) Snorri gives the genealogy of Yngvifreyr's line and in ch. 17 (*ÍF* XXVI, 34) that of Rígr father to Danpr, grandfather to Drótt and great-grandfather to Dyggvi. Again, in *Landnámabók* (*ÍF* I, 40) the three sons of Atli are Hásteinn, Hersteinn and Hólmsteinn, although these could be historical. Keil (1931, 60–70) suggests that the choice of names in the Icelandic sagas was also partly influenced by alliteration and other similar factors.

Considering the specific names in *Guta saga*, the name *Hafþi* might possibly be linked with the parish name *Havdhem* on southern Gotland as Wessén (*SL* IV, 302) implies. It is more than likely, however, that the parish name preceded the writing of that portion of *Guta saga*, and that the name *Hafþi* is secondary to that. It is necessary to accept the possibility that personal names appearing in legends could have been invented as a result of the existence of place-names with an *apparent* genitive form and/or with a second element that invited such an assumption. Another example of this possibility is *Lickershamn*, discussed below, p. xliv. Olsson (1984, 26) interprets *Havdhem* as relating either to the Gotlandic *haued*, 'head', or to *havde*, 'raised grass bank at haymaking'. Schütte (1907, 136), however, relates the name *Hafþi* itself to 'head', suggesting he was the 'head-man', with the mystical wife, Huitastierna. The place-name *Havdhem*, although it could have suggested the name *Hafþi*, is not mentioned in *Guta saga*. The name *Huitastierna*, apart from alliterating with *Hafþi*, leads Läffler (1908–1909, Part 1, 171–172) to note that it reminds one of the 'cow-name', and to consider that the two might originate in an alternative creation myth, representing animal deities; cf. above, p. xix, in relation to Inishbofin.

### F *Dreams about snakes*

The dream that Huitastierna has on her wedding night, of the three snakes issuing from her womb or breast, has folklore parallels. The motif of pregnant women dreaming of events connected with the birth of their children is very commonplace. There is, for example, a tale concerning William the Conqueror's mother who is said to have dreamed that a great tree grew from her womb. Equally, dreams concerning snakes are not unusual and the combination of the two motifs (with the snakes proceeding from some part of a woman's anatomy) is also encountered. Henning Feilberg (1886–1914, IV, 316, s. v. *orm*) mentions a motif concerning a snake growing out of a young girl's back and coiling itself around her neck. Snakes also figure largely in Celtic myth in various guises: as protectors, as fertility symbols and in connection with the underworld and death. The snake motif is common on Gotlandic picture-stones and one in particular, from Smiss in Gotland, is of interest; see Note to 2/8. It is therefore possible that a literary or oral motif concerning a pregnant woman's dream has been combined with snake iconography to give this version of the tradition. What the true source is for the dream-sequence it is probably not possible to know: it could have been a folk-tale applied in a particular case or it could have been a specific story associated with the island's settlement, perhaps linked to some native or foreign mythological element. It could even have been an invented story based on the seeds of an idea sown by some artefact similar to the disc found in a woman's grave at Ihre, Gotland; cf. Note to 2/8.

## G *Predictive verse*

Huitastierna tells her husband the dream and he interprets it, by means of a verse. The verse is delivered in two half-strophes, each of three lines. The first half-strophe is a confirmation of the power of fate, a reassurance and a statement of belief in the future. The verse is in all probability older than *Guta saga* itself, i. e. not the work of the author of *Guta saga*, and thus possibly the kernel of an oral tale. In the second half-strophe, Hafþi gives his offspring names 'unborn as they are': Guti, Graipr and Gunfiaun, and indicates that they will be born in that order, with the first taking the lead in ruling Gotland. The place-names *Gute* (in the parish of Bäl), *Gothem, Gothemhammar, Gothemån*, as well as *Gotland* itself, would be apparently explained by this tale; cf. Note to 2/1. There are no major place-names that obviously relate to the names of the two other sons, and indeed it has been maintained by Wessén (*SL* IV, 302) amongst others that the name *Gunfiaun* is unknown outside *Guta saga*, although the element *Gun-* occurs in many Scandinavian names. Schütte (1907, 194) suggests that it may be a name plucked out of the air to complete the expected trinity of names, and that the whole episode expresses a parochial view of events. The name *Graipr* occurs, but only rarely, in Old Norse literature. In the parish of Garde, however, there are remains said to be of 'Graipr's house' and 'Graipr's grave-mound' (*rör*). There is also a ruin in the parish of Ardre with the name 'Gunnfiaun's chapel', which is probably from the fourteenth century and therefore, like the other remains, very possibly secondary to the legend, if not to *Guta saga* itself; cf. *SL* IV, 302–303. As Schütte (1907, 194) also points out, the three alliterating names must in any event be regarded as a pure fiction, on the pattern of the three sons of Borr, the three sons of Mannus and other examples. In *Guta saga*, the names could be being used merely as an explanation for the division of the island into thirds. In fact what immediately follows is a contradiction of the verse just quoted, a not uncommon phenomenon in Old Norse literature when an older verse is incorporated into a prose work by a later author. In the verse, *Guti* is presented as the first and most important son, who will own all Gotland, whereas the prose following cites *Graipr* as the eldest son, with *Guti* taking the central position. The fact that the middle third of Gotland contains Roma, later the site of *gutnalþing*, the assembly for the whole island, could have influenced this version of events, and show that it might represent a later tradition in which Guti was associated with the middle third; cf. Notes to 2/19; 2/27; 6/21–22. In this case, as Wessén suggests (*SL* IV, 302–303), the only 'error' in the prose text of *Guta saga* is in the naming of Graipr as the oldest son.

The strophe with which Hafþi interprets his wife's dream may well be part of a longer poem and the alliteration in the prose surrounding the verse (e. g. *sum hit Hafþi, sum þaun saman suafu, droymdi henni draumbr, slungnir saman, skiptu siþan Gutlandi, lutaþu þair bort af landi*) suggests that the material in it appeared in the lost verse; cf. Notes to 2/12–14, 16–18. Lindquist (1941, 12, 39, 51) has discussed in detail the lists of bishops and lawmen that appear as supplements to *Västgötalagen* and argues convincingly, by only slightly rewording the prose, that they are the remnants of now lost verses. It is possible that a similar literary source lies behind at least this early part of *Guta saga*. If there were two versions extant, differing slightly in the tradition they represented, this would explain the apparent contradiction in the text.

H *The division of the island*

One possible explanation for the discrepancy between the verse and the prose describing the division of the island has been given above. Läffler (1908–1909, Part 1, 172–177), on the other hand, argues that the verse carries a separate tradition from that behind the prose, and that it has been included here in order to follow Saxo's example of larding his texts with verse. Authors such as Strelow (whose chronicle of Gotland, *Cronica Guthilandorum*, was designed to show that the island had been settled by, and always subject to, the Danes, in particular the *Jutar*) have even more imaginative ideas, based on surmise from place-names; see Strelow, 1633, 20–21. Strelow, in fact, names the two younger sons as *Grippa* and *Gumphinus*. There *may* have been several versions of an oral genealogy and associated stories of the division of the island, but the straightforward explanation, given above, is preferable to a more complicated one. The connection between the three sons of Hafþi and the three administrative districts had certainly been made by the time the verse source was composed.

The division of the island of Gotland into three is first recorded in 1213 (*DS* I, 178, no. 152) in a letter from the Pope to the deans of the northern and southern thirds ('prepositis de Northlanda et de Sutherlanda') and to the abbot of Gotland ('abbati de Gothlanda'), who would have been in spiritual charge of the middle third; see Yrwing, 1978, 81. A recent study by Hyenstrand (1989) questions the age of the *þriþiung* division, however, and argues that the original division of Gotland was not into thirds. He suggests that the original division was into 12 *hundari* and that this was older than that into *þriþiungar*, although it is only mentioned in *Guta lag* and not elsewhere; cf. *GLGS*, 46. He notes that the number 12 appears frequently in *Guta saga*, and suggests that the original administrative division of the island was into 12 *hundari*, each divided into eight, which *later* gave rise to the division of the island into sixths, *settingar* (Gutnish pl. *siettungar*), and thirds; see Hyenstrand, 1989, 108, 136 and cf. Note to 2/19. Both *hundaris þing* and *siettungs þing* are referred to in *Guta lag*.

The motif of the division of an island, in this case Ireland, occurs in Giraldus Cambrensis (1867, Part 3, 143–147), where successions of brothers, some with alliterating names, divide up the land between them, before one becomes king of the whole of Ireland.

## I *Emigration as a remedy for over-population*

The enforced emigration resulting from the overpopulation of Gotland may have been a historical reality and possibly the subject of oral tradition, as is discussed below. On the other hand there are so many instances of similar events in the history of various peoples that the possibility that the author was adapting a literary motif must also be considered. Weibull thinks that this whole episode is a formula tale, 'en lärd transponering på ett nytt folk av en urgammal utvandringsberättelse'; see Weibull, 1963, 27, 34–35. He considers it to be derived ultimately from authors such as Herodotus (Book 1, §94), in which the author writes of the King of Lydia dividing the people into two groups, determining by lot which group should emigrate and which stay at home. Weibull argues that, as the tale appears so frequently in other sources, it cannot be true in the particular case of Gotland. A similar story, indeed, occurs in Book 8 of Saxo's *Gesta Danorum* (written around 1200), with the added twist that the original suggestion was to kill the old and the very young and to send away those below arms-bearing age; cf. Saxo Grammaticus, 1931–1957, I, 237–238. By general agreement this plan is rejected and there is a ballot, after which it is the stronger members of the community who must stand in for the weaker members in exile. They set off from Denmark, stopping in Blekinge and, coincidentally, anchor off Gotland on their way eastwards. They are instructed by divine intervention to change their name to *Langobardi* and eventually reach Italy, where they impose their name upon the existing inhabitants. Saxo refers directly to Paulus Diaconus's history of the Langobardi (written at the end of the eighth century), where there is a similar account, including mention of *Nigilanda* or *Ingolanda* (or 'Golanda', derived from *Golhaida*) as one of the places visited on the way to Italy; cf. Paulus Diaconus, 1878, 54. There is another version of the motif, but this time relating to the young men of Dacia under Rollo, in Dudo of St Quentin's History of the Normans, written about 1014 (Part 2, §1–2, 5). There are certainly considerable similarities between these stories, of which the one in *Guta saga* was most probably the latest in written form, but this does not necessarily mean that its writer consciously borrowed from those cited, or from any similar source.

If, on the other hand, the possibility of the episode recording details of an *actual* exodus is accepted, the question of when that exodus occurred has to be considered. One wonders if over-population might not, in some areas, have been a cause of Viking activity, although archaeological studies have led scholars to date the exodus from Gotland, certainly, several centuries earlier than the Viking Age. The archaeological evidence points to a sharp reduction in population between circa 475 and 550, as indicated by the paucity of grave finds and by the number of abandoned settlements; cf. Nerman, 1963, 19. At the same time, the instances of imported goods from Gotland increased in the countries around the eastern Baltic; cf. *KL*, s. v. *Vikingetog*, cols 49–51. If the exodus did occur, the story in *Guta saga* probably relates to folk-tales generated from this period. It is possible that some of the banished Gotlanders or their descendents came back years later with exotic goods and tales of the East, but of this there is no remaining direct evidence. From finds in Gotland, it appears that during the ninth and tenth centuries the coins imported were principally from the Caliphate, and there are very few from Byzantium itself. Later, coins seem to have come chiefly from western Europe. If there was any group returning from exile, it does not appear to have been a large one. Hadorph (1687, viii) considers the emigration episode to be important in relation to the start of the great Scandinavian expeditions, but this is not supported by the available evidence.

Nils Tiberg (1946, 44) suggests it would have been natural for both the author of *Guta saga* and the composer of the material he used to have had patterns in mind. Having received an oral tale that he wanted to record, the author might expand it to some extent on the basis of similar written material. The opposing argument in favour of purely literary sources has been discussed, but it seems probable that behind the tale presented here there is some genuine oral material that relates specifically to Gotland. One point worth noting in the story as told by Paulus Diaconus is that he writes, of the island of Scandinavia (variously Scadinavia and Scadanavia), that it is covered by the waves that run along its flat shores; see Paulus Diaconus 1878, 48–49, 52, 54; Goffart, 1988, 385. This, or some similar tale, is another possible source of inspiration for the discovery legend. Cf. also Olaus Magnus, 1909–1951, I, Book IV, ch. 6.

## J *Torsburgen and Fårö*

According to the text, the people who were balloted away declined in the end to depart and installed themselves in Torsburgen, called *Þorsborg* in *Guta saga*. This immense prehistoric fortification, the largest of Sweden's hill-forts, utilises one of the few high places on the island, so that man-made fortification was only required along half its perimeter. Considerable archeological research has been done into the dating and use of Torsburgen, and it is certainly possible that it was used in the way suggested in *Guta saga*. It is impressive in scale and could have supported several thousand people. Engström (1984, abstract on title verso, 123, 124–126; *GV*, 76) has estimated that about 100–200 men could complete each two-kilometre length of wall in approximately two months. The date of construction has been disputed, but as a result of radiocarbon dating and other techniques, Engström has dated the two phases of the fort to the periods between AD 300 and AD 400, the end of the Roman Iron Age, and between AD 800 and AD 1100, the end of the Viking Age. These were periods of vigorous Scandinavian expansion, combined with social and climatic change, which might have been the cause of unrest. The position of Torsburgen, near to the coast and to administrative centres, would lend itself to use in the defence of the island, as well as in any internal conflicts. The suggestion (Engström, 1979, 127–128) is that Torsburgen was constructed as a defensive fort from which the islanders sortied to fall upon invaders. It is possible that this successful strategy lies behind the later episode concerning the 'many kings' who attacked Gotland, but the author does not mention Torsburgen specifically in connection with these attacks. Engström rejects the suggestion that Torsburgen was a general place of refuge, since it lay too near the coast from which danger might come, but does not dismiss the idea that it might have been built by a group of Gotlanders threatened with expulsion. The findings are, in general, consistent with the emigration story as recorded in *Guta saga*, which gives the clear impression that Torsburgen was established well before the emigrants fled there, and was not built by them. There is also evidence that at least one of the walls has been augmented after its initial construction. However defensible their position was, the emigrants were not permitted to stay at Torsburgen and decamped to the island of Fårö, where they again failed to set up a permanent residence; cf. Note to 4/1.

   One might expect an edifice of the size and prominence of Torsburgen to attract oral traditions, but it has a relatively low-key role in the story as told in *Guta saga*. In the sixteenth- and seventeenth-century chronicles of Gotland the forced emigrants are led by one *Tore*, and Torsburgen is said in one tradition to have been named after him; cf. Strelow, 1633, 32. It seems more likely, however, that the name relates to a cult place dedicated to Thor and that later authors have combined the place-name and the emigration story and invented a name for the leader of the emigrants. There are legends linking Torsburgen to Thor, describing how he could look out from its highest point over the sea, and of the god avenging himself on the farmer who dared to try to build on it; cf. Nihlén, 1975, 82–85.

## K *Traces of emigrants abroad*

When the author describes the temporary settlement on Dagö (Estonian Hiiumaa), he mentions a fortification, which '*enn synis*'. It is possible that the author himself visited Dagö, but if not, his knowledge of the fortification must either have come from an oral tradition or from a written account. According to information from the State Historical Museum in Tallinn (private communication), however, no such construction is now evident. The fortress, although it might still have been extant at the time of writing, and may have attracted oral tradition, seems not to have survived.

If it is accepted that there *was* a forced emigration from Gotland in the fifth century, or at some other time, it is perhaps natural that it would have been eastwards, and there is no doubt that parts of Estonia have been settled by Swedish speakers at various times. The two large islands off the coast of Estonia, Dagö and Ösel (Estonian Saaremaa), lie north-east of Fårö, in the mouth of the Gulf of Riga, and this may have been a more likely direction to take than to the nearer coast of Latvia. One might also speculate upon the reason that the emigrants could not stay there. Apparently their numbers must have been so great that the area where they landed was not able to support them and some, but not all, continued eastwards. The island of Dagö is not large, smaller in area than Gotland, and much of the centre is low-lying. It is possible to imagine that it would not have supported a large influx of people. The author's sketch of the onward journey to Greece follows the route customary for the time; see Note to 4/6.

## L *The tricking of the king*

This passage distinguishes the emigration episode as told in *Guta saga* from the more generalised accounts in the written sources discussed above, pp. xxv–xxvii, and contains such a remarkable number of alliterative phrases (*so fierri foru þair, baddus þair byggias, ny ok niþar, maira þan ann manaþr, þissun þaira viþratta* and so on) that it seems probable that some lost poetry lies behind the story. If so, it is likely to have been of the orally-transmitted variety. One would expect to find parallels to the episode of the word-play used to trick the Byzantine emperor in ballads or folktales, the purpose of them being to show the superiority of one group of people over another. The emigrants from Gotland are in this case seen to outwit the monarch in one of the centres of learning of the then known world. The fact that the empress is involved in the dispute and successfully intercedes on behalf of the immigrants perhaps reflects a Scandinavian social pattern, in which women were more the equals of men than in other parts of Europe. Examples of influential women may be found in *Landnámabók* and in several of the Icelandic sagas, for example *Laxdœla saga*. No close parallels to this story have come to light, but there are similar tales extant of ordinary people tricking monarchs (e. g. the ballad of *King John and the Abbot of Canterbury* (Child no. 45 B) where the disguised shepherd says, in reply to the king's 'Tell me truly what I do think', 'You think I'm the Abbot of Canterbury'). There are also a number of land-claiming tricks, for example ones in which permission to claim only as much land as could be covered by a hide is circumvented by cutting the hide into a thin strip and using that to encircle the land claimed. One version of the story relates that Birger Magnusson, who had been beaten by the Gotlandic farmers at Röcklingebacke in 1313, was taken to Visby. There he asked for as large an amount of land as a calf-skin would cover. When permission was granted, he had the calf-skin cut into strips and with these surrounded a considerable area, on which he had an impressive royal residence built. This is said to be the origin of Kalvskinnshuset in Visby, but this is probably more likely to have been built as a symbol of Swedish power by Magnus Ladulås, who was in a much stronger position than Birger. No king has ever lived there and there are several more likely explanations for the name; cf. Pernler, 1982. The motif itself probably goes back to ancient methods of measuring land, perhaps with a ceremonial aspect; cf. Söderberg, 1959, 48–49. Another example of the trick is related by Saxo, in relation to Ívarr, the son of Ragnar loðbrók, and King Ella of the Danelaw. Ívarr cut a horse-hide or ox-hide into narrow strips and so was able to claim the land on which London was founded; cf. Saxo Grammaticus, 1931–1957, I, 263; *Ragnars saga loðbrókar*, 1954, ch. 16–17.

A further clue to the origin of the particular tale in *Guta saga* might lie in its final sentence: the people there still have 'some of our language'. To which people does this statement refer? Not the Greeks, certainly, but perhaps the Goths or *Getae*, and this provides another perspective on the emigration story. Weibull (1963, 33), suggests that the reason for the choice of destination by the author of *Guta saga* is that the *Getae*, who lived on the borders of the Byzantine empire, *Grekland* in Scandinavian sources, were linked to the Goths and thus, by implication, to Gotland. It was, in other words, an attempt at a folk-etymology of the name of *Gotland*. According to one of what Gust Johansson (1968, 4) calls the 'norröna trosartiklarna', the Swedes of the Viking Age were directly descended from those peoples who moved into the area as the ice drew back. Johansson challenges this and favours the idea of the later invasion by the Goths via Finland. This would appear to turn the whole of the Gotlandic emigration story on its head, as it is at about the time of the supposed exodus that Johansson assumes that the Goths, beaten westwards by the Huns, moved *into* Sweden. The claim that some people of eastern Europe 'still have some of our language' would then refer to the *source* of the language in Gotland. It has been remarked that there are similarities between Gutnish and Gothic; cf. Bugge, 1907. It is unlikely, however, that the author himself would have been able to make the comparison, so consideration must be given to what justification the author can have for the statement. It could be merely an invention to complete the narrative, or some report might have come back with later travellers to Constantinople or Jerusalem of a people they had met in the east, who spoke a language reminiscent of their own, namely Gothic. This in turn could have led to the invention of the emigration story, based on the tradition current amongst the Black Sea Goths of their origins on the island of *Scandza*, as recorded by Jordanes (1997, 33, 37, 81); cf. Tacitus, 1914, 195; *GU*, x–xi; Wolfram, 1988, 36 and references. Alternatively, the incident could merely be an adaptation of a later movement eastwards with a resultant integration of culture and language. Wessén, however, thinks it more likely that there already existed an emigration tradition, and that this was combined with a tradition amongst the Black Sea Goths, relating to their origins, either by the author of *Guta saga* or earlier. Until the end of the eighteenth century, there were the remnants of an East Gothic community on the Crimean peninsula; see *SL* IV, 300.

## M *Heathen beliefs and practices*

The heathen beliefs and practices described parallel to a degree those proscribed in *Guta lag* (*GLGS*, 7). The source of the author's information could have been tradition, but there are a number of written accounts which, while they would not have been the specific ones used by the author, might suggest that his information came from written material.

Belief in sacred groves (*hult*) is recorded by Tacitus (1914, 51, 190) and in Adam of Bremen's description of the temple at Uppsala (1961, 471–477) amongst others, and is so well documented that no special source need be sought for this piece of information. A respect for the howes (*haugar*) of ancestors is also a commonplace and the numerous stories in Norse literature of magical events associated with burial mounds are ample evidence of a cult related to them. The meaning of *stafgarþar* is discussed in the Note to 4/18.

One of the most dramatic of the Gotlandic picture-stones (Hammars I, preserved in the Bunge museum near Fårösund in the north of Gotland, but originally from Hammars in Lärbro parish in northeast Gotland) shows what appear to be preparations for a human sacrifice, with a figure lying across what seems to be an altar. Gustaf Trotzig (*GV*, 370–371) writes of the figure, who is apparently being threatened by a spear, that he is particularly badly placed ('ligger illa till'). It might be significant that the potential victim is considerably smaller than the other figures depicted; see Lindqvist, 1941–1942, I, fig. 81; II, 86–87. Beyond him an armed man seems about to be hanged, once the branch to which he is tied is released, although Trotzig asks why, in that case, he is armed. Adam of Bremen gives an account of human as well as animal sacrifice at Uppsala, so one could accept that this picture-stone carries evidence of heathen practice as well as belief. On a stone from Bote, in Garde parish in central Gotland, there is a procession of men who appear to have ropes around their necks and could be about to be sacrificed. This particular scene is, however, open to other interpretations. According to *Guta saga* human sacrifices were offered for the whole of the island, whereas the thirds had lesser sacrifices with animals, and there were also sacrifices on a smaller scale more locally, possibly centred round the home of an influential farmer, which later became the centre of a parish; cf. Schück, 1945, 182. This structured organisation could well be a later imposition of order upon what was a much more haphazard arrangement, but there is no evidence for this either way. Steffen (1945, 232–239) argues that the *treding* was a medieval division and not a prehistoric one, with the original division of the island being into two, but Schück (1945, 179–180) disagrees. Hyenstrand's study of the subject is referred to above, p. xxv.

Ibn Fadlan describes in detail the sacrifice of a servant girl at the cremation of her Rus master, and the Russian Primary Chronicle has a reference specifically to the sacrifice of their sons and daughters by the people of Kiev, to idols set up by Vladimir, Jaroslav's father; see Birkeland, 1954, 17–24; *RPC*, 93–94. The victims of human sacrifice were often slaves, criminals or prisoners of war, and the means of death was frequently hanging as described by Ibn Rustah and Adam of Bremen; see Birkeland, 1954, 16–17; Adam of Bremen, 1961, 471–473. The king, who represented a god, was sometimes sacrificed in time of particular hardship, for example if the harvest failed, and Håkon jarl offered his son Erling during the Battle of Hjørungavåg in 986.

The subject of the extent and significance of human sacrifice is discussed by, amongst others, Mogk and Ström. Mogk (1909, 643) summarises his opinion as that the Germanic sacrifice was not an act of punishment and that a cult act was involved, whereas Ström (1942, 277–278) does not regard the death penalty as sacred, but thinks that superstitions related to the *act* of killing led to rituals, which gave a quasi-religious appearance to the deaths, making them appear to have been self-inflicted. This does not, however, explain the sacrifice of the king by the Swedes in time of need; cf. Gordon, 1962, 256–257. Whichever is the case, the author of *Guta saga* must have been aware of heathen traditions, since laws forbidding them were incorporated into *Guta lag*.

## N Gotland's treaty with Sweden

The successful negotiations by Avair Strabain with the king of Sweden and the resulting treaty do not appear in any other known source, but in King Alfred's ninth-century translation of Orosius' History of the World there is a description by a traveller named Wulfstan of a voyage across the Baltic from Hedeby to Truso. Wulfstan records that Gotland belongs (*hyrað*) to Sweden; see *Orosius*, 16, line 28. This must be treated with caution, since he also states that Blekinge did (*Orosius*, 16, line 27), and certainly by the eleventh century the latter belonged to Denmark. On the other hand, Rydberg (*STFM* I, 40) uses Snorri's narrative in *Heimskringla* to argue that Gotland was independent of Sweden at the time of Olaf Skötkonung and Olaf Tryggvason, that is in the tenth century. Gotland was said by Snorri in *Óláfs saga Tryggvasonar* (*ÍF* XXVI, 254–255) to have been the subject of a Norwegian attack (unlikely if Gotland belonged to Sweden, as the two kings were allies) and Rydberg's argument, based on this account and another in the same saga (*ÍF* XXVI, 337), places the treaty after the time of Olaf Tryggvason. From the dating of a runic inscription on the Torsätra stone in Uppland (U 614), it appears that some sort of tribute was being paid to Sweden in the second half of the eleventh century. The inscription records that Skuli and Folki had the stone raised in memory of their brother Husbiorn, who fell sick abroad (**usiok uti** 'vas siukʀ uti') when they were taking tribute in Gotland. It is dated to the 1060s or 1070s on account of its attribution to the rune-master Vitsäte, who appears to have been active about this time; see Jansson, 1987, 88. Codex Laur. Ashburnham, the so-called Florens-dokument, dated to circa 1120, mentions *Guthlandia* as one of the 'insulae' (literally 'islands', though the list includes non-insular districts) of Sweden, but as it contains a number of very obvious errors, its testimony on this point must be questionable; cf. Delisle, 1886, 75; *DS, Appendix* 1, 3, no. 4; Tunberg, 1913, 28; *GV*, 449–451.[1]

Whenever the treaty was negotiated, it seems possible that the author of *Guta saga* had access to some written information about the arrangements as they stood in his time and that there was then some annual tax being paid to the Swedish crown. In 1285, King Magnus Birgersson Ladulås issued an edict that each year the Gotlanders should pay a levy tax in addition to the tribute, whether or not a muster of ships were commanded. This seems not to have been the case as described in *Guta saga*, where a levy tax is only

---

[1] Various alternative theories have been advanced about the dating of the incorporation of Gotland into Sweden. Nerman (1923, 67; 1932, 163–167; 1963, 25) argues from archaeological evidence of periods of disturbance on Gotland and from finds at Grobin, Latvia, where Swedish and Gotlandic artefacts from similar periods were found side by side, for an early dating, around 550. Wessén, however, rejects this in favour of a date not long before St Olaf's visit in 1029; cf. *SL* IV, 306. Lindqvist (1932, 78) suggests that the ninth century is a more likely period for the incorporation to have occurred, since this was a time of Swedish expansion, and would have offered advantages to Gotland of trade with the East.

demanded if the Gotlanders for some reason fail to provide the ships for the levy, so the annual tax would have been separate. These taxes would have been in silver, a material not available in the migration period; see Nerman, 1932, 167. If, as has been suggested by Sjöholm (1976, 108), *Guta saga* was written as a legendary history with the purpose of arguing the case for Gotland's autonomy, it would be necessary to demonstrate that the agreement had been first entered into freely and not under duress, as a symbiotic relationship that did not involve Gotland relinquishing its sovereignty. Written sources for an early agreement seem unlikely and the possibility of oral sources is further discussed below. The treaty terms themselves probably relate more closely to those of the author's day than to those of 200 years or more previously and the change from the preterite to the present tense in the text might support this argument.

If the interpretation put by Wessén on the expression *fielkunnugr* is to be accepted, and Avair Strabain was skilled in 'magical' arts, this would, according to Wessén, place the treaty in the heathen period; see *SL* IV, 306 and Note to 6/9–11. Any details about it must therefore have come from oral rather than written tradition, possibly a narrative verse. There is no hint as to where the author found his story, and no other record of an *Avair*, but it is possible, one might suggest, that he had heard poetry concerning a much-respected heathen who might have acted as intermediary in such a negotiation. Schütte (1907, 83) compares Avair Strabain in *Guta saga* to a character in a tale told about Charlemagne who succeeded in getting a law agreed upon where others had failed. He suggests that this could have been a model for the episode in *Guta saga*. The man in this story later disappears without trace, as mysteriously as he appeared, but the information about Avair seems to be more circumstantial. He is given a home parish, a wife and a son, and extracts a promise of compensation should his mission miscarry. As Wessén remarks, the alliterative phrase *faigastan ok fallastan* ('doomed and ill-fated') suggests an oral tale behind the speech Avair delivers, if not behind the whole story; see *SL* IV, 306. The use of such phrases is not, of course, confined to poetry and there would be no reason for particularly assuming that a lost verse lay behind this episode, were it not for the proliferation of alliterative phrases throughout the passage, for example: *sipan sentu gutar sendimen, fikk friþ gart, gierþi fyrsti friþ.* The use of parallelism is a further indication of possible poetic origin for this part of the narrative. Similarly, the details of the actual treaty contain evidence of an oral source. Phrases such as *frir ok frelsir, hegnan ok hielp* and *stepi til sykia* may well have had their origin in verse, although they may have been in written form when used by the author of *Guta saga*, possibly as a set of legal formulae.

It is dangerous to rely on place-names to support oral traditions and there seems little doubt that names such as *Ava, Avagrunn* and *Avanäs* lack any connection with Avair, particularly as they are all on Fårö, and as the names are repeated on the Swedish mainland. A village named *Awirstadha* in the parish of Askeby, Östergötland, was mentioned in a manuscript from 1376 (designated 9/10 in Linköpings stifts- och landsbibliotek, but probably destroyed in a recent fire); see *Sveriges medeltida personnamn*, 1974– , s. v. *Aver.* Hilfeling (1994–1995, I, 184) records the existence of a *Strabeins grav* in Alva parish and provides a sketch of it, but the designation of this *kämpargrav* to Avair is, as he says, not historical. Even if it is accepted that Avair was a historical figure, which is by no means certain, firm evidence is still lacking for the dating of the treaty. One also wonders if, in the figure of Ívarr beinlauss of West Norse tradition, there is any sort of parallel to Avair Strabain. Cf. also Note to 6/4.

## O *The Visit of St Olaf*

### 1 BACKGROUND TO THE VISIT

The history of the conversion of Gotland has been extensively studied and there are several theories concerning its approximate date.[2] One of the central episodes in *Guta saga* is that concerning

---

[2] Both Ochsner (1973) and Pernler (1977) have produced detailed analyses of the evidence surrounding the conversion of Gotland to Christianity. While they both consider the role played by St Olaf to be exaggerated, Pernler rejects all suggestion of a full conversion to Christianity before the eleventh century. The fact that *Guta saga* gives an inconsistent account and chronology, however, seems to support such a possibility. First Olaf arrives and converts Ormika, then Botair, in a seemingly totally heathen community, builds two churches, which are followed by others when Gotland becomes generally Christian. Finally, after a delay, Gotland is incorporated into the see of Linköping. Ochsner (1973, 22) points to graves without grave goods dating from the eighth century as an indication of the possible commencement of conversion and this view is also put

St Olaf's visit. The story, as it is told, contradicts the explicit statement in *Heimskringla, Óláfs saga helga* (*ÍF* XXVII, 328), that Olaf travelled *um sumarit ok létti eigi, fyrr en hann kom austr í Garðaríki á fund Jarizleifs konungs ok þeira Ingigerðar dróttningar*, although Bruno Lesch (1916, 84–85) argues that Olaf did stop in Gotland on that journey and that his stay was simply unknown to Snorri. *Guta saga* does not, understandably, mention the visit in 1007, during which the twelve-year-old Olaf intimidated the Gotlanders into paying protection money and subsequently stayed the winter; see *Óláfs saga helga* (*ÍF* XXVII, 9). On that occasion he proceeded eastwards on a raid on Eysýsla (Ösel), the Estonian Saaremaa. It has been suggested that the visit described in *Guta saga* is actually the one mentioned in *Óláfs saga helga* (*ÍF* XXVII, 343), when Olaf is said to have visited Gotland on his way *home* from Russia in the spring of 1030, a view supported by Finnur Jónsson (1924, 83) as the correct one. It does not seem very likely, however, that Olaf would make a prolonged break in his journey at that time. Other sources do not mention Gotland at all in this connection (e. g. *Fagrskinna, ÍF* XXIX, 198–199), and in those that do, Olaf only seems to have stopped for news of Earl Hákon's flight and to await a favourable wind. Clearly not all the accounts of the journey to Russia can be correct and it is probably impossible to discover which, if any them, is the true one. It is, however, very likely that St Olaf visited Gotland while he was king, since a coin with his image on it was found at Klintehamn, Klinte parish, on the west coast of Gotland, and that this visit would have given rise to

---

forward by Nerman (1941a, 39–40), who argues from artefacts that have been found that there was a conversion, albeit not a complete one, in the eighth or ninth century, as a result of a missionary effort from Western Europe, followed by a reversion, such as occurred at Birka, in the tenth, and a re-introduction of Christianity in the eleventh century; cf. Stenberger, 1945, 97. Holmqvist (1975, 35–39) has also noted possible Christian motifs in early artefacts; cf. Note to 2/8. It is remarkable that neither Rimbert's biography of Ansgar nor Adam of Bremen's writings mention Gotland, which could mean that the Hamburg–Bremen mission did not take any substantial part in the conversion of Gotland; cf. Holmqvist, 1975, 39, 51, 55; Pernler, 1977, 43–44. Pernler, throughout, argues for a gradual conversion, culminating in the incorporation of Gotland into the see of Linköping, rather than a concerted mission; see Notes to 8/1–10, 8/7–8, 8/14, 8/28–29, 10/21.

traditions; cf. Dolley, 1978. The missionary visit to Gotland, if it occurred, can be placed between 1007 or 1008, when Olaf made his earlier visit, and 1030. Given the discrepancy between the accounts in *Heimskringla* and *Guta saga*, it seems unlikely that Snorri was the author's source for this episode and there is internal evidence that some sort of oral tale was the primary inspiration; see pp. xl–xli. Cf. also *SL* IV, 306–311 and references; Note to 8/4. Akergarn, in Hellvi parish, where Olaf is said to have landed, is now called S:t Olofsholm. Although the account in *Guta saga* may have originated in an early oral tradition, other traditions exist, which make it difficult to identify those which were current at the time *Guta saga* was written. For example, there is a tradition from S:t Olofsholm, recorded by Säve (1873–1874, 249), of Olaf either washing his hands or baptising the first Gotlanders he came across in a natural hollow in a rock. This hollow is still visible and is called variously *Sankt Oles tvättfat* and *Sankt Oläs vaskefat*; see *Gotländska sägner* 1959–1961, II, 391; Palmenfelt, 1979, 116–118; *Sveriges Kyrkor: Got(t)land*, 1914–1975, II, 129. Tradition further holds that there is always water in the hollow, but such tales are common in relation to famous historical figures.

Strelow (1633, 129–132) includes a number of elements in his account of St Olaf's visit that in all probability had their origins later than *Guta saga*. He mentions (1633, 132) the apparent existence at Kyrkebys, in the parish of Hejnum, of a large, two-storey, stone house, called *Sankt Oles hus*, in which Olaf's bed, chair and hand basin (*Haandfad*), set in the wall, could be seen. According to Wallin (1747–1776, I, 1035) these were still visible in the eighteenth century, although Säve (1873–1874, 249–250) admits that by the nineteenth century the original building was no longer there, the stone having been used for out-buildings. Wallin also says in the same context that for a long time one of Olaf's silver bowls, his battle-axe and three large keys could be found, but this contention is in all probability secondary to *Guta saga*. Of the wall-set hand basin mentioned by Wallin, Säve (1873–1874, 250) says that what was intended was probably a vessel for holy water but that the object that was referred to in his time was a large limestone block with a round hollow in it, which was much more likely to have been an ancient millstone.

On the west coast of Fårö, south of Lauter, there is also a *S:t Olavs kyrka* and there was a tradition amongst the local population, recorded by Säve (1873–1874, 252), that Olaf landed near there, at Gamlehamn (Gambla hamn). This is now shut off from the sea by a natural wall of stones, boulders and gravel. The stone includes *gråsten,* which is not otherwise found in the area, and which Olaf is said to have brought with him. Some 70 metres south of the harbour, Säve continues, there was a nearly circular flattened low dry-stone wall surrounding *Sant Äulos körka,* or a remnant of it. The church-shaped wall was still visible with what could have been the altar end pointing more or less eastwards and human remains in the north of the enclosure. Fifty metres to the east and up a slope was, according to Säve, *Sant Äulos källda,* which is also said never to dry up, and which was traditionally said to have been used to baptise the first heathens Olaf encountered. Nearby on the beach are two abandoned springs, *Sant Äulos brunnar.* They are about two metres apart and the saint is said to have been able to lie with a hand in each, which feat put an end to a severe drought; see Säve, 1873–1874, 253, after Wallin. A further addition to this folklore is the mention of a hollow in the chalk cliff a little to the north of this area, about 1.8 × 0.9 metres, called *Sant Äulos säng.* Säve saw all these features and discussed them with the local people. They are considered by Fritzell (1972, 40) to be related to a heathen cult associated with a local spring, which has a depression resembling a bed or a bath.

There is no mention in *Guta saga* of any of these traditions, and it seems probable that they are later inventions to give, in W. S. Gilbert's words, 'artistic verisimilitude to an otherwise bald and unconvincing narrative'. The wealth of tradition on Fårö, as recorded by Säve, and the fact that the more natural landing-site for Olaf would be on the west coast if he were coming *from* Norway as *Guta saga* states, could mean, however, that he did at some time land in Gotland and effect a number of conversions.

Strelow (1633, 131) carries an altogether more violent version of the conversion and gives an account of a battle at a place he calls Lackerhede (Laikarehaid in the parish of Lärbro, about 10 kilometres north-west of S:t Olofsholm), which resulted in the acceptance of Christianity by the Gotlanders. This account has been generally rejected by scholars, and was certainly not a tradition that the author of *Guta saga* used, although Säve (1873–1874, 248) suggests that Olaf might have applied some force to convert a small number of the islanders on his way eastwards. The legend could, as Pernler (1977, 14–15) suggests, have arisen through confusion with the battle between the Gotlanders and Birger Magnusson at Röcklingebacke, both sites being just east of Lärbro parish church. Many of the details mentioned, such as the existence of the iron ring to which Olaf was said to have tied up his ship, are clearly not factual; cf. Strelow, 1633, 130.

The greatest mystery surrounding the missionary visit relates to the fact that nowhere in the mainstream of the Olaf legend is the conversion of so important a trading state as Gotland mentioned, either in Snorri or elsewhere. This seems strange, if Olaf did in fact convert Gotland, and points to the episode in *Guta saga* being the product of local tradition, centred around a number of place-names and other features, as well as the likelihood that Olaf did actually visit Gotland at least once, if not twice, and that he was taken as Gotland's patron saint. The importance of St Olaf to the medieval Gotlanders is emphasised by their dedicating their church in Novgorod to his name. There is also a suggestion that the church laws in *Guta lag* resemble those of Norway and that they could have been formulated under the direct or indirect influence of St Olaf; cf. *SL* IV, 310.

## 2 ORMIKA'S GIFTS

The motif of important leaders who start as adversaries exchanging gifts when their relationship changes is a common one, but it is worth noting the iconographical connection between the *braipyx* and *bulli* and St Olaf, and the fact that the author of *Guta saga* must have seen images of the saint with just those objects. The description of the exchange of gifts between Olaf and Ormika of Hejnum raises the possibility of one or a pair of drinking vessels and/or a battle-axe being extant at some time, which the author was led to believe had some connection with this incident. Perhaps he, or someone known to him, had seen a bowl of the type called a *bulli*, which was said to have been a gift from St Olaf to a Gotlander on the occasion of his acceptance of Christianity. One of St Olaf's attributes, which he is depicted as carrying in some images, is a ciborium (the lidded bowl in which the communion host is carried). Nils Tiberg (1946, 23) interprets the *bulli* as just such a covered vessel, and Per Gjærder (*KL*, s. v. *Drikkekar*) states that the *bolli* type of drinking-bowl not only had a pronounced foot but was sometimes furnished with a lid. Such a vessel could have been in the possession of the chapel at Akergarn and have been associated with St Olaf's visit. The *braipyx* is the other attribute of St Olaf and it would be even more natural that a connection should be made between St Olaf and such a weapon. Perhaps one was kept in the church at Akergarn at the time the author wrote the text, and he linked the building to an earlier chapel on the site, one said to have been built by Ormika. There might also have been a tradition that a man named Ormika travelled the 20 kilometres from his home south of Tingstäde träsk to meet St Olaf, some considerable time after he had landed, at the request of the people of his district. The fusing of the two traditions then produced the version of events that survives. The interpretation of the name Ormika as a feminine form, which led Strelow (1633, 132) to represent the character as female, is almost certainly incorrect. It is possible that the Gotlandic pronunciation of the feminine personal pronoun, which is more like that of the masculine than on the Swedish mainland, combined with the -*a* ending, led to confusion, particularly if the story had been transmitted orally.

In the light of *Heimskringla*, however, another interpretation can be put on the Ormika episode: the mention of the giving by Ormika of 12 wethers 'and other costly items' to Olaf could possibly be regarded as the payment of some sort of tribute, as described by Snorri. It might be that the tradition that protection money was paid to Olaf at one time or another was combined with a tradition that he occasionally offered gifts in return, perhaps merely as a pledge of good faith. A gift of sheep would no doubt be a natural one from a Gotlander, but equally sheep have been a substitute for money in many societies, ancient coins being marked with the image of a sheep. Fritzell (1972, 30) points out that the number 12 is associated with taxes extracted by the Danes in the Viking period. It may also be linked to the 12 *hundari* proposed by Hyenstrand (1989, 119). The name *Ormika* occurs in an inscription found at Timans in the parish of Roma; see Note to 8/3.

### 3 THE ORATORY AT AKERGARN

According to *Guta saga* Ormika *gierþi sir bynahus i sama staþ, sum nu standr Akrgarna kirkia.* A chapel was certainly in existence at Akergarn by the thirteenth century, since it is mentioned in several letters from bishops of Linköping; see Note to 8/9. It was in ruins by the seventeenth century but had by that time become the centre for a number of traditions about St Olaf to be found in contemporary folklore, and in Strelow's description of the conversion of Gotland; see *SL* IV, 308, 311; *Sveriges Kyrkor: Got(t)land,* 1914–1975, II, 128–130.

## P *Church building*

### 1 BOTAIR AND LIKKAIR

There is in *Guta saga* what might be considered to be an alternative account of the conversion, not involving St Olaf and Ormika, but Botair and his father-in-law, Likkair. In this version, Gotlandic merchants come into contact with the Christian religion as a result of their trading voyages, and some are converted. This intercourse has been dated to the tenth century, that is before St Olaf's first visit to Gotland; cf. *SL* IV, 312. Priests are brought back to Gotland to serve these converts and Botair of Akebäck is said to have had the first church built, at Kulstäde. According to tradition, the foundations of the church can still be discerned, lying SW–NE and with dimensions of 30 metres by 12 metres; see Pernler, 1977, 20 and references. This identification was called into question as early as 1801 by C. G. G. Hilfeling (1994–1995, II, 145–146) who considers the remains to be comparable to that of a so-called *kämpargrav,* and this opinion is to a certain extent supported by Fritzell (1974, 14–16), on account of the generous dimensions and the existence of a door in the west gable. Fritzell maintains that Kulstäde *was* the site of the church mentioned in *Guta saga,* but that it was also a cult site prior to this. Pernler, however (1977, 20), and with some justification, is wary of making such an assumption, when there is no evidence of the actual date of the event described. Together with Gustavson (1938, 20), he suggests that the church-building story could have its basis in a place-name saga. If this were the case, it is possible that the saga formed the basis of the account in *Guta saga.*

Botair builds another church near Vi, just when his heathen countrymen are having a sacrifice there. Gustavson (1938, 36) cites Lithberg as saying that no place of sacrifice existed near Visby and that the passage in *Guta saga* is based on folk-etymology. Although Hellquist, despite his earlier doubts (1918, 69 note), noted by Knudsen (1933, 34), accepts the traditional view and dismisses other interpretations, it may still be disputed whether the name *Visby* was connected with the existence of a pagan holy site or *vi* in the area. It is possible that the author of *Guta saga* had heard a tradition about the building of the first church that was allowed to

stand in Gotland and placed it, not unnaturally, in the neighbourhood of Visby; see Hellquist, 1980, s. v. *Vi*; 1929–1932, 673. This
argument seems defensible, despite Olsson's assertion (1984, 20)
that it 'förefaller inte särskilt troligt, att författaren skulle ha diktat
ihop dessa uppgifter, inspirerad av namnet *Visby*'. The idea that the
first Christian church that was allowed to stand should have been
built on the site of a pagan holy place has not been universally
accepted and, in his study of *stafgarþr* place-names, Olsson (1976,
115, note 58; 121) specifically rejects the link between cult places
and the later building of churches. In an earlier thesis (1966, 131–
133, 237–238, 275) based largely on sites in Denmark, Olaf Olsen
came to the conclusion that great care must be taken in assuming
a continuity in the use of sites for burial from the Bronze Age
through the Viking Age, particularly when based on place-names,
but that in certain cases, the church at Gamla Uppsala for example,
there might have been a transition from immediately pre-Christian
to Christian use; cf. Foote and Wilson, 1979, 417–418; Lindqvist,
1967, 236. There are, however, several examples of churches being
built on the sites of Stone-Age and Bronze-Age barrows. These
barrows might have been used by Viking-Age pagans as cult sites
(rather in the way that *stafgarþar* were possibly used), but when
churches were built there, it could have been the fact that they were
situated on high ground that led to the choice of site, rather than
any other reason; cf. Olsen, 1966, 274–275. Considerable rebuilding has taken place on the site of the churches of S:t Hans and
S:t Per in Visby and it is possible that some remains (graves,
for example) carried a tradition of there having been an older
church there; see Notes to 8/27 and 8/28. Any wooden church
would of course long since have disappeared and Wessén (*SL* IV,
312) suggests that it would probably have dated from a period prior
to the foundation of Visby itself. Cf. also Notes to 8/18 and
8/25–26.

   The story in *Guta saga* of Likkair, and his success in saving both
his son-in-law and his church, contains certain inconsistencies.
The reason he gives to the heathens that they should not burn this
edifice is that it is in *Vi*, presumably a heathen holy place. This
would not seem to be a very plausible reason to give, and to be
even less likely for the heathens to accept; cf. Note to 8/18. The
fact that the church is said to be dedicated to All Saints, whereas
the church present in the author's day, of which part of a wall is

still visible as a ruin, incorporated into S:t Hans's ruin, was called
S:t Pers also suggests that there may have been a half-understood
tradition, perhaps not related to Visby at all. It is possible, however, that the place-name *Kulasteþar* gave rise to oral tradition
about the building of a church there, which was reduced to char-
coal, and that *Stainkirchia* relates to a later stone church of a more
permanent nature. Botair's second church was also obviously wooden,
since it was threatened with the same fate as the first. Likkair
seems to have been a local hero, and there are other tales about
him; see Notes to 8/22 and 8/23. Conversion stories tend naturally
to be told about people who are presented as having the respect of
both the converted and heathen communities. Another example of
this is Þorgeirr Ljósvetningagoði in *Njáls saga* (ch. 105; *ÍF* XII,
270–272). Likkair's soubriquet, *snielli*, is reminiscent of those
given to wise counsellors in the Icelandic sagas and he may have
been the equivalent of a *goði*, since he is said to have had 'most
authority' at that time.

There appear to be no place-names that might have suggested the
name *Botair* to the author and although the farm name *Lickedarve*
from Fleringe parish in the north-east of Gotland could be connected with someone called Likkair, he might not be the character
referred to in the story; cf. Olsson, 1984, 41, 131 and Note to 8/22.
In the churchyard of Stenkyrka church, however, there is an impressive slab which is known as *Liknatius gravsten*; see Hyenstrand,
1989, 129. It might indicate a medieval tradition connecting Likkair
to Stenkyrka. There is at least one other tale, certainly secondary
to *Guta saga*, told about Likkair Snielli, and several place-names
(e. g. *Lickershamn*, a harbour in the parish of Stenkyrka on the
north west coast of Gotland) are said to be associated with him.
The folk-tale, recorded by Johan Nihlén in 1929, concerns Likkair's
daughter and the foreign captive, son of his defeated opponent,
whom he brought home as a slave. The daughter falls in love with
the foreigner and Likkair is violently opposed to the relationship,
not least because the young man is a Christian, and he has already
lost one of his daughters (Botair's wife) to the new faith. He has his
daughter lifted up to the top of a high cliff and the prisoner is told
that if he can climb up and retrieve her, he will be given her hand,
otherwise he will be killed. The young man manages the climb, but
as he comes down with the girl in his arms, Likkair shoots him with
an arrow and they both fall into the sea. At Lickershamn there is

a cliff called *Jungfrun* which is said to be the one from which the lovers fell; see Nihlén, 1975, 102–104. Wallin records a different tale in connection with this rock, however, relating it to a powerful and rich maiden called *Lickers smällä*, said to have built the church at Stenkyrka; see *Gotländska sägner,* 1959–1961, II, 386. Lickershamn is about five kilometres north-west of Stenkyrka itself but, although it is tempting to regard this as suggestive of a connection between Stenkyrka and Likkair, it is probable that the name of the coastal settlement is secondary to the tradition and of a considerably later origin than the parish name.

2 OTHER CHURCHES

Church building is one of the categories of tale that Schütte (1907, 87) mentions as occurring in ancient law texts, forming part of the legendary history that is often present as an introduction. In *Guta saga* churches are assigned to the three divisions of the country, followed by others 'for greater convenience'. The three division churches were clearly meant to replace the three centres of sacrifice and in fact were not the first three churches built. (The one built by Botair in Vi was the first to be allowed to stand, we are told.) There could well have been some oral tradition behind this episode, linked to the division of the island, and it is hard to believe that everything would have happened so tidily in reality. As no bishops have been mentioned at this stage, it is difficult to understand who could have consecrated these churches, and it seems more likely that they started off as personal devotional chapels, commissioned by wealthy converts such as Likkair. There are no authenticated remains of churches from the eleventh century, but there were certainly some extant in the thirteenth century when *Guta saga* was written. The tradition of rich islanders building churches, and the relatively high number of those churches (97) highlights the wealth of medieval Gotland; cf. *SL* IV, 313.

   Church-building stories form an important part of early Christian literature and there is often a failed attempt (sometimes more than one) to build a church followed by a successful enterprise at a different site; cf. *KL*, s. v. *Kyrkobyggnassägner* and references. The combination of these motifs with a possible oral tradition, and the placing of the three *treding* churches, has been built by the author into a circumstantial narrative, which to some extent conflicts with the Olaf episode in accounting for the conversion of Gotland.

So far the possible sources discussed have been in the nature of oral traditions or literary parallels as models. The remainder of *Guta saga* is of a more historical character and the suggested sources for these sections tend to be in the form of legal or ecclesiastical records, even if in oral form.

## Q *Conversion of Gotland as a whole*

Within the description of the early church-building activity is a short statement concerning the acceptance of Christianity by the Gotlanders in general. It is reminiscent of the passage describing the subjugation to the Swedish throne. The one states that *gingu gutar sielfs viliandi undir suia kunung,* the other that the Gotlanders *toku þa almennilika viþr kristindomi miþ sielfs vilia sinum utan þuang.* The similarity leads one to presume that a written or oral model lies behind both, particularly as the statements differ in style from the surrounding narrative. The models do not, however, appear to have survived.

## R *Ecclesiastical arrangements*

### 1 TRAVELLING BISHOPS

The formula for the acceptance of Christianity mentioned above appears to come out of sequence in the text since the next episode, that of the travelling bishops, apparently takes place before the general conversion. If, as has been suggested, the author was a cleric, he might have felt it necessary to legitimise Gotland's early churches by inserting a tradition, of which he had few details, to explain the consecration issue. Gotland was a stepping-stone on the eastwards route as described in the Notes to 4/6, 8/10 and 10/16 and it would be more than likely that travelling bishops stopped there. If so, they might have been unorthodox, of the type mentioned in *Hungrvaka* (1938, 77). Wessén (*SL* IV, 318) suggests that the importance of Gotland as a staging post might have emerged at the same time as its trading importance, in the twelfth century. The consecration of priests is not mentioned, but there would be little point in having hallowed churches and churchyards if there were no priests to say holy office in the churches or bury the dead in the churchyards. The priests whom the Gotlanders brought back with them from their travels would hardly be sufficient to satisfy a growing Christian community, however. The obvious explanations

for the omission are, either that the author did not know and had
no available source to help him, or did not think it of importance.
The possibility of there having been a resident bishop on Gotland in
the Middle Ages is discussed by Pernler (1977, 46–56), but he reaches
the conclusion that there is no evidence to support such an idea.

## 2 ARRANGEMENTS WITH THE SEE OF LINKÖPING

The formal arrangements made with the see of Linköping read like
a more or less direct copy of an agreement drawn up at the time.
There is a considerable amount of contemporary corroboration for
the arrangements, including a letter dated around 1221 from Archbishop Andreas Suneson of Lund and Bishops Karl and Bengt of
Linköping; cf. *DS* I, 690, no. 832; *SL* IV, 313–314. The letter
enables one to interpret more accurately the Gutnish text. Again,
the author of *Guta saga* lays emphasis on the voluntary nature of
the arrangement, a stress probably intended to demonstrate Gotland's
effective independence from the Swedish crown. The fact that the
financial arrangements between the Gotlanders and the bishop of
Linköping were relatively lenient to the former, in comparison to
those with other communities in the same see, seems to support the
author's claim; cf. Schück, 1945, 184. The actual dating of the
incorporation of Gotland into the see of Linköping is less certain,
but could not be much earlier than the middle of the twelfth
century. The manuscript Codex Laur. Ashburnham (*c.*1120) names
both Gotland and 'Liunga. Kaupinga', but there is some doubt as
to whether the latter refers to Linköping at all; cf. Delisle, 1886,
75; *DS, Appendix* 1, 3, no. 4; Envall, 1950, 81–93; 1956, 372–385;
Gallén, 1958, 6, 13–15. It seems probable that Gotland was incorporated into the see in the second half of the twelfth century,
during the time of Bishop Gisle, but there is no direct evidence of
the date, or of the relationship between this event and the absorption of Gotland into the Swedish kingdom; cf. Pernler, 1977, 65.
Bishop Gisle, in collaboration with King Sverker the Elder and his
wife, introduced the Cistercian order into Sweden. The Cistercian
monastery of the Beata Maria de Gutnalia at Roma was instituted,
although by whom is not known, on September 9th, 1164 as a
daughter house to Nydala in Småland; cf. Pernler, 1977, 57, 61–62;
*SL* IV, 306 and references; Note to 6/21–22. It seems possible that
Gisle was behind the foundation, and that Gotland had by that time
been included into the see of Linköping. It is not certain that Gisle

was the first bishop of the see, but there is no other contrary evidence than a list of bishops, dating from the end of the fourteenth century and held in Uppsala University library. This list mentions two earlier bishops (Herbertus and Rykardus) but nothing further is known of them; see Schück, 1959, 47–49; Pernler, 1977, 58; *SRS* III, 102–103, no. 5; 324, no. 15.

## S *Levy arrangements*

The establishment of an obligation to supply troops and ships to the Swedish crown and the levy terms associated with this obligation have been dated by Rydberg (*STFM* I, 71) to around 1150, but placed rather later by Yrwing (1940, 58–59). Once again, contemporary letters corroborate to a large degree the content of *Guta saga* in respect of this material. Despite several protestations within *Guta saga* of the independence of Gotland from foreign domination, the other statutes mentioned at the end of the text suggest that this independence was being slowly eroded, and that Gotland was gradually becoming a province of Sweden. The *ledung* was mainly called out for crusades against the Baltic countries, and there are several contemporary sources recording these expeditions and the reaction of the Gotlanders to the summons; see Notes to 12/23. Wessén points out (*SL* IV, 319) that Magnus Ladulås in 1285 established a different arrangement, according to which a tax was payable annually, rather than merely as a fine for failing to supply the stipulated ships when they were summoned; cf. *DS* I, 671–672, no. 815; *STFM* I, 290–291, no. 141. Wessén and other scholars use the fact that the author of *Guta saga* does not seem aware of this change to postulate that he must have been writing before 1285; see below, pp. l–lii.

## T *Relationship with the King*

The final sentences of the text, concerning the Gotlanders' obligations in the event of a *coup d'état*, and the necessity for all communication on the king's business to be sealed, have a disconnected character. They are most probably quotations from edicts issued in response to contemporary events and the sentence regarding the retention of tax provides a possible *terminus post quem* for the text as a whole, when considered in relation to events in Sweden, and give some hint as to the intention of the author, both of which aspects are discussed below, pp. l–liii.

## (vi) *Date and place of composition*

When attempting the dating of a written work there are several factors to be considered. The following might give a *terminus ante quem*: the date of the oldest preserved manuscript; mention of the work in question in another work, if the second work can be dated more accurately; negative evidence in the form of a lack of knowledge of certain facts or events exhibited in the work. The following might be used to give a *terminus post quem*: direct or indirect reference within the work itself to events that can be dated; quotations from other works for which a date of composition is known with some certainty; external events that may have triggered the writing of the work and could provide a likely date range. Finally, the palaeographic and linguistic evidence of the text in the manuscript could point to a date range by comparison with works of a known date, although this must be treated with caution.

Scholars in general agree with Schlyter (*CIG*, i) when he dates the manuscript B64 to the early to middle of the fourteenth century, and this can therefore be taken as a starting-point for a *terminus ante quem* for *Guta saga*. The mention of St Olaf dates *Guta saga* to at least as late as 1030 and the account of the church-building and the arrangements concerning the bishop of Linköping advance that by a further century or so, since the first recorded bishop was Gisle, who took office in 1139. This gives a *terminus post quem* of circa 1140 for the saga's composition.

The first serious attempt at dating *Guta saga* was made by Schlyter (*CIG*, ix). He argues on the basis of the short passage concerning the action to be taken regarding the taxes in the event of a king being driven out of Sweden, that it be withheld for three years, but then paid in full, maintaining that this refers to Birger Magnusson who fled to Gotland in 1318; see above, p. ix.

Säve questions this theory on the basis that the passage in question has the appearance of being a later addition. He does not, however, offer an alternative dating, although he dates *Guta lag* to the late twelfth or early thirteenth century (*GU*, ix–x).

Läffler (1908–1909, Part 1, 161) does not think that the passage is a later addition. He notes that Schlyter's opinion has been supported (1908–1909, Part 1, 137–138), but argues that, since Birger was still within his own realm, and in all probability received funds for his military expeditions, the withholding of tax could not apply to that incident, particularly in view of the letter from King Magnus in 1320 cancelling the increase in taxation; cf. *DS* III, 473–475, no. 2255. Läffler (1908–1909, Part 1, 145) discusses the possibility that the reference to a deposed and exiled king refers to Sverker Karlsson, who was defeated at the Battle of Lena in 1208, the year after Archbishop Andreas Suneson visited Gotland, and was succeeded by Erik Knutsson. He concludes that this is the most probable explanation, since three years passed between the Battle of Lena and Sverker's death. In connection with the fact that *Guta saga* refers specifically to a *crowned* king, whereas there is no documentary evidence of Sverker's having been crowned, he suggests that the crowning could be inferred from papal letters (1908–1909, Part 1, 149; Part 2, 125).

Läffler sets the *terminus ante quem* as 1226, the date of a letter from the papal legate, William of Modena, in which he confirms visitation arrangements between Gotland and the bishop of Linköping (1908–1909, Part 1, 162). He does not think that the relevant passage in *Guta saga* can be a translation of the letter from Archbishop Suneson (dated 1220–1223), as Schlyter (*CIG*, vi, note 28) maintains, since it contains details not to be found there. Läffler (1908–1909, Part 1, 165–167) also rejects the idea that the Latin text could be a translation of the Gutnish. As further support for his dating, Läffler (1908–1909, Part 1, 142) points out that the new levy agreement between Magnus Birgersson and the Gotlanders, drawn up in 1285, is not mentioned. He concludes (1908–1909, Part 1, 167; Part 2, 123) that *Guta saga* was composed on Archbishop Suneson's suggestion, shortly after 1220.

The omission of any mention of the new levy arrangements is also noted by Pipping (*GLGS*, ii–iii), Jacobsen (*GGD*, 123), and Yrwing (1940, 51–52), although the last does not think that the date Läffler proposes as a *terminus ante quem* is any more than a possibility. Both Wessén (*KL*, s. v. *Gutasagan*) and Yrwing (1978, 19) repeat these views a number of years later and other authors, for example Schück (1959, 265), have supported their conclusions. Although Rolf Pipping (1943, 67) proposes a date of composition of circa 1318, he concedes that the traditions *Guta saga* contains are older.

Since the two manuscripts of *Guta lag* (in Gutnish and Low German), to which the complete texts of *Guta saga* are appended, give us, according to Wessén (*LG*, xxxii), two traditions independent of each other, it may be assumed that there are at least three independent traditions of *Guta saga*, since one more is represented by the range of partial texts; see above, pp. xii–xiii. The existence of this last tradition would indicate that the work had a separate history from *Guta lag*. But is *Guta saga* a 'natural complement to the law' and thus written down not long after the former, as Wessén (*LG*, xxxiv) claims? Wessén states that the text must be later than *Guta lag*, but offers no evidence for this assertion. He also deems that it must be earlier than 1285, since the author seems unaware of the changes to the levy laws made by Magnus Birgersson (*SL* IV, 297), but places it *after* certain letters by Archbishop Andreas Suneson (*SL* IV, 313–315), concluding that it was probably written around 1220, on Suneson's inspiration. He bases this on the arguments put forward by Läffler noted above, and proceeds to use this to date *Guta lag*, which he also places around 1220 (*SL* IV, lxxii), although he quotes from letters by Archbishop Suneson that indicate that the law was *not* written down before about 1220, but was codified subsequently, as a result of his own encouragement and admonition. A study by Skov (1946, 114–116), comes to the conclusion that Suneson was instrumental in the codification of the law of Gotland and that it occurred at some time after 1220 but before 1223 when the archbishop resigned his position.

More recently, Elsa Sjöholm (1976, 94) has out forward alternative arguments for a considerably later dating. She dismisses the earlier dating adhered to by Wessén and others as a regression, and continues by maintaining that Andreas Suneson was probably *not* involved in the codification of *Guta lag*. She also postulates that *Guta saga* very probably had Latin models for substantial parts of its early material (1976, 99–100, 102). She further rejects Yrwing's argument for a dating of *Guta saga* prior to 1285 on the basis of the change in the *laiþingslami* contained in the letter from Magnus Birgersson. Her argument is that, for Yrwing's interpretation to be correct, the letter of 1285 would have to differentiate fundamentally between a compulsory levy and a previous voluntary one, whereas she reads it merely as a difference of emphasis, in that the Gotlanders still have the right to remain at home if they need to defend the island. Accordingly, there is nothing in either *Guta saga* or the letter that would prevent the former from being later than the latter. She maintains that the sources from 1320 give no evidence that would conflict with the taxation and levy arrangements described in *Guta saga*, and that 1285 cannot therefore be used as a *terminus ante quem* (1976, 104–105). In 1320 Magnus Eriksson removed the increases in tribute which Birger Magnusson had imposed in 1313, but the sources do not mention the *laiþingslami,* which Sjöholm therefore argues must have been paid as normal. She claims that *Guta saga* was written with the purpose of supporting Gotland's claim to independence in the face of Birger Magnusson's tax increases (1976, 105–110).

This opinion has not been discussed by any later writers, e. g. Yrwing (1978) and Mitchell (1984, 151), although the latter refers to the other two main opinions as represented by Läffler and Yrwing, nor is it mentioned in, for example, either *Medieval Scandinavia* (1993, s. v. *Guta saga*) or *National encyklopedin* (1989–1996, s. v. *Gutasagan*). Only in a review by Ole Fenger (1979, 117) is any mention made of Sjöholm's arguments. Fenger, in passing, appears to accept them, but without any reference to the counter-opinions, or giving a reason for the endorsement other than that they appear reasonable.

As far as is known, *Guta saga* is not mentioned in any work that is earlier than the manuscript in which it first appears, although it is referred to in fifteenth-century sources; hence there is no external information available concerning its date. On the other hand, the fact that *Guta saga* does not form part of AM 54 4to cannot be used to argue that it was composed after the exemplar that Bilefeld used to create that copy; cf. *GLGS,* xviii.

One further piece of evidence that can be put forward to suggest a relatively early date of composition is the fact that the *jarl* is referred to several times. In 1275 the position of *jarl* was replaced by that of *sveahertig* and it seems unlikely that, if that date were long passed, the author would have used the outmoded term to describe the king's right-hand man. The period at the start of the reign of Magnus Birgersson seems to have been a time of great fluctuation in the relationship between Gotland and the Swedish crown and would thus be a natural time for the production of a short history to assert the independence and rights of the Gotlanders. In 1288 the civil war between Visby and the rest of the islanders led to further changes, including a promise by the citizens of Visby not to act without the king's permission, but there is nothing in *Guta saga,* apart from the passing reference to the king's oath, to indicate that it post-dates the war; cf. *STFM* I, 300–303, no. 144 and Note to 14/22–23. It thus seems reasonable to propose a *terminus ante quem* for the composition of *Guta saga* of 1275 or very shortly thereafter, with a *terminus post quem* of 1220 as agreed by the majority of scholars. The place of composition of *Guta saga* is less open to debate. It seems fairly clear that it was composed and first written down in Gotland, and in the Gutnish in which it survives. There is internal evidence in two places for the first of these assumptions:

Þair sendibuþar aigu friþ lysa gutum alla steþi til sykia yfir haf, sum Upsala kunungi til hoyrir, ok so þair, sum þan vegin aigu hinget sykia. (6/22–25)

and

Kunnu hetningar eþa dailumal varþa, sum biskupi til hoyra at retta, þa a hier biþa biskups quemdar ok ai yfir fara, utan þuang reki til ok mikil synd sei, et ai ma proastr loysa. (12/14–17)

It seems probable from these two passages that the author was in Gotland at the time of writing, even if he were not a Gotlander himself. Argument has been put forward by Pipping (*GLGS*, iv) that the text was originally a Latin one, translated and augmented into the form in which we have it. Despite the fact that some of the phrases used resemble Latin constructions, for instance, the 'dative absolute' in *siþan gangnum manaþi* (4/10), the balance of probability is surely against this, and it is much more likely that a text with the pro-Gotlandic bias that *Guta saga* exhibits would have been conceived and written in Gutnish from the outset, albeit influenced by Latin written sources; cf. Läffler, 1908–1909, Part 1, 177.

### (vii) *Authorship and circumstances of authorship*

It is not possible to say who the author of *Guta saga* was, and no suggestions have been made in this respect. The supposition that he was a cleric is not without attraction, in view of the detailed account of the rights and duties of the bishop of Linköping, and the generally pious sentiment; cf. *SL* IV, 297. Certain elements of the earlier narrative, such as the description of pilgrims consecrating churches and the building of the first *treding* churches, also indicate a clerical interest. If, as has been suggested, the work was written at the instigation of Andreas Suneson, it would also be natural that a priest should have undertaken the task. There is nothing in the text that contradicts such a general assumption and in want of other evidence it seems the most likely authorship.

### (viii) *Value as a source of history*

There are two aspects to the historical value of an old text. First, there is the value of the content of the text as factual information about the period it is supposedly describing, and secondly there is the incidental value of the text as information about the period in which it was most probably composed. In the first instance, we are poorly placed to make anything other than a very tentative judgement in the case of *Guta saga*, since the existence of supporting evidence is not to be expected. In the second instance we must be careful to avoid circular arguments of the type: 'This text is assumed to have been written at this time. Such a thing is known to have happened at this time, therefore this text must have been written as a reaction to this thing, and was thus written at this time.' That is not to say, however, that no conclusions can be drawn about the historical events at the time of composition, or about what the Scandinavians, borrowing from German, call the *tendens* behind it.

Taking the simple story-line presented in *Guta saga,* it is possible to dismiss considerable sections of it as clearly unhistorical or legendary in character. Such elements have been discussed in detail in connection with the sources and the details need not be rehearsed here. It is with the Avair Strabain episode that the author moves nearer to the description of a historical event. Arguments have been presented above (pp. xxxiii–xxxvi) about the dating of the apparently voluntary treaty with Sweden; cf. *SL* IV, 304–306. From the early medieval arrangements between the central administration and other Swedish districts, it seems possible that some sort of loose and symbiotic union was entered into at a time preceding the composition of *Guta saga*, which gradually involved more commitment from Gotland to Sweden in terms of tax; cf. Tunberg, 1940, 106–107. The inclusion of a description of the earliest treaty is triggered by the need to stress the original independence of the Gotlanders in the face of ever more intrusion by the Swedish crown.

The second event presented as historical is the arrival of St Olaf on the island. There is no serious dispute about the suggestion that he actually did visit Gotland at least once, but there is much discussion about how many times, for how long, with what result, and which of his supposed visits is intended to be represented here. The actions described (exchanges of gifts, agreement by a local representative to baptism, building of a chapel) suggest more the buying-off and placating of a harrying warlord than at the submission to a concerted and overtly peaceful missionary attempt. Ormika's name may only have been a useful peg on which to hang the conversion story, like Avair Strabain's in the previous episode. It would be more convincing historically if either the conversion of Gotland were mentioned elsewhere in the St Olaf hagiography, or the author had not given a slightly different version of the introduction of Christianity almost immediately afterwards, involving Botair and his father-in-law Likkair. Once again, there seems to be a *tendens* behind this: Gotlanders were converted of their own volition and no one forced them. This has parallels in the conversion of Iceland as told in *Íslendingabók* (*ÍF* I, 14–18). Olaf comes to the Gotlanders as an exile, not as the Church Militant, and his influence is limited to a personal conversion (of Ormika), which had no immediate effect elsewhere on the island.

The historicity of the church-building that is said to have immediately preceded and followed Likkair's conversion does not allow of proof either way. The first churches were no doubt of wood and there are no remains of so old a church at Stenkyrka. What is interesting is the description of what existed in the author's day. S:t Per's church in Visby is reduced to just a small section of wall absorbed into the later S:t Hans's church. Of other, older, churches in Visby there is no sign. This raises the possibility that the author was attached in some way to S:t Per's church and was anxious to further its claim to be on the site of the oldest church that was allowed to stand on the island. The placing of the next few churches so conveniently in the three 'thirds' of the island says, one imagines, more about the administrative arrangements at the time of the composition of *Guta saga* than about any known building activities in the eleventh century.

The passage leading up to and covering the absorption of the island into the see of Linköping is reminiscent of the earlier passage describing the treaty with the king of Sweden: various bishops take a hand in Gotland's ecclesiastical affairs, but the islanders finally select for themselves the bishop whose authority they will accept. It may not reflect the historical course of events. The final effect was a historical one, well-documented and indisputable, but its execution might in actual fact have demonstrated less well the independence of the Gotlanders. What does have a historical basis, since there is a episcopal letter to support it, is the description of the actual arrangements for the bishop's visitations. Here, however, the text in *Guta saga* provides little additional historical information.

The following passage, setting out the levy obligations of the Gotlanders with respect to the Swedish king, is of a similar nature to that covering the relationship with the bishop, much of the evidence being available elsewhere, in letters, and it is thus of no independent value as a historical source.

The final sentences have been discussed in connection with the dating of *Guta saga* and their value historically can only be seen in relation to this; see above, pp. l–lii.

To summarise: there is a relative paucity of solid historical material in *Guta saga* as regards the events of the period it purports to describe. Where the attitude and needs of the author are concerned, we get a little more information, but this is largely by induction, based on our knowledge of the events at or around the time we deduce him to have lived, and hence these surmises are subject to the very caveat mentioned at the start of this section. The final verdict on the historical value of *Guta saga* must be that there is none proven.

### (ix) *Language*

Comments on some individual aspects of the language and of the current translation appear in the Notes. Pipping (*GLGS*, xxiii–cxiv) has presented a detailed analysis of the language and forms of both *Guta lag* and *Guta saga*, and there are further studies, notably those by Söderberg (1879) and Gustavson (1940–1948). Gustavson (1940–1948, I, vii) argues that there is a case for regarding Gutnish as a separate language alongside Old Swedish, Old Danish, Old Norwegian and Old Icelandic. The noticeable features of Gutnish in comparison to Old Swedish are: (a) the presence of diphthongs, retained where Old Swedish lacks them (*hoyra*); (b) the fronting and rounding of certain vowels in particular positions (*dyma*, cf. Swedish *döma*); (c) the retention of Common Norse short *u* where Old Swedish has short *o* (*gutar*, *fulk*); (d) more instances of *i*-umlaut than in other Scandinavian languages (*segþi*, cf. Old Icelandic *sagði*); (e) the lack of breaking in certain instances (although there are no examples given from *Guta saga*). The case system is conservative and there are particular forms, such as the genitive singular of weak feminine nouns (e. g. *kuna*, gen. *kunur*) and the pronouns (*hann*, 'he', *han*, 'she') that differ from those in Old Swedish. The vocabulary also has differences (*lamb*, 'sheep' rather than 'lamb'); see *KL*, s. v. *Forngutniska* and references.

Some scholars have, as a result of the phrase used at the end of the emigration episode, *sumt af varu mali*, looked for similarities between Gothic and Gutnish, and Bugge (*NIÆR* I, 152–158) notes a number of further examples. He concedes, however, that the evidence is inconclusive and that there could be other explanations than that a form of Gothic was at one time spoken in Gotland. Nevertheless, of all the Scandinavian languages, Gutnish is the one that most resembles Gothic.

The language of *Guta saga* in B64 is similar to that of the latter portion of *Guta lag* and the text would thus seem to have been available to the scribe in a version dating from later than that of the earlier parts of *Guta lag*, although the same scribe is responsible for the whole of B64. In any case, *Guta saga* has, in all probability, a separate author from that of *Guta lag*. Pipping (*GLGS*, iii) and others, including Sjöholm (1976, 105), suspect that the scribe who produced B64 did not wholly understand the language of *Guta saga*. Pipping's emendations, indicated in the footnotes and discussed in the Notes, draw attention to some of the places where this is apparent.

### (x) *Editions of* Guta saga

A *Previous editions, translations, etc.*

The first printed edition of *Guta lag* and *Guta saga*, entitled *Gothlandz-Laghen på gammal Göthiska*, was produced in 1687 by Johan Hadorph, who was at that time the secretary of Antikvitetskollegiet. In the dedication, dated 1st February, 1690, Hadorph records that the manuscript had been found a few years previously 'uthi en Kyrckia der på Landet ibland orenligheet, såsom en förkastat Ting, och omsider hijtkommen till sin rätta Herre och Konung'. His edition contains a translation into contemporary Swedish and some added section rubrics, as well as an introduction and a word-list, with occasional glosses. In the introduction there is a section on Gotlandic runic inscriptions. The rubrics inserted by Hadorph at the listed points in the text, with his page numbers, are:

2/1   Om Gothlandz Första Upfinnelse och bebyggiande samt Afgudadyrkan i hedendomen (p. 47).

4/17  Om Götenas afguda dyrkan (p. 48, marginal note).

Schlyter (*CIG*, xx–xxi) considers that the translation, although good for the time, is inaccurate in a number of places and that the text has many misprints, some caused by a misreading of the manuscript. This seems to be a fair judgement.

An apparently accurate text of the first chapter of *Guta saga*, followed by a Latin translation, was published by Peringskiöld (1699, 442–445), but the next complete edition to be produced was that by Karl Schildener in 1818 (*G-L*), entitled *Guta-Lagh das ist: Der Insel Gothland altes Rechtsbuch*. The B64 text is presented in parallel with the medieval German translation (B65) and a contemporary German translation. The B65 text is, however, missing for much of *Guta saga*, as Schildener was using a copy by Hammarsköld that was incomplete; cf. *CIG*, xxiii. This edition retains some of the errors contained in Hadorph's edition, corrects some and introduces others.

In 1852 Schlyter, as the seventh volume in a series covering the Swedish district laws (*CIS*), produced what might be regarded as the first scholarly edition of *Guta lag* and *Guta saga* (*CIG*). His introduction discusses the various manuscripts still preserved, although as Ljunggren (1959, 10–11) notes, he does not appear to be aware of the Old Swedish translation (in Codex Holmiensis D2). Schlyter presents the text with a parallel translation into contemporary Swedish. His apparatus is in Latin, but he includes Swedish footnotes with his translation. He divides the work into six chapters, Chapter 2 covering the visit of St Olaf and Chapter 5 covering the travelling bishops and the visitation arrangements. These chapter divisions have been used in all subsequent editions. Schlyter includes a glossary and an index of proper names. The final volume of the series (*CIS* XIII) is also a glossary, covering the complete set of law texts as well as *Guta saga*.

In 1859 Carl Säve produced an academic thesis, *Gutniska urkunder* (*GU*), part of which is an edition of *Guta lag* and *Guta saga*. Säve discusses the language and acknowledges the previous edition by Schlyter, offering a number of alternative readings.

The most thorough study of the language of *Guta saga* is presented in the edition produced by Pipping (*GLGS*). This edition contains a detailed introduction on the language of B64 and AM 54 4to, a diplomatic text and a full glossary showing all instances of each word. The emendations Pipping makes are signalled and cross-referenced to those made by previous editors.

In 1945, volume five of *Corpus codicum Suecicorum medii aevi* was published, containing a facsimile of *Guta lag* and *Guta saga* as preserved in B64 and B65 (*LG*). It includes an introduction in both Swedish and English by E. Wessén.

The translation of *Guta lag* and *Guta saga* into Swedish, produced by Åke Holmbäck and Elias Wessén in *SL* IV, includes an introduction, discussing in detail the preservation, dating, content and historical background of both *Guta lag* and *Guta saga*, as well as very full explanatory notes on the text and content, with extensive references. It does not discuss the language of the original, but refers frequently to editions that do.

Of the translations into languages other than Swedish and German, Lis Jacobsen's translation into Danish, *Guterlov og Gutersaga* (*GGD*), published in 1910, contains the fullest commentary. It is based on Pipping and draws attention to the rich alliteration in the texts. No complete edition has previously been published in English, but there is an extract (in Gutnish, with glossary entries) contained in Gordon (1962, 175–177, first published in 1927) and an English translation by Adolph Burnett Benson of the same extract, deriving from Gordon, in Leach (1946, 312–314, 349). A translation into French of the whole of *Guta saga*, including an introduction and commentary, was produced by Jean Marie Maillefer (1985). Ljunggren's critical edition covering the surviving Old Swedish and Danish translations of fragments of *Guta saga* (1959) contains a comparison of these with the text in B64 and a proposed stemma based on these comparisons.

## B *The present edition*

The text is presented as in B64 but with a number of emendations, some following Pipping (*GLGS*), signalled by an asterisk. The readings of the manuscript and earlier editions are shown in the footnotes. Characters and words apparently accidentally omitted from the manuscript are indicated by angled brackets. The text is normalised in spelling, sometimes following suggestions in Pipping's footnotes. Nasal strokes and emendations by the scribe have been expanded or applied without comment, both in the text and the notes. Punctuation and capitalisation have been inserted following, as far as possible, modern Swedish practice and paragraph divisions have been made where they have seemed appropriate. The four chapter divisions marked in the manuscript have been retained; details of the chapter headings and marginal notes in the manuscript have been included in the Notes.

The translation, which faces the original text, has retained, where possible, changes in tense and mood that characterise the legal sections of the text, but idiomatic English expressions have been substituted for those in the original. Place-names are given their modern English equivalent where they exist, otherwise the modern Swedish equivalent has been used. Personal names are given in a single nominative singular form (adopting Pipping's emendation where relevant). Punctuation and capitalisation follow modern English practice.

*Guta saga*

*The history of the Gotlanders*

## [1]

Gutland hitti fyrsti maþr þann, sum Þieluar hit. Þa var Gutland so eluist, et þet dagum sank ok natum var uppi. En þann maþr quam fyrsti eldi a land, ok siþan sank þet aldri.

5 Þissi Þieluar hafþi ann sun, sum hit Hafþi. En Hafþa kuna hit Huitastierna. Þaun tu bygþu fyrsti a Gutlandi. Fyrstu nat, sum þaun saman suafu, þa droymdi henni draumbr, so sum þrir ormar varin slungnir saman i barmi hennar, ok þytti henni sum þair skriþin yr barmi

10 hennar. Þinna draum segþi han firir *Hafþa, bonda sinum. Hann *reþ draum þinna so:

'Alt ir baugum bundit.
Boland al þitta varþa,
ok faum þria syni aiga.'

15 Þaim gaf hann namn allum ofydum:

'Guti al Gutland aiga,
Graipr al annar haita,
ok Gunfiaun þriþi.'

Þair skiptu siþan Gutlandi i þria þriþiunga, so et Graipr,
20 þann elzti, laut norþasta þriþiung ok Guti miþal þriþiung. En Gunfiaun, þann yngsti, laut sunnarsta. Siþan af þissum þrim aukaþis fulk i Gutlandi so mikit um langan tima, et land elpti þaim ai alla fyþa. Þa lutaþu þair bort af landi huert þriþia þiauþ, so et alt skuldu þair aiga ok
25 miþ sir bort hafa sum þair ufan iorþar attu. Siþan vildu þair nauþugir bort fara, men foru innan Þorsborg ok bygþus þar firir. Siþan vildi ai land þaim þula utan raku þaim bort þeþan.

10 Hafþa *G-L*, 106; *CIG*, 94, note 8; *GLGS*, 62, note 5; hasþa *MS*.
11 raiþ *GLGS*, 62, note 6; riaþ *MS*.

# THE HISTORY OF THE GOTLANDERS

## Chapter 1

Gotland was first discovered by a man named Þieluar. At that time the island was so bewitched that it sank by day and rose up at night. That man, however, was the first that brought fire to the island, and afterwards it never sank again.

This same Þieluar had a son named Hafþi, and Hafþi's wife was called Huitastierna. These two were the first to settle in Gotland. The first night that they slept together, she dreamed a dream. It was just as if three snakes were coiled together within her womb, and it seemed to her as though they crawled out of her lap. She related this dream to Hafþi, her husband, and he interpreted it as follows:

'Everything in rings is bound.
Inhabited this land shall be;
we shall beget sons three.'

He gave them each a name, while they were still unborn:

'Guti shall Gotland claim,
Graipr the second by name
and Gunfiaun the third.'

They later divided Gotland into thirds, in such a way that Graipr the eldest inherited the northern third, Guti the middle third and Gunfiaun the youngest inherited the southernmost. Subsequently, from these three men, the population of Gotland increased so much over a long period of time that the land was not able to support them all. Then they cast lots to send every third person away from the island, on the understanding that they should have a right to keep, and take away with them, everything that they owned in the way of moveables. But then they were unwilling to move away, and went instead into Torsburgen, and lived there. Later the people of the island were not prepared to tolerate them, but drove them away from there.

Siþan foru þair bort i Faroyna ok bygþus þar firir. Þar
gatu þair ai sik uppi haldit, utan foru i aina oy viþr
Aistland, sum haitir Dagaiþi, ok bygþus þar firir ok
gierþu burg aina, sum enn synis.

5 Þar gatu þair ok ai sik haldit, utan foru upp at vatni,
þy sum haitir Dyna, ok upp ginum Ryzaland. So fierri
foru þair, et þair quamu til Griklanz. Þar baddus þair
byggias firir af grika kunungi um ny ok niþar. Kunungr
þann lufaþi þaim ok hugþi, et ai *maira *þan ann manaþr
10 vari. Siþan gangnum manaþi, vildi hann þaim bort visa.
En þair *annsuaraþu þa, et ny ok niþar vari e ok e, ok quaþu,
so sir vara lufat. Þissun þaira viþratta quam firir drytningina
um siþir. Þa segþi han: 'Minn herra kunungr! Þu lufaþi
þaim byggia um ny ok niþar. Þa ir þet e ok e, þa matt
15 þu ai af þaim taka.' So bygþus þair þar firir ok enn
byggia, ok enn hafa þair *sumt af varu mali.

Firir þan tima ok lengi eptir siþan troþu menn a hult
ok a hauga, vi ok stafgarþa ok a haiþin guþ. Blotaþu
þair synum ok dytrum sinum ok fileþi miþ mati ok
20 mungati. Þet gierþu þair eptir vantro sinni. Land alt hafþi
sir hoystu blotan miþ fulki. Ellar hafþi huer þriþiungr
sir. En smeri þing hafþu mindri blotan miþ fileþi, mati
ok mungati, sum haita suþnautar, þy et þair suþu allir
saman.

9 ai maira þan *CIG*, 95, note 11; *GU*, 32, line 14; *FL*, 153; ain
niþ *GLGS*, 63, note 3; ai miþ *MS*. *See Note to 4/9.*

11 annzsuaraþv þa *GLGS*, 63, note 4; annzsuaru *with* suaraþv þa
*inserted above the line MS*.

16 sumt *CIG*, 95, note 13; *GLGS*, 63, note 6; suint *MS*.

They then went away to Fårö and settled there. They could not support themselves there, but travelled to an island off Estonia called Dagö, where they settled, and built a fortification, which is still to be seen.

They could not support themselves there either, but travelled up by the watercourse called the Dvina, and forward through Russia. They travelled for such a distance that they came to the Byzantine empire. There they asked permission of the Byzantine emperor to live 'for the waxing and waning'. The emperor granted them that, thinking that this meant no more than a month. After a month had passed, he wanted to send them on their way. But they answered then that 'the waxing and waning' meant 'for ever and ever' and said that was just what they had been promised. This dispute of theirs came at last to the notice of the empress. She then said, 'My lord emperor, you promised them that they could settle for the waxing and the waning of the moon. Now that continues for ever and ever, so you cannot take that promise away from them.' So there they settled and still live. And, moreover, they retain some of our language.

Prior to that time, and for a long time afterwards, people believed in groves and grave howes, holy places and ancient sites, and in heathen idols. They sacrificed their sons and daughters, and cattle, together with food and ale. They did that in accordance with their ignorance of the true faith. The whole island held the highest sacrifice on its own account, with human victims, otherwise each third held its own. But smaller assemblies held a lesser sacrifice with cattle, food, and drink. Those involved were called 'boiling-companions', because they all cooked their sacrificial meals together.

## [2]

Mangir kunungar stridu a Gutland, miþan ha‹i›þit var. Þau hieldu gutar e iemlika *sigri ok ret sinum. Siþan sentu gutar *sendimen manga til Suiarikis, en engin þaira fikk friþ gart, fyr þan Avair strabain af Alfa sokn. 5 Hann gierþi fyrsti friþ viþr suia kunung.

Þa en gutar hann til baþu at fara, þa suaraþi hann: 'Mik vitin ir nu faigastan ok fallastan. Giefin þa mir, en ir vilin, et iek fari innan slikan vaþa, þry vereldi: att mir sielfum, annat burnum syni minum, ok þriþia kunu.' Þy 10 et hann var *snieldr ok *fielkunnugr, so sum sagur af ganga, gikk hann a staggaþan ret viþr suia kunung. Siextigi marka silfs um ar huert, þet ir skattr guta, so et Suiarikis kunungr ‹hafi› fiauratigi markr silfs af þaim siextigi, en ierl hafi tiugu markr silfs. Þinna *staþga 15 gierþi hann miþ lanz raþi, fyr en hann haiman fori. So gingu gutar sielfs viliandi undir suia kunung, þy et þair mattin frir ok frelsir sykia Suiariki i huerium staþ utan tull ok allar utgiftir. So aigu ok suiar sykia Gutland firir utan kornband ellar annur forbuþ. Hegnan ok hielp 20 skuldi kunungr gutum at vaita, en þair viþr þorftin ok kallaþin. Sendimen al ok kunungr ok ierl samulaiþ a gutnalþing senda ok lata þar taka skatt sin. Þair sendi-buþar aigu friþ lysa gutum alla steþi til sykia yfir haf, sum Upsala kunungi til hoyrir, ok so þair, sum þan 25 vegin aigu hinget sykia.

1 haiþit *GU*, 32, line 29; *GLGS*, 64, note 2.
2 sigri *CIG*, 96, note 3; *GLGS*, 64, note 3; siþri *MS*.
3 sendimen *GU*, 32, line 31; *GLGS*, 64, note 4; sendimenn *GU*, 67, note; sendumen *MS*.
10 snieldr *CIG*, 96, note 4; *GLGS*, 62, note 6; senieldir *MS*.
fiel-kunnugr *GU*, 32, line 37; fielkunnugr *FL*, 154, §7; fiel cunnugr *AL*, 39, §18; *GLGS*, 64, note 7; fiel kunungur *MS*.
13 hafi *CIG*, 97, note 6; *GLGS*, 64, note 9.
14 staþga *CIG*, 97, note 7; *GLGS*, 64, note 11; staþgaþ *MS*.

## Chapter 2

Many kings fought against Gotland while it was heathen; the Gotlanders, however, always held the victory and constantly protected their rights. Later the Gotlanders sent a large number of messengers to Sweden, but none of them could make peace before Avair Strabain of Alva parish. He made the first peace with the king of the Swedes.

When the Gotlanders begged him to go, he answered, 'You know that I am now most doomed and ill-fated. Grant me then, if you wish me to expose myself to such peril, three wergilds, one for myself, a second for my begotten son and a third for my wife.' Because he was wise and skilled in many things, just as the tales go about him, he entered into a binding treaty with the king of the Swedes. Sixty marks of silver in respect of each year is the Gotlanders' tax, divided so that the king of Sweden should have forty marks of silver out of the sixty, and the jarl twenty marks of silver. Avair made this statute in accordance with the advice of the people of the island before he left home. In this way, the Gotlanders submitted to the king of Sweden, of their own free will, in order that they might travel everywhere in Sweden free and unhindered, exempt from toll and all other charges. Similarly the Swedes also have the right to visit Gotland, without ban against trade in corn, or other prohibitions. The king was obliged to give the Gotlanders protection and assistance, if they should need it and request it. In addition the king, and likewise the jarl, should send messengers to the Gotlanders' general assembly and arrange for their tax to be collected there. The messengers in question have a duty to proclaim the freedom of Gotlanders to visit all places overseas that belong to the king in Uppsala and, similarly, to such as have the right to travel here from that side.

Eptir þet siþan quam helgi Olafr kunungr flyandi af
Norvegi miþ skipum ok legþis i hamn, þa sum kallar
Akrgarn. Þar la helgi Olafr lengi. Þa for Ormika af
Hainaim ok flairi rikir menn til hans miþ giefum sinum.
5 Þann Ormika gaf hanum tolf veþru miþ andrum klenatum.
Þa gaf helgi Olafr kunungr hanum atr agin tua bulla ok
aina braiþyxi. Þa tok Ormika viþr kristindomi eptir
helga Olafs kennidomi ok gierþi sir bynahus i sama
staþ, sum nu standr Akrgarna kirkia. Þeþan for helgi
10 Olafr til Ierslafs i Hulmgarþi.

[3]

Þau et gutar hainir varu, þau silgdu þair miþ kaupmannaskap innan all land, baþi kristin ok haiþin. Þa
sagu kaupmenn kristna siþi i kristnum landum. Þa litu
sumir sik þar kristna ok fyrþu til Gutlanz presti.
15 Botair af Akubek hit þann sum fyrsti kirkiu gierþi, i
þan staþ, sum nu haitir Kulasteþar. Þet vildi ai land þula
utan brendu hana. Þy kallar þar enn Kulasteþar. Þa eptir
þan tima var blotan i Vi. Þar gierþi kirkiu aþra. Þa samu
kirkiu vildi land ok brenna. Þa for hann sielfr upp a
20 kirkiu þa ok segþi: 'Vilin ir brenna, þa skulin ir brenna
mik miþ kirkiu þissi.' Hann var rikr sielfr ok *rikasta
manz dotur hafþi hann, sum hit Likkair *snielli, boandi
þar, sum kallar Stainkirkiu. Hann reþ mest um þan tima.
Hann halp Botairi, magi sinum, ok segþi so: 'Herþin ai
25 brenna mann ella kirkiu hans, þy et han standr i Vi, firir
niþan klintu.' Miþ þy fikk þaun kirkia standa obrend.
Han var sett þar miþ aldra helguna namni, innan þan
staþ, sum nu kallar Petrs kirkiu. Han var fyrsti kirkia i
Gutlandi, sum standa fikk.

21 rikasta *G-L*, 111; *CIG*, 99, note 7; *GLGS*, 65, note 6; ricasca *MS*.
22 snielli *CIG*, 99, note 8; *GLGS*, 65, note 7; snilli *with* e *above*
*the* i *MS*.

Later, after this, King Olaf the Saint came fleeing from Norway with his ships, and laid into a harbour, the one called Akergarn. St Olaf lay there a long time. Then Ormika of Hejnum, and several other powerful men, went to him with their gifts. Ormika gave him twelve yearling rams along with other valuables. St Olaf then reciprocated and gave him in return two round drinking vessels and a battle-axe. Ormika subsequently received Christianity according to St Olaf's teaching and built himself an oratory at the same location as Akergarn church now stands. From there St Olaf travelled to visit Jaroslav in Novgorod.

## Chapter 3

Although the Gotlanders were heathen, they nevertheless sailed on trading voyages to all countries, both Christian and heathen. So the merchants saw Christian customs in Christian lands. Some of them then allowed themselves to be baptised, and brought priests to Gotland.

Botair of Akebäck was the name of the one who first built a church, in that place which is now called Kulstäde. The islanders were not prepared to tolerate that, but burned it. For that reason the place is still called Kulstäde. Then, later on, there was a sacrifice at Vi. There Botair built a second church. The people of the island also wanted to burn this particular church. Then Botair went up on top of the church himself and said, 'If you want to burn it, you will have to burn me along with this church.' He was himself influential, and he had as his wife a daughter of the most powerful man, called Likkair Snielli, living at the place called Stenkyrka. Likkair carried most authority at that time. He supported Botair, his son-in-law, and said as follows, 'Do not persist in burning the man or his church, since it stands at Vi, below the cliff.' As a result, that church was allowed to stand unburnt. It was established there with the name of All Saints, in that place which is now called St Peter's. It was the first church in Gotland to be allowed to stand.

Siþan um nequan tima eptir, lit suer hans Likkair
sn‹i›elli sik kristna, ok husf‹r›oyu sina, barn sin ok
hiskep sin allan. Ok gierþi kirkiu i garþi sinum, þar nu
kallar Stainkirkiu. Han var fyrsti kirkia a landi uppi i
5 norþasta þriþiungi. Siþan gutar sagu kristna manna siþi,
þa lydu þair Guz buþi ok lerþra manna kennu. Toku þa
almennilika viþr kristindomi miþ sielfs vilia sinum utan
þuang, so et engin þuang þaim til kristnur.

Siþan en menn orþu almennilika kristnir, þa gierþis
10 kirkia annur a landi i Atlingabo. Han var fyrsti i miþal-
þriþiungi. Siþan varþ þriþi gar a landi i Farþaim i
*sunnarsta þriþiungi. Af þaim briskaþus kirkiur allar i
Gutlandi, þy et menn gierþu sir kirkiur at mairu maki.

Fyr en Gutland toki steþilika viþr nekrum biskupi, þa
15 quamu biskupar til Gutlanz, pilagrimar til helga lanz
Ierusalem ok þeþan haim foru. Þan tima var vegr oystra
um Ryzaland ok Grikland fara til Ierusalem. Þair vigþu
fyrsti kirkiur ok kirkiugarþa, miþ byn þaira, sum giera
litu kirkiur.

20 Siþan en gutar vendus viþr kristindom, þa sentu þair
sendibuþa til hoygsta biskups i Leonkopungi, þy et
hann var þaim nestr, so et miþ steddum ret quami hann
til Gutlanz þan reþskep giera miþ þaim forskielum, et
biskupr vildi kuma af Leonkopungi þriþia huert ar til
25 Gutlanz miþ tolf mannum sinum, sum hanum skuldin
fylgia um land alt miþ bonda hestum, so mangum ok ai
flairum.

So a biskupr um Gutland fara til kirkiu vigsla ok
gingerþa sinna taka: þry borþ ok ai maira at kirkiu vigsl
30 huerri, miþ þrim markum; at alteris vigsl att borþ, miþ
tolf oyrum, en alteri ainsamt skal vigias; þa en baþi iru

---

2 snielli *GU*, 33, line 38; *GLGS*, 66, note 3. *See footnote to 8/22.*
husfroyu *G-L*, 111; *CIG*, 99, note 10; *GLGS*, 66, note 4.
12 sunnarsta *CIG*, 100, note 14; *GLGS*, 66, note 7; sunnarnasta *MS*.

Then, at some time after that, his father-in-law Likkair Snielli had himself baptised, together with his wife, his children, and all his household, and he built a church on his farm, in the place now called Stenkyrka. It was the first church on the island up in the northernmost third. After the Gotlanders saw the customs of Christian people, they then obeyed God's command and the teaching of priests. Then they received Christianity generally, of their own free will, without duress; that is no one forced them into Christianity.

After the general acceptance of Christianity, a second church was built in the country, at Atlingbo; it was the first in the middle third. Then a third was built in the country, at Fardhem in the southernmost third. From those, churches spread everywhere in Gotland, since men built themselves churches for greater convenience.

Before Gotland allied itself to any bishop permanently, bishops came to Gotland who were pilgrims to Jerusalem, in the Holy Land, and were travelling home from there. At that time the route eastwards was to cross through Russia and the Byzantine empire to Jerusalem. In the first place they consecrated churches and graveyards, according to the request of those who had caused the churches to be built.

After the Gotlanders became accustomed to Christianity, they then sent messages to the Lord Bishop of Linköping, since he resided closest to them, to the effect that he should come to Gotland, by a confirmed statute, to lend his support, on the following conditions: that the bishop would come from Linköping to Gotland every third year together with twelve of his men, who would accompany him around the whole country on farmers' horses, just that many and no more.

Thus the bishop has a duty to travel around Gotland to church consecrations and to collect his payments in kind, three meals and no more for each consecration of a church, together with three marks; for an altar consecration, one meal together with twelve öre, if the altar alone is to be

ovigþ, alteri ok kirkia saman, þa skulu baþi vigias firir
þry borþ ok þriar markr penninga. Af presti andrum
huerium a biskupr gingerþ taka, um tilquemda siþ, þry
borþ ok ai maira. Af andrum huerium presti, sum ai
5 gierþi gingerþ a þy ari, taki biskupr af huerium lausn, so
sum kirkiur iru til skuraþar. Þair sum ai gingerþ gierþu
at þy bragþi, þair skulu gingerþ giera, þegar biskupr
kumbr atr at þriþia ari. En hinir aigu loysa, sum fyrra
bragþi gingerþ gierþu.
10    Kunnu dailur varþa, sum biskupr a dyma, þaar skulu
lendas i sama þriþiungi, ‹þy› et þair menn vita mest af
sannundum, sum þar nest boa. Varþr ai þar þaun daila
lent, þa skal han skiautas til aldra manna samtalan ok ai
af þriþiungi i annan. Kunnu hetningar eþa dailumal
15 varþa, sum biskupi til hoyra at retta, þa a hier biþa
biskups quemdar ok ai yfir fara, utan þuang reki til ok
mikil synd sei, et ai ma proastr loysa. Þa skal yfir fara
millan Valborga messur ok helguna messur, en ai þar
eptir um vintrtima til Valborga messur. Biskups sak i
20 Gutlandi ir ai *hoygri þan þriar markr.

[4]

Siþan gutar toku sir biskup ok presti ok viþr fulkumnum
kristindomi, þa toku þair ok viþr at fylgia suia kunungi
i herferþ miþ siau *snekkium ufan a haiþin land, ok ai
ufan kristin. So þau, et kunungr a biauþa gutum laiþing
25 eptir vittr ok manaþar frest firir liþstemnu dag, ok þau
skal liþstemnu dagr vara firir missumar ok ai siþar. Þa
ir laglika buþit, ok ai ellar. Þa hafa gutar val um at fara,

11 þy CIG, 101, note 11.
20 hoygri CIG, 102, note 13; GLGS, 68, note 4; hoyþri MS.
23 snekkium GLGS, 68, note 6; snieckium MS.

consecrated; but if both are unconsecrated, altar and church together, then both shall be consecrated for three meals and three marks in coin. From every second priest the bishop has a right to collect payment in kind as a visitation tax, three meals and no more. From every other priest, who did not make payment in kind in that year, the bishop is to take a fee from each one, as is laid down for churches. Those who did not make payment in kind at that time, they shall make payment in kind as soon as the bishop comes back in the third year. And the others have a duty to pay a fee, who the previous time had made payment in kind.

Should disputes arise that the bishop has a duty to judge, they shall be resolved in the same third, since those men know most about the truth who live nearest to it. Should the dispute not be resolved there, it shall then be referred to the consideration of all men, and not from one third to another. Should hostilities or matters of conflict occur, which belong to the bishop to judge, one has an obligation to await the bishop's arrival here and not travel over to the mainland, unless necessity force it, and it be such a great sin that the rural dean cannot give absolution. Then one shall travel over between Walburga's Day and All Saints' Day, but not after that during the winter, until the following Walburga's Day. A fine to the bishop, in Gotland, is to be no higher than three marks.

## Chapter 4

Since the Gotlanders accepted bishop and priest, and completely embraced Christianity, they also undertook, on their part, to follow the Swedish king on military expeditions with seven warships, against heathen countries, but not against Christian ones. It had to be in such a way, however, that the king should summon the Gotlanders to the levy after winter, and give them a month's respite before the day of mobilisation and, furthermore, the day of mobilisation shall be before midsummer, and no later. Then it is a lawful summons, but not otherwise. Then the Gotlanders have the choice of travelling,

en þair vilia, miþ sinum *snekkium ok atta vikna vist,
en ai maira. Þa en gutar efla ai fylgia, þa gialdin fiauratigi
marka penninga firir hueria *snekkiu, ok þau at andru
ari ok ai at þy sama ari, sum buþit var. Þet haitir
5 laiþingslami.

I þaim manaþi, þa skal aina viku buþkafli um fara ok
þing nemnas. Þa en mannum sembr et laiþingr skal ut
ganga, þa skal siþan halfan manaþ til ferþar boas. En
siþan siau netr firir liþstemnu skulu laiþings menn garlakir
10 vara ok byriar biþa. Þa en so kann varþa, et ai kumbr
byr i þairi viku, þa skulu þair enn biþa siau netr eptir
liþstemnu dag. Þa en ai kumbr byr i þairi frest, þa aigu
þair haim fara at saklausu, miþ þy et ai gatu þair roandi
yfir haf farit utan siglandi. Kuma laiþings buþ i minnum
15 frestum þan manaþar, þa a ai *fara utan haima sitia at
saklausu.

Ir so et kunungr vil ai troa, et buþ quamin olaglika eþa
byr hindraþi at retum frestum, þa aigu sendimenn kunungs,
sum skatt taka a þy þingi, sum nest ir eptir Sankti Petrs
20 messu, taka tolf nemdamanna aiþ, sum sendimenn kunungs
nemna vilia, et þair miþ laglikum forfallum haima satin.

Engin gief‹s› nemda aiþr i Gutlandi utan kunungs
aiþr. Kann so illa at bieras, et krunaþr kunungr varþr
miþ nequaru valdi bort rekinn af sinu riki, þa aigu ai
25 gutar skatt ut giefa utan haldi hanum um þry ar. Ok þau
aigu þair e huert ar skatt saman giera ok liggia lata, en
þa ut giefa, þa en þry *ar iru ut gangin, þaim sum þa
raþr Suiariki.

Lykt bref miþ kunungs insigli skal at allum kunungs
30 ret sendas, ok ai *ypit.

1, 3 snieckium, snieckiu *MS*; *cf. 12/23.*
15 fara *GLGS*, 69, note 3; faras *with the* s *above the line MS.*
22 giefs *GLGS*, 69, note 5 *after* Bugge, 1877–1878, 261–262.
27 ar *G-L*, 115; *CIG*, 104, note 9; *GLGS*, 69, note 9; ar ar *MS*.
30 ypit *GU*, 35, line 38; *GLGS*, 69, note 11; ypit *MS, altered to* vpit.

if they wish, with their longships and eight weeks' provisions, but no more. Nevertheless, if the Gotlanders are not able to take part, then they are to pay a fine of 40 marks in coin, in compensation for each longship; but this, however, is at the following harvest and not in the same year that the summons was made. This is called the 'levy-tax'. In that month the summoning-baton shall pass around for one week and an assembly be announced. When people are agreed that the expedition shall go out, they shall then further arm themselves for the voyage for a fortnight. And afterwards, for a week before the mobilisation, the men on the muster ought to be prepared and wait for a favourable wind. But if it should happen that no favourable wind comes during that week, they shall still wait seven nights after the day of mobilisation. If, however, no favourable wind comes within that specified time, they then have the right to go home freed from obligation, since they are not able to cross over the sea rowing, only under sail. Should the levy summons come within a shorter period than a month, they do not have to go, but may remain at home with impunity.

Should it be the case that the king is not willing to believe that the summons came unlawfully, or that the wind hindered them at the proper specified times, the king's messengers, who collect the tax at that assembly which is next after St Peter's mass, have a duty to take an oath from twelve commissioners, whom the king's messengers wish to select, that they remained at home for lawful reasons.

No commissioned oath shall be given in Gotland apart from the king's oath. Should the misfortune occur that the crowned king is by some force driven away from his kingdom, the Gotlanders then have the right not to hand over their tax, but retain it for three years; but they nevertheless have a duty to continue to collect the tax together each year and allow it to lie, and then hand it over when three years have passed, to the one who at that time rules Sweden.

A sealed letter with the king's authority shall be sent concerning all the king's law, and not an open one.

# NOTES

The manuscript lacks headings to the chapters, which are apparently signalled by larger initial letters and indentation. Chapter numbers have been inserted by a later hand in the margin. These divisions have been adhered to in this edition. The marginal headings, which have been added to the manuscript by a later hand, are given in these Notes. Previous editors have inserted further chapter divisions and headings; see Introduction, pp. lvii–lix.

Place-names on Gotland, in Sweden and the Baltic, and in Russia that are mentioned in the notes are shown on the maps on pp. 98–100. Those occurring in the text are italicised on the maps and appear in the Index.

## Chapter 1

2/1. In the manuscript, a sixteenth-century hand has added in the margin 'Quomodo Gotlandia inuenta et culta', that is 'How Gotland was discovered and inhabited'.

The earliest instance of the name Gotland is from the end of the ninth century, in *The Old English Orosius* (*Orosius*, 16). Here Gotland is mentioned in Wulfstan's account of his voyage from Hedeby to the mouth of the Vistula (Weichsel). Wulfstan states that he passed Gotland to port along with Blecingaeg, Meore and Eowland (Blekinge, Möre and Öland), and this is almost certainly a reference to Gotland. For the question of the political position of the island, see the Note to 6/5 in connection with Avair Strabain's negotiations with Sweden. Olsson (1984, 13–18) summarises the theories so far put forward about the origin of the name Gotland as (a) that it was given to the island by outsiders and is related to the tribe name *gautar* (*götar*), used of the people from Väster- and Östergötland, which gave rise to *gutar* for the inhabitants of Gotland, and *gotar* for the Goths, (b) that it can be traced more directly to an early settlement on Gutån (earlier Guteån) in the parish of Bäl, or Gothemån in the parish of Gothem, and is related to such words as *gjuta*, 'pour out', independently of *götar*; cf. Hellquist, 1980, s. v. *göt*; Lindroth, 1914a and 1941. Olsson's investigation of place-names and their physical location, for example two farms called Gute in the parish of Bäl, led him to conclude that features in Gotland gave rise to the name *gutar*. The alternative is that the name was adopted because of the origin of the inhabitants, in Väster- or Östergötland. Another explanation of the name, relevant to the story of Gotland's discovery, might be that it is related to the concept of *Landit góða*, explained by Nansen (1911, 282–283) as *huldrelandet* or *usynlighetslandet*; cf. Introduction, pp. xviii–xx; Note to 2/2.

Läffler (1908–1909, Part 1, 170) and Gordon (1962, 199, 255) are of the opinion that the name *Þieluar* is probably related to *Þjálfi*, the name of Thor's follower; cf. Introduction, pp. xvii–xviii. Gordon gives the meaning of the name *Þjálfi* as 'one who seizes and holds', which would correspond well to the function of Þieluar in *Guta saga*. Hadorph (1687, v–vi) notes a variant of the name on two inscriptions from stones in Öster Skam in Östergötland, unfortunately now disappeared. They read as follows (Ög 27): **þuriʀ. sati. stain. at. þialfar. faþur. sin. iaʀ. stranti. a. kautaun.** (Þurir raised this stone after Þialfar, his father, who came to land on *kautaun*); (Ög 28): **. . . sun. iaʀ. buki. a. kautaun . . . truista. sina.** ( . . . son, who lived at *kautaun* . . . his dearest). The significance of *kautaun* is uncertain and it seems possible that the name has been misread; cf. *SL* IV, 300. Hadorph is cautious of identifying *kautaun* with Gotland or *þialfar* with the Þieluar of *Guta saga*, but both Peringskiöld (1699, 445) and Schlyter (*CIG*, 317) do so. Säve (*GU*, viii), however, rejects the idea that *kautaun* could be Gotland and questions whether the name *þielfar* is to be taken as *þiel-uar* or *þielu-ar*.

2/2. The word *eluist* is problematic. The reading of it as *eliust* by Hadorph (1687, 47), misinterpreting the position of the dot over the *i*, has led to his translation 'okunnigt' ('unenlightened'). Schildener (*G-L*, 259) follows Hadorph, breaking the word down into the negative particle *e* and *lius*, 'light', and translating it 'unscheinbar'. Schildener also discusses an alternative explanation, based on the Old High German *ellen* meaning 'power' and the suffix *-lös*, giving the meaning 'powerless', which could relate to the island's enchanted state. He rejects this interpretation, however, and points to the statement that the island was only above water at night and was therefore, naturally, 'dark'. Schlyter (*CIG*, 93) also favours Hadorph's reading. He uses the translation 'dunkelt', but adds other possibilities in his glossary. He thinks that the word may be a form of *oliust*, 'dark', or *eldlaust*, 'without fire', and that it might indicate that there was no fire on the island. These interpretations are possible, but a meaning related to 'elf' seems more probable; see Introduction,

p. xx. Bugge (1877–1878, 260–261), referring to Lyngby (1858–1860, 269), gives several examples of similar words in Scandinavian, English and German, which have meanings like 'bewitched' or 'visited by trolls'. He argues, however, that the form of the word as it occurs here is defensible if *eluist* were a neuter form, standing for *elvitskt* (derived from *\*elvitskr* or *\*elviskr*, rather than from *\*eluiscr* as proposed by Lyngby). Wadstein (1892, 152–153) also takes the word as being related to similar ones in English meaning 'elfish' and considers the form of the word to be in accordance with this interpretation. Wessén (*SL* IV, 301) summarises these and later theories and translates *eluist* as 'förtrollat', best rendered by the English 'bewitched', which carries all the relevant connotations.

2/2–3. There is evidence of a rise in the level of the land in certain areas of the Scandinavian peninsula, initially very rapid; see *KL*, s. v. *Niveauforandring*. Certainly, when Gotland was first inhabited, it was much smaller and had more inlets that it has today, although even now most of the island is less than 30 metres above sea-level; cf. Öhrman, 1994, 8–13, 14; Introduction, pp. xviii–xix.

2/3. The importance to a farm of its first inhabitant and the probably unrelated concept of a protective spirit (*hustomte*) are noted by Landtman (1922, 20, 46). The link between the efficacy of fire as a protection, the protection believed to be offered by Thor, and the belief that fire would not burn in a house inhabited by someone possessed by evil spirits, are also recorded by Landtman (1919, 776). See also Introduction, p. xx.

2/5. *Hafþi*. Perhaps from the place-name *Havdhem*; see Introduction, pp. xxi–xxii.

2/7–8. *droymdi henni draumbr*. The word 'dream' is nominative and the dreamer apparently dative; cf. the English expression 'a dream came to her'; see Söderwall, 1884–1973, s. v. *dröma*. On the motif of a pregnant woman's dreams, see Perkins, 1974–1977, 224; Introduction, pp. xxii–xxiii.

2/8. *þrir ormar*. In 1955 a picture-stone was found on a grave site at Smiss in När parish, in eastern Gotland. On the basis of its chisel shape, it has been thought to date from the seventh century (although this is not undisputed); see Nylén, 1978, 13; Nylén and Lamm, 1987, 40–41. It depicts in its lower third a seated woman, who appears to be naked apart from a headdress, holding up two wriggling snakes. The woman's head is large in proportion to her body, and the snakes are also large compared to her arms. The upper section of the stone shows a triskelion consisting of the heads of three creatures. Each creature is different, although at first glance one might get the impression that the image depicted three serpents. The first appears to be a boar, the second, by comparison with similar representations on other stones, possibly a serpent or dragon of some kind, and the third a bird of prey, or possibly a ram-headed serpent. Ram-headed serpents appear frequently in Celtic iconography and the curve of the head of the creature concerned could either be a beak or a roman nose. Snake-women appear in Celtic and other mythology, and there are representations of a number of different goddesses holding one or more snakes. One example probably represents Verbeia, the spirit of the River Warfe in Yorkshire; see Green, 1992, 227. This image, found near Ilkley, also has a disproportionately large head, but this is the only real similarity. No other picture-stone has been found in Gotland with a similar motif to the one from Smiss, although snakes occur quite frequently, as do female figures. The triskelion is also a commonly-occurring motif on picture-stones, although few are as detailed and zoomorphic as this one. A different interpretation has been put on the stone by Wilhelm Holmqvist (1975, 35–39), and he considers that it might represent Daniel in the lions' den, and so be post-conversion; cf. Introduction, p. xxxvi, note 2. A picture-stone from Sandegårda in Sanda parish, just inland from Västergarn on the west coast of Gotland, is similar in shape and dating to the stone at Smiss and carries as its main motif a large serpent in a figure of eight; see Lindqvist, 1941–1942, I, fig. 48; II, 110. The serpent is supported (in the heraldic sense) by two more naturalistic snakes which writhe up the inside of the borders of the design. The similarity of the central creature to one of the three in the Smiss stone and of the snakes to those held by the snake-witch is striking. A small disc with a pierced decoration, about two and a half inches in diameter, was found in a woman's grave at Ihre in Hellvi parish, north-eastern Gotland, and seems to depict three intertwined serpents. The grave is dated, on the evidence of other finds within it, to the beginning of the ninth century. Nerman, however, on the basis of similar finds from that parish and elsewhere, has dated it to around AD 650–700. Jan Peder Lamm of Statens Historiska Museum, Stockholm has suggested in private correspondence with the writer (14/4/1999) that the article in question might have been an antique when it was buried and this raises the possiblity of such decorative discs having been heirlooms passed from mother to daughter. See Nerman, 1917–1924, 59–60, 86–88; 1969–1975, II, Plate 174, figure 1451. In addition, there is a type of pendant, again often associated with women's graves, in the form of a spiral with a snake's head at its outer end, and one such object forms part of the tenth-century Eketorpsskatten from Örebro län, Sweden; cf. *VABC*, s. v. *Ormspiralshängen*; *Från stenålders-jägare*, 1986–1987, 88–90. Pendants of this kind might have been worn at the breast as amulets both to protect the wearer (the snake as a source of danger) and to promote fertility (the snake as a phallic symbol). The danger against which the amulet was to provide protection could have been that of a difficult labour, with the snake as a mimetic charm, much in the same way that certain fruits and stones that contained a core that rattled and thus imitated the child in the womb were used to assist in labour; see *KL*, s. v. *Barsel*; *Encyclopaedia of religion and ethics*, 1908–1926, III, s. v. *Charms and amulets*, 394, 419, 422. A further type of snake amulet has been found in Gotland, consisting of a copper locket ('dosa') containing the coiled skeleton of a snake, or possibly a slow-worm; cf. Magnusson, 1976, 113. The imagery of a coiled creature in a closed space again suggests that this object was an amulet worn either to procure pregnancy or to ease childbirth. The snake's sloughing of its skin could be taken as a metaphor for the latter. Snakes' tongues were used as amulets against black magic and illness as late as the fourteenth century, and snakes were sacred to the Baltic peoples, being particularly associated with marriage and birth; see *KL*, s. v. *Amulettar*; Gimbutas, 1963, 203.

According to Hellquist, 1980, s. v. *slunga* (1), *slunga* corresponds to Swedish *slingra*, 'entwine (oneself)', but he also considers it related to the Middle Low German *slingen*, with the additional meaning 'plait', and to Anglo-Saxon *slingan*, 'creep'. The images of the disc and the amulet mentioned above correspond to the former interpretation. If one assumes that it was common for a pregnant woman to wear a snake spiral or some such amulet, it is possible that the dream represents the movement of the snake or snakes from the amulet into her body, as well as the birth itself. The phrase *slungnir saman* would then be being used in two meanings: 'crept together' and 'coiled together', with respectively the past and passive participles.

2/9. *barmi*: 'womb' in this instance, although the usual translation is 'breast' or 'bosom'. The Swedish *sköte*, which is also used as a synonym for *barm* has, additionally, the connotation *moderssköte*, 'womb', and despite Hellquist's dismissing this interpretation of *barm* as hardly tenable (1980, s. v. *barm*), it seems possible in the present context. The natural site from which the snakes representing Huitastierna's three sons would emanate is, it might be suggested, her womb. *SAOB* (s. v. *barm* (2)) gives *moderlif, kved*, 'womb', as an obsolete meaning, with an example of its use in 1614. This is in fact one of the oldest citations included in the entry and gives a strong indication that 'womb' may have been the principal medieval meaning. That the word was also used in Old Danish in this sense is indicated by Falk and Torp (1903–1906, s. v. *Barm*). Kalkar (1881–1918, s. v. *Barm*) gives *moderliv*, 'womb', as the primary meaning and cites *barmbroder* as meaning *halvbroder på mødrene side* which would correspond to the same interpretation. Schlyter in his glossary to *Guta lag* (*CIG*, 243) gives *sinus* as the Latin equivalent for *barm*. This can mean 'breast' but also 'lap', 'curve', 'fold', 'hiding place'. Peringskiöld (1699, 443) translates *barmi* as Latin *gremio*, 'lap', 'breast' and 'womb'. One possibility is that ambiguity is intended and that the dream is an example of a 'pun' dream with the ambiguity between 'breast' and 'womb' being an extension of the pun implicit in the phrase *slungnir saman*, mentioned in the Note to 2/8; cf. Perkins, 1974–1977, 211–213.

2/12–14, 16–18. The metre of the verse is irregular. Lines 12–13 and 16–17 are like *dróttkvætt*, but there is no alliteration in lines 14 and 18. The alliteration in the passage leading up to the verse suggests that the six lines are all that survive of a longer poem. The rings (*baugum*) of the verse echo the coiling of the snakes, as well as the rings that appear frequently on picture-stones. *Alt* could refer to the future of Gotland as a whole, or simply to 'everything', and the binding in rings could be a reference to the interconnection of various events, or to the idea that the future of Gotland is to be determined by the coiling of the snakes (Hafþi's and Huitastierna's sons). The word *boland* could mean either 'inhabited land' or, possibly, 'farming land', that is cultivated land. Nerman (1958) offers a different explanation for the significance of *baugum*, suggesting that they refer to the rings worn by both men and women during the Migration period (*c.*400–*c.*550), although not during the Vendel period immediately following. From this he infers that the traditions behind the verse date from before AD 550. See also Introduction, pp. xxiii–xxiv.

2/19. The division of an area into three administrative districts seems to have been a common one in Scandinavia, occurring both on Öland and in Närke by the thirteenth and fourteenth centuries, as well as in Norway; see Tunberg, 1911, 48. There is also evidence in the oldest law for Dalarna that it was divided into three; see Tunberg, 1911, 135–138. In the case of Gotland, it appears that the word *landet* was used of the whole island and that the *Gutnal þing* or *Gutnalþing* or *Gutna alþing* was the overall authoritative body; cf. Tunberg, 1911, 138; Note to 2/27. Each of the subordinate thirds had its own *þriþiungs þing.* The thirds themselves were divided into *siettungar*, two within each third, and each *siettungr* into a number of *hundari*, the smallest administrative area, of which there were 20 on the island by the Late Middle Ages; see *KL*, s. v. *Hundare*. The arithmetic behind the arrangement is discussed by Steffen (1945, 252) who explains the fact that the middle third had only six *hundari*, whereas the other two had seven, by arguing that the island was originally divided into two along a northwest-southeast line, with 10 *hundari* in each. The *hundari* also had *þing*, 10 in each half of the island. The northern half had its main *þing* place at Tingstäde and the southern half at Suderting, now Ajmunds, in the parish of Mästerby. The word *þriþiung* itself is related to the English *riding* as an administrative division. See also Note to 6/21–22; Introduction, p. xxv.

2/23–24. There is evidence of a population reduction at the end of the fifth and in the first half of the sixth centuries. The period of emigration could have extended over a number of decades and then have been followed by a time of unrest in Gotland and attack by outside powers, culminating in the assimilation of Gotland into Sweden; see Note to 6/1; Introduction, pp. xxv–xxvii; Nerman, 1963, 19–21, 23.

2/25. *sum þair ufan iorþar attu*: literally 'that they owned above ground'. This phrase would be translated in Swedish legal language by *lösöre*, 'moveables' or 'chattels' as opposed to land. The corresponding Old Swedish expressions were *lösöre, lösa pänningar, löst goz,* but in *Guta lag* the term used is simply *oyrar*; cf. *GLGS,* 32; *KL,* s. v. *Lösöre* and references. In *Grágás* two sections concerning the finding of property refer specifically to whether it was above or below the ground. In the former case it usually passed to the ownership of the finder. It is possible that the emigrants were forbidden to dig up anything buried on their land; cf. *Grágás,* Ib, 75; 185–186; *KL,* s. v. *Hittegods.*

2/26. The first element of the name *Þorsborg* itself is probably related to the name of the god *Þórr,* one of the most popular deity-names used as place-name elements, and the place was possibly named in the late Middle Ages. At least three other examples of the place-name *Torsborg* are found in Sweden: in Uppland, between Sigtuna and Skokloster, in Härjedalen, and on Öland, east of Torslunda. This last has a *fornborg* just to the east of it; cf. Hallberg, 1985, 91. See also *KL,* s. v. *Fornborgar* and references; Introduction, pp. xxvii–xxix.

2/27. It has been suggested by Steffen (1945, 246) that *land* is here being used to mean the *alþing* and this seems to make some sense. The decision to ballot away a third of the population would probably have been taken by the *alþing* in this instance, and they would thus have the responsibility for ensuring that the edict was obeyed. The *gutnal þing* is referred to as *land alt* in a passage in *Guta lag;* cf. *GLGS,* 46.

4/1. The modern form of the place-name, *Fårö,* might suggest that it is related to Swedish *får,* Old Swedish *far,* 'sheep'. The word for sheep in Gotland, however, was and is *lamb.* An alternative derivation is from *fara* ('travel', 'fare', 'go on one's way'). This might, it has been suggested, refer to the crossing of the sound between Gotland and Fårö, in this case by the emigrants. Olsson (1984, 98–100) agrees and states that if the name had anything to do with *får* it could not have been given to the island by the inhabitants, but must have been given by outsiders. When P. A. Säve made his unpublished study of dialect in the nineteenth century, he noted that the islanders used the pronunciation /farö/ with a long *a,* rather than /fårö/. Säve's findings have been used by, among others, Adolf Noreen, Danell and Schagerström, and Herbert Gustavson; see Noreen, 1879, 336; *GO;* Gustavson, 1940–1948, I, 96; 1977, 12. On Fårö, at Vardabjerget, just south of Fårö church, there are remains of a prehistoric fort, which had a simple earth wall, as opposed to the more substantial limestone

construction at Torsburgen. It is suggested by Nordin (1881, 97–
99) that this fort may have been raised by the evacuees. Cf. also
Olsson, 1984, 136–137.

4/3. Estonia, like Gotland, has a chalky landscape, and is mainly
low-lying, being less than 320 metres above sea-level at its
highest point. From at least the time of Tacitus, one of the Baltic
tribes, probably the Lithuanians or Letts, was designated *Æstii*,
but this term was later transferred to the Finno-Ugric tribes in
Estonia and Livonia; cf. Tacitus, 1914, 54, 198. The origin of the
word is not known, but could be Germanic; see Hellquist, 1980,
s. v. *est.* Hellquist considers the place-name *Aistland* to be secondary to the name of the tribe, and thus of no significance in
determining the origin of the element *est* itself.

Dagö, Estonian *Hiimuaa*, is a flat, low-lying island with a
marshy, sparsely-populated interior, only the southern part being
fertile, and having harbours only on its northern coast. The
second element of its name as recorded in *Guta saga* does not,
however, appear to mean 'island'. Tamm (1890–1905, s. v. *ed*)
has Swedish *ed* as 'det gamla namnet för "näs" i detta ords nutida
mening = "isthmus", vanligt i svenska ortnamn'. The same word
lies behind the dialect word *ed* (*eda* or *ida* according to Hellquist,
1980, s. v. *ida*) meaning 'ställe i en fors, där vattnet strömmar
tillbaka'. Tamm takes it to be related to Old Swedish *ēþ* n. 'ställe
där den som färdas på en vatten-farled måste för naturhinder taga
vägen över en kortare sträcka land, t. ex. över ett näs (landtunga)
eller förbi ett vattenfall'. It has the same meaning as Old Icelandic *eið* (n.), and according to Tamm means 'gång' or 'ställe över
hvilket man går fram' as opposed to *sund*, 'ställe där man simmar
över'. There is a narrow wooded promontory, now called *Köppo*,
stretching from the western edge of Dagö and it is possible that
it was this promontory that was referred to here. The island of
Viðoy in the Faeroes has a promontory joined to it by an isthmus
called Viðareiði. The name *Dagaiþi* could thus be a *pars pro toto*.
Svensson (1919, 9), however, relates the suffix to a proposed
*-haiþi*, which, he argues, persisted in Estonian ('Estlands finska
dialekt') in the Middle Ages, although he gives no examples. He
relates this suffix to that in names such as *Finnhed*, which as a
result of confusion came to refer to several different parts of the
Baltic seaboard. The name *Dagaiþi*, if it implies a heath-like
landscape, would also be consistent with the island of Dagö as it

appears on maps today. Carl Säve (1852, 163, note 4) suggests that the name may be related to a personal name *Dagr*, or to the fact that eastward-bound travellers were accustomed to stop there for a day, at some ness or promontory. He also notes the name *Kylley* or *Kyllaj*, a harbour on the east coast of Gotland, in the parish of Hellvi. This is pronounced as *Kyllai, Kyll-aid* by the older generation, that is with a similar second element to that in *Dagaiþi*. Johansen (1951, 125, 278, 280–281) mentions that the western peninsula is called *Dagerort*. He also gives several different spellings of the name for the island (*Dageyden, Dagden, Dageden*), all of which seem to point to *Dagaiþi* being very close to the original form. In 1228, the form *Dageida* (translated as *insula deserta*) is recorded, and Johansen is of the opinion that, with the lack of any archaeological finds on the island from that period or earlier, this interpretation of the name seems possibly to be justified.

4/4. There is no existing evidence for a fortification on Dagö.

4/6. The Western Dvina formed the first part, undertaken by boat, of one of the major trade routes to Byzantium. The route continued by land across to the River Dnieper, then by boat, passing the river rapids by portage, and finally across the Black Sea under sail to Byzantium. Three other sources mention the routes taken by Scandinavians to the East. The passing of the rapids of the Dnieper is described in Constantine Porphyrogenitus's *De administrando imperio* (1962–1967, I, 57–61; II, 38–52). Here the 'Russian' names of the rapids are given interpretations of Scandinavian origin. In the *Russian primary chronicle* the route between the Varangians and the Greeks (the people of the Byzantine Empire) is described, starting from Greece, as being along the Dnieper, via portage to the River Lovat and thence to Lake Ilmen. From there, the River Volkhov flows into Lake Neva (Ladoga), which eventually opens into the Varangian Sea (the Baltic), as does the Dvina. The latter is called 'the route to the Varangians'. The Varangians are described as a tribe related to the Swedes, Normans, Gotlanders, Russes, English and others; see *RPC*, 52, 53, 59. Thirdly, Adam of Bremen mentions that there was a route from Sweden to Greece and that it was followed by ship. The reference by him to an island called *Iumne*, described as Christian and belonging to Denmark, has given rise to speculation that Gotland might be intended. He states that the island has a safe harbour for ships being despatched to the barbarians and to Greece. Adam also describes a route from Denmark via Birka to Russia; see Adam of Bremen, 1961, 252, 254, 460, G Schol. 126. The Arabic writer, al-Masudi, writing in about 956, mentions a people called *al-Kūd.kānāh*, a name that has been interpreted as 'northmen' and, tentatively, 'Gotlanders' (*al-Kūḏlānah*). Reference is also made to *Baḥr Warank*, the Varangian Sea; see Birkeland, 1954, 30–42, 142. Another Arabic writer, Ibn Rustah, records the trade routes of the Rus (*ar-Rusiya*) down the Volga to an island or peninsula in a lake (probably Novgorod); see Birkeland, 1954, 15–16, 135, notes 5 and 6. In Gotland, a small stone carrying a runic inscription was found at Bogeviken, in Boge parish in north-east Gotland (Pilgårdsstenen). The inscription, which has been dated to the late tenth century, includes the words **kuamu uitiaifur**, which Krause (1953) interprets as 'De kommo långt i Aifur'. It is possible that *Aifur* refers to the fourth and largest of the rapids described by Constantine Porphyrogenitus, of which *Aifur* was the Scandinavian name; see *GV*, 427–429. The trade route along the Dvina was important during the ninth and tenth centuries, but trade with Kiev was replaced by trade with Novgorod in the following century. See also Foote and Wilson, 1979, 224–229; *KL*, s. v. *Rysslandshandel* and references.

4/7. *Grikland*. The Byzantine Empire is meant here, rather than Greece, and the 'king' referred to, the Byzantine emperor. *Grikland* is mentioned on several runestones, including one in Gotland, the slipstone from Timans in Roma parish (G 216). This is the only inscription found in Gotland that mentions *Grikland*, a fact which Svärdström does not think, however, to be of any special significance; cf. *GR* II, 235. See also Note to 8/3.

4/8. The phrase *ny ok niþar* refers to the new and the waning moon. It was used as a legal term in the oldest laws, for example *Gulaþingslǫg* (*NGL* I, 29), and the older and later *Västgötalagar*, in connection with the sale of slaves. The seller was responsible for the slave being free of hidden faults for a 'waxing and waning' after the sale; cf. *Codex iuris Vestrogotici*, 1827, 60, 176. In other law texts 'month' is used for the same time period; cf. *NGL* I, 25; *KL*, s. v. *Ny og ne* and references.

4/9. Pipping, in rejecting Schlyter's emendation of *ai miþ ann* to *ai maira þan*, and putting forward the otherwise unsupported reading, *ain niþ ann*, presents the idea that a 'waning' was used to designate a complete month. One waning occurs each month, but the period of the waning itself occupies only half a month. A slightly more radical change to the text would seem to have some justification; cf. Pipping, 1904, 14–15; *GLGS*, 63 note 3; *CIG*, 95; *AL*, 38, §31.

4/11. The phrase *e ok e* also occurs as *ee ok ee* and *ä ok ä*; cf. *Konung Alexander*, 1855–1862, II, 319, line 9854; *Erikskrönikan*, 1963, 227, line 3958. The expression seems to have been borrowed into Middle English; cf. *a33 occ a33* in *The Ormulum*, 1852, line 3212; Olszewska, 1933, 76, 80.

4/16. Trade between Gotland and the Goths flourished during the first century, but the Weichsel (Vistula) route through to the Donau (Danube) was blocked by the Slavs in the third century, and more westerly routes gradually replaced it in importance; cf. Lindqvist, 1933, 58–61. Points of similarity between Gutnish and the Gothic language are discussed by Bugge (*NIÆR* I, 152–158) in connection with a runic inscription on a silver clasp from Etelhem parish in central Gotland, although he does not conclude that the medieval inhabitants were ethnically Goths. Examples he gives of possible influence or remains are Gutnish and Gotlandic *lamb*, 'sheep' and the form of the ending in *Ormika*. He suggests that the Gothic spoken in Gotland before the arrival of Swedish-speakers coloured the development of the Swedish used on the island; cf. *NIÆR* I, 157. Carl Säve (*GU*, x–xi) wonders if visitors from Gotland to the Byzantine empire or Jerusalem could have encountered people calling themselves *gutans*, and been struck by the similarity of their language to their own. See also Introduction, pp. xxx–xxxi.

4/17. In the manuscript, a sixteenth-century hand has added in the margin 'cultus idololatricus', that is 'the cult of idolatry'.

4/17–18. The punctuation here follows that suggested by Wessén (*SL* IV, 292). Earlier editions, that of Hadorph (1687, 48) for example, take *hauga* to qualify *vi* and insert a full stop after *stafgarþa*, or at least include *a haiþin guþ* as part of the following clause (referring specifically to the sacrificing of their sons and daughters). On the grounds of rhythm alone the former punctuation seems preferable, and there is no need to lose the meaning of *hauga* as 'howe' by taking it as an adjective to qualify the 'holy places'. Hadorph (1687, 48) also translates *vi* as 'Nääs', which he then interprets as 'Åsar'. *Ás* is the name of the place at which the first church in Iceland was built; cf. Notes to

8/18 and 8/25. The phrase is apparently formulaic, since it also occurs in *Guta lag* in a slightly different form; cf. *GLGS*, 7.

4/18. Olsson (1976; 1992), having studied over 40 places in Gotland with names apparently related to the word, comes to the conclusion that *stafgarþar* were sites of abandoned Iron-Age dwellings, which became the subject of an ancestor cult. This explanation seems probable.

Other alternatives which he rejects are: (1) that a *stafgarþr* was a fenced area, surrounded by staves, which was a cult site of some sort, (2) that it was an enclosed cult site containing one or more raised wooden pillars, (3) that it was a secular area fenced in a certain manner and (4) that it was a place where wood was collected. Olsson admits the third of these to be linguistically justifiable. There could, he thinks, be a connection between *stafgarþr* and the Swedish dialect *skidgård*, 'gärdesgård', the area immediately surrounding the dwelling on a farm and marked off from the agricultural land. *Stafgarþr*-names, however, always seem to be associated with the sites of Early Iron-Age house foundations. Olsson rejects the fourth suggestion, that *stafgarþar* were places where wood was gathered, or permitted to be gathered, for a similar reason. He considers the first two interpretations together, and argues that their supporters are inferring, from *Guta lag* and *Guta saga*, a meaning which has no other justification. He also suggests that, since the retention of a place-name is dependent upon continuous habitation, and since all the Early Iron-Age sites concerned seem to have been abandoned before AD 600, it seems unlikely that memories of cult use before that time would have been retained in the place-names up to 1500 years after the sites had been abandoned; see Olsson, 1976, 18, 97–100. His overall conclusion is that *stafgarþr* is 'ett gammalt gotländskt ord för "(plats med) järnåldershusgrund(er)"' and that certain of these sites, but probably not all, had become places of worship, just as certain *hult* were cult sites, but by no means all groves of trees; see Olsson, 1976, 101–103. In a later article, Olsson (1992, 95–96) initially rejects Måhl's suggestion (1990, 23–24) that *stav* had the meaning *bildsten*, and that *stavgarþr* [sic] thus meant a place or enclosure with a picture-stone, on the grounds that this meaning was secondary to the existence of places with the name *stavgard*. He then cites a private communication from Gösta Holm (3/11/1976) in which the latter suggests that the old foundations were used as enclosed areas, *gardar*, within which, perhaps, cult pillars were raised. If these pillars were of stone, then Måhl's suggestion of an enclosure containing picture or other stones would be linguistically acceptable, and the etymology of *stafgarþr* explained.

4/18–19. Evidence for human sacrifice in Scandinavia exists in archeological material, art and literature, both native and foreign. The Oseberg ship-burial is an example of a 'double grave' in which one of the occupants did not, apparently, die a natural death. In the period of conversion in Iceland sacrifices were made, perhaps, to prevent the spread of the new religion; see *Kristnisaga*, 1905, ch. 12. Cf. also *KL*, s. v. *Blot*; *Menneskeoffer*; *Offer* and references; Introduction, pp. xxxii–xxxiii.

4/19–20. The term *filepi* would have included horses and a description in *Hákonar saga góða* in *Heimskringla* (ch. 14; *ÍF* XXVI, 167–168) gives circumstantial details of a sacrificial meal centred around boiled horse-meat. The *matr* referred to would probably have been food derived from home-grown crops, a tradition continued in the Christian harvest festival. *Mungat* was a specially-brewed ale for times of celebration; see *KL*, s. v. *Øl*, col. 693. It was possibly drunk in connection with ritual dedications to the gods, for a good harvest, for the dead, etc. as described in *Hákonar saga góða*. Again, the custom of brewing ale and drinking it at times of celebration continued into the Christian era, and is written, for example, into the law of the Gulathing district of Norway (*NGL* I, 6). Cf. also Foote and Wilson, 1979, 401–402; *KL*, s. v. *Hästkött*; *Minne* and references; Magnusen, 1829, 4, 13.

4/20–21. It might have been customary for the annual sacrifice on behalf of the island to have been held at the *alþing*. If the origin of the name *Roma* is taken to be *rum* 'area, open place' (Olsson, 1984, 47), it could be that the central cult and administrative sites were one and the same; cf. *KL*, s. v. *Ting på Gotland*; *Tingsted* and references.

4/21–22. *Ellar hafþi huer þriþiungr sir.* These were probably interim, seasonal sacrifices. Magnusen (1829, 3–15) gives details of the times of sacrifice at which strong ale was brewed by guilds, which were gradually taken over by the Christian festivals, for example the feasts of All Saints (November 1st), Christmas, Walburga (Valborg, May 1st) and St John (S:t Hans, June 24th).

4/22–23. The lesser assemblies were probably the *hundaris þing* and *siettungs þing*; see Note to 2/19.

4/23. The first element of *supnautr* is related to Gutnish *saupr*, 'spring, brook', Old Icelandic *soð*, 'meat broth', *suð*, 'simmering' and ultimately *sjóða*, 'cook'. It is also associated with Old Swedish *söper*, 'sheep' and Gutnish *soypr*, 'beast', which are in turn related to Gothic *saups*, 'sacrifice'. The second element is related to the Old Icelandic *nautr*, 'companion', Old Swedish *nöter*, 'someone who enjoys something together with'; see Hellquist, 1980, s. v. *sjuda*; *njuta*; *nöt* (2). Possible archaeological support for the practice of holding communal sacrificial meals is suggested by Nerman (1941b); see Note to 4/19–20. See also Introduction, pp. xxxii–xxxiii.

## Chapter 2

6/1. In the margin of the manuscript the following is added: 'pacis conditio cum Rege sveciæ facta. et Tribvtum Anniuersarium', that is 'peace agreement made with the king of the Swedes and the annual tribute'.

*stridu a Gutland.* This could possibly refer in part to the raids against Gotland made by Olaf Haraldsson; see Note to 8/4.

6/2. The Swedish name for the islanders of Gotland is *gotlänningar*, but the term *gutar* persisted throughout the Middle Ages. See Note to 2/1.

6/4. Avair's nickname, if it is interpreted as 'straw legs' (i. e. one who wrapped his legs in straw), is reminiscent of the derogatory name *birkibeinar* given to the Norwegian supporters of Eystein Meyla who in 1174 rose up against Magnús Erlingsson. It is assumed that they were given this name because they were so poor that they used birch leggings instead of boots. The negative connotation of the name had disappeared by 1217–1218, when they joined with the clerical party in the Norwegian civil war in support of a hereditary monarchy; cf. *KL*, s. v. *Birkebeiner*, cols 600, 610. Other possible meanings might be 'straw bones' ('för sina smala bens skull' as suggested in *VABC*, s. v. *Avair Strabain*), 'tall and thin-legged' (Öhrman, 1994, 62) or perhaps 'straw-straight', if *bein* means 'straight' (Hellquist, 1980, s. v. *ben*). Other -*bein* nicknames recorded are *þiokkubeinn* 'thick-legs', *sperribein* 'stiff in the feet' and *krakabein* 'thin-legged' (a name used by the Danes of Olaf Tryggvason); cf. *Sveriges medeltida personnamn*, 1974– , s. v. *Aver*; Lind, 1920–1921, s. v. -*bein*.

The name *Alfa* could be related to *alv*, 'jordlager under matjorden'

and to the German dialect word *alben*, 'ett slags lös kalkjord';
see Hellquist, 1980, s. v. *alv*. The geology of considerable areas
of Gotland might be consistent with this interpretation. Olsson
(1984, 43) suggests an alternative, that *Alva* is related to *alver*,
'flackt, trädlöst, öppet, öde fält'. Neither of these etymologies
can be supported by reference to other Gotlandic place-names.

6/5. This is the only record of the first treaty between Gotland and
Sweden, but it was probably drawn up during the eleventh century. It is possible that Gotland passed in and out of Swedish
control at various times from the sixth to the twelfth centuries,
with its incorporation only being recorded officially in the thirteenth century. Certainly the author of *Guta saga* assumes that
the first agreement was put in place in heathen times, but not so
far in the past that a firm tradition did not exist; cf. *SL* IV, 304–
306; Introduction, pp. xxxiii–xxxv, esp. p. xxxiv, note 1.

From the later mention of Uppsala, it is evident that the king
of the Svear is being referred to here. The Svear inhabited the
eastern part of Sweden, around Lake Mälaren. Tacitus's use of
the name Suiones in the late first century is assumed by Hellquist
and others to have included all the Scandinavian Germanic tribes,
and so may Jordanes's *Suehans* in the sixth century, although this
has been disputed; cf. Hjärne 1938, 14–19. By the ninth century,
however, the corresponding name most probably referred only to
the inhabitants of eastern Sweden; cf. Tacitus, 1914, 53, 196;
Jordanes, 1997, 39; Hellquist, 1980, s. v. *svear*; *KL*, s. v. *Svear*
and references.

6/7. The original meaning of the Old Swedish *fēgher*, 'condemned
to death', is retained in Swedish dialect and, with various other
meanings, in the related Scottish word 'fey'; see Hellquist, 1980,
s. v. *feg*. The Old Swedish *fallin*, 'suitable for', and possibly by
extension 'destined for', might be a relevant meaning for *fallastan*
in this instance; cf. Hellquist, 1980, s. v. *falla*.

6/8. The wergild laid down in Gutnish law (*GLGS*, 19) is three
marks of gold (equivalent to 24 marks of silver or 96 marks in
money), so in this case Avair was stipulating a value of nine marks;
cf. *SL* IV, 259. A proportionally high valuation (in this instance
six hundreds as compared with the more usual two hundreds for
a man of standing) was placed on the life of Hǫskuldr Hvítaness-
goði in *Njáls saga*, ch. 123 (*ÍF* XII, 312). For a more detailed
discussion of compensation for loss of life, cf. *KL*, s. v. *Mansbot.*

6/9–11. *Þy et . . . af ganga.* This could refer either to the preceding speech or to the following negotiations. If the former, the author is admiring Avair's foresightedness in making provision for his family should his mission miscarry; if the latter he is explaining to some extent why Avair succeeded in his negotiations where others had failed. The former interpretation has a certain immediacy about it, but the balance of the syntax (the inversion of subject and verb in the following sentence) and the generally more objective tone, would favour the latter interpretation in the absence of other evidence. Although Hadorph (1687, 49) punctuates and translates the clause as belonging to the previous sentence and Gordon (1962, 177) as belonging to the following sentence, Schlyter (*CIG*, 96), Säve (*GU*, 32), Noreen (*AL*, 38, §§18–19) and Wessén (*SL* IV, 292) all treat the clause as a separate sentence, thereby retaining the ambiguity of the original. The adjective *snieldr* can mean: 'wise', 'clever', 'brave' or 'eloquent'. In connection with the expression *fielkunnugr* it could be noted that in Icelandic *fjǫlkunnigr* has specific connotations of supernatural powers, of being 'skilled in the black arts'; cf. C–V, s. v. *Fjöl-kunnigr*; *ÍO*, s. v. *fjölkyn(n)gi.* Pipping (*GLGS, Ordbok*, 23), however, translates it merely as 'mångkunnig'. It is possible that the phrase *so sum sagur af ganga* refers to tales relating to Avair's supposed supernatural powers, which the author thought were not relevant to the immediate narrative, or not helpful to his argument. See also Introduction, pp. xxxv–xxxvi.

6/12. The mark of silver was a unit of weight rather than money; cf. *KL*, s. v. *Mark.* Lindquist (1984, 139–144) investigates the implications of the amount of tax agreed upon for the islanders. In particular, he relates the tax level to the imposition of the *ledung* in the latter part of the twelfth century and the severe increases in taxation brought in by Birger Magnusson in 1313. His conclusion is that until the start of the fifteenth century the resulting tax was not particularly onerous, and in fact very much lower than that in, for example, the Lake Mälaren area. The increases brought in by Birger Magnusson were cancelled during the minority of Magnus Eriksson, in letters dated August 25th, 1320, as a recognition of the loyalty shown by the Gotlanders since the death of Magnus's father, Erik; see *DS* III, 473–475, nos 2255–2256.

6/14. The term, *svearnas jarl* in full, denoted the king's highest officer, a position recorded in Sweden from the mid-twelfth to the mid-thirteenth century. The jarl was responsible for the *ledung*-fleet; see Note to 12/24–25. Probably the most famous holder of the title was Birger Jarl (†1266) who was appointed in 1248 by Erik Eriksson (†1250), the last king of his line. Birger held the position of regent from 1250 until his own death and the title *jarl* was replaced by (*svea*) *hertig*; cf. *KL*, s. v. *Jarl. Sverige.* The jarl's position in this case probably related directly to Gotland's association with Sweden and may be an argument for dating the absorption of Gotland into Sweden to no earlier than the middle of the twelfth century. The mention of the jarl at this point in the narrative could, however, be an anachronism introduced by the author. See also Introduction, p. lii.

6/16. The phrase *sielfs viliandi* is intended to stress that the Gotlanders were not subjugated by the Swedes, but entered into a mutually advantageous arrangement. The apparent low level of taxation, as discussed in the Note to 6/12, would seem to support the supposition that the full subjugation of Gotland to Sweden did not occur with the first payment of tax, but only later.

6/17. The alliterative phrase *frir ok frelsir* could be a quotation from the legal document drawn up between Sweden and Gotland; cf. *KL*, s. v. *Handelsfred.* See also Introduction, p. xxxv.

6/18. Toll payments for the movement of goods were common throughout the Middle Ages in Scandinavia; see *KL*, s. v. *Told.*

6/19. *kornband*: literally, 'corn prohibition'. In 1276 Magnus Ladulås confirmed the freedom of Gotlanders to import corn (barley) from Sweden, except in those years when there was a general export ban; see *STFM* I, 273–274, no. 126; *PRF* I, 1; *KL*, s. v. *Kornhandel.* The fact that this edict is described as a 'confirmation' could indicate that the arrangement existed earlier on a more informal basis.

The word *hegn*, Old Swedish *hægn*, is related to the English 'hedge' in the sense of 'hedge around, protect'; cf. Hellquist, 1980, s. v. *hägn.* Olszewska (1937–1945, 242) notes the corresponding Middle English *help and hald*, 'help and protection'.

6/21–22. The *gutnalþing*, the general assembly of Gotland, was held at Roma in the centre of the island during the Middle Ages. The form *gutnalþing* is problematic, because of the -*n*-, and Schlyter (*CIS* XIII, 241, s.v. *gutnal þing*) comments that *guta alþing* would be the expected form, and that no explanation can be offered for the -*n*-. Bugge (*NIÆR* I, 152), however, suggests that *Gutna* was an older form of *Guta*, the genitive plural of *Gutar* (cf. Old Norse *goti*, genitive plural *gotna*). The adjective *gutnisk* refers to the language, etc. of Gotland, as opposed to the people; cf. *SAOB*, s. v. *gutisk*. Lindroth (1915, 73) has put forward an alternative view, that *Gutnal* was a place-name, meaning 'gutarnas helgedom' and that this was Latinised to *Gutnalia*. He cites several instances in which the element -*al* could mean 'helgedom'. The expression *gutnal þing* would then mean simply 'the assembly at Gutnal', with no implication that it was from the outset an assembly for the whole of the island. Cf. also Olrik and Ellekilde, 1926–1951, I, 540–541. Roma itself is not mentioned in the oldest manuscript of *Guta saga*, nor in *Guta lag*, although it is referred to in the Low German translation (manuscript dated 1401) where it says, 'czu gutnaldhing das ist czu Rume'; see *CIG*, 164. Roma seems first to have come to prominence when it became the site of the Cistercian monastery, called *Beata Maria de Gutnalia*; cf. Steffen, 1945, 250; Introduction, p. xlvii. This form of the name occurs as early as the twelfth century; cf. Yrwing, 1978, 166–167 and references. The place-name *Roma* might possibly be related to the name *Rome* itself, but more likely to the place-name element *rum*, signifying an open place; see Hellquist, 1980, s. v. *rum*; Olsson, 1984, 47. Cf. also *KL*, s. v. *Ting på Gotland*; Note to 4/20–21.

6/23. *friþ lysa*. This could also be interpreted as referring to a formal declaration of truce at a public meeting, perhaps for a particular period of time; cf. *KL*, s. v. *Fridslagstiftning*; Magnusen, 1829, 14.

6/24. Gamla Uppsala was the administrative and cult centre of Sweden until the start of the eleventh century, but already appeared in tenth-century sources. The kings at first had the title *Uppsalakonung*, but were later called *sveakonung*, to differentiate them from the rulers of the *götar* from the south and west. It was in Gamla Uppsala that the temple, described by Adam of Bremen as late as 1070, was raised and the kings buried. When the first Swedish bishopric was established at the instigation of Olaf Skötkonung around 1000, it was at Skara in Västergötland, rather than in Uppsala. It is reasonable to suggest that this indicates the strong pagan influence which still pervaded Uppsala, making it unsuitable as a see. One might also infer that the Götar had at this time accepted the overlordship of the Uppsala kings. When a bishopric was founded in Uppland in 1050 it was at Sigtuna, and not until 1164 was the archbishopric at Uppsala established, after the bishopric of Sigtuna had moved there in the 1130s. In 1273 or 1290 the see and the name *Uppsala* were transferred to the site of the modern town; see Adam of Bremen, 1961, 470–473; Foote and Wilson, 1979, 25–34, 389–391, 418; Kumlien, 1967, 13–15, 18–21; Lindqvist, 1967.

8/1–10. The narrative concerning St Olaf (or *Óláfr* as his name is usually given in Old Norse texts) has the following added, in a sixteenth-century hand, in the top margin of the manuscript: 'De S. OLAO', that is 'Concerning St Olaf'. Most editions record this paragraph as chapter 3.

This passage is the first mention in written sources of the conversion of Gotland to Christianity. Gotland is not included in the general legends concerning Olaf, and Söderberg (1922, 224, 227–228) states that there is evidence from runic inscriptions that Christianity was well established in Gotland by 1050, and that this would be unlikely if it were first introduced in 1028. Cf. also Lindqvist, 1960–1962, 87; Introduction, p. xxxvi, note 2. On the other hand, P. A. Säve (1873–1874) records legends about Olaf in Gotland, particularly from the northern part of the island; see Introduction, pp. xxxviii–xxxix. Nihlén (1975, 154–155) also gives an account of a number of tales in some of which Olaf seems to take over the role of Thor as the protector of the people from giants and trolls. Olaf's importance on the island could possibly be more the result of his being the first Scandinavian 'saint' (although never officially recognised in Rome) than of any particular missionary effort; cf. Ochsner, 1973, 26–28. One suggestion proposed is that this episode is a later insertion into *Guta saga*; cf. Söderberg, 1922, 235–236; Lindqvist, 1960–1962, 110, 114; Fritzell, 1971, 20. Cf. also Introduction, pp. xxxvi–xl.

8/1–2. Olaf was driven into exile by King Knut of Denmark through the agency of Hákon jarl in 1028–1029; cf. *Óláfs saga helga*, ch. 181 (*ÍF* XXVII, 328–330). According to Snorri Sturluson the principal reason for the revolt against him was that he curtailed the common practice amongst powerful Norwegians of harrying the coast of Norway.

8/3. The name *Akrgarn*, which fell into disuse in the seventeenth century, seems to be composed of two elements that occur quite frequently in place-names. The first, *acr* or *aker*, is the Gotlandic form of Swedish *åker*, 'field'. The second, *garn*, is related to a word meaning 'gut' or 'intestines', but has come also to have the meaning 'yarn'. Hellquist (1980, s. v. *Garn* (2)) suggests that in place-names it could relate to an older meaning 'något långsträckt' and this interpretation seems likely here (a place with a string of fields, for example, or a peninsula with fields). Harry Ståhl (*KL*, s. v. *Svear*) suggests that the word means 'långsträckt holme', while Lindroth (1914b, 125–126) puts forward alternative interpretations: (1) that it could mean 'långsträckt vattendrag', which would be consistent with places such as *Gammelgarn* and *Östergarn*, and (2) that the meaning 'klippholme' had been imported from the Swedish mainland and applied to places like *Akrgarn* and *Grogarn*. Olsson (1984, 49–50) rejects this latter and points to the narrow sound between the peninsula and the mainland in the case of *Akrgarn*, and the narrow gravel ridges in the case of *Grogarn*, as more likely origins of the name. Since this interpretation appears to correspond best to the original meaning of the word *garn*, it seems to be a more probable explanation than Lindroth's second one. Akrgarn, which was a port in the Middle Ages, is now no longer on the coast. The coastline there is barren and it is some way from agricultural land. Like S:t Olofshamn (also known as Gamlehamn) on Fårö, and Hau Gröno in Fleringe parish on the sound between Fårö and Gotland, Akrgarn has the remains of a medieval chapel, and like S:t Olofshamn might have been used in prehistoric times. During the Middle Ages it was possibly a fishing port, particularly a refuge for long-distance fleets; see Lundström, 1983, 108–116.

The name *Ormika* also occurs in a cryptic runic inscription on a slipstone from Timans, in the parish of Roma (G 216). Alongside the personal name **ormiga** is the name **ulvat** (or **ulfuair**), and the place-names **krikiaʀ**, **iaursaliʀ**, **islat** and **serklat**. These are usually interpreted as Greece (the Byzantine empire; see Note to 4/7), Jerusalem, Iceland and the Islamic Caliphate. The inscription, dated to the second half of the eleventh century, could refer to the actual travels of two merchants or pilgrims; see *GV*, 436; von Friesen, 1941, 12–14. There is no reason, however, to assume, as von Friesen does, that the *Ormiga* mentioned in the inscription is idential to the *Ormika* of *Guta saga*. Cf. also *NIYR* III, 305 note 2. Bengt Söderberg (1971, 41–42) contends that such an assumption is historically untenable, but one wonders if it is not possible, as Elisabeth Svärdström (*GR* II, 237) suggests, that the inscription is an imaginative assembly of names (two famous Gotlanders and four exotic places), not referring to any particular event. The form of the name is unusual and Svärdström (*GR* II, 235) suggests that the suffix -*ika* is a diminutive derived from West Germanic, in particular Anglo-Saxon or Frisian, similar to that found in Old Swedish *Svænke*, but retaining the original intermediate vowel. It has also been suggested by Bugge (*NIÆR* I, 156–157) that the form of the name reflects a Gothic origin. See also Introduction, p. xli.

8/4. The first element of *Hainaim* is related to the Swedish dialect word *häjd*, interpreted as 'stängsel' (enclosure); see Hellquist, 1980, s.v. *hejd*. The second element, -(*h*)*aim*, probably relates to a word meaning 'settlement'. The place-name might, if it were pre-Christian, refer to an enclosed community, possibly with some sort of cult background; cf. *stafgarþr*, Note to 4/18. A relationship to a cult site might be supported by the fact that in the north of the parish lies Bjärs, where there is a large burial ground, with finds ranging from the first century to around AD 1050; cf. Nylén, 1966, 196–198. On the other hand, Olsson (1984, 26) relates the first element to \**haiþnir*, \**hainir*, 'hedbor' (heath-dwellers), and points for support to the many heaths and sparsely-vegetated areas in the parish. Hadorph (1687, 50) spells the name *Hainhem*; cf. Note to 10/11.

The episode described here, in which tribute is offered to Olaf, could have its origin in Olaf's visit to Gotland in 1007; cf. Pernler (1977, 13). Tribute was paid on that occasion by Gotlandic representatives to prevent Olaf from harrying Gotland, and this would probably have involved the extended stay that Snorri records. Pernler thinks that this incident might have been confused by the author of *Guta saga* with a later visit, related to Olaf's return from Russia in 1030, which would have been very much shorter; cf. *Óláfs saga helga*, ch. 192 (*ÍF* XXVII, 343); Introduction, pp. xxxvi–xxxviii.

8/5. According to Hellquist (1980, s. v. *vädur*) *veþur* was often used in, for example, biblical language, and originally denoted a yearling male sheep or other animal, as indicated by the fact that the Gothic *wiþrus* is used to translate the Greek word for 'lamb'. *Veþur* does not have the sense of the Modern English cognate *wether*, 'a castrated male sheep'. In Old English and other Germanic languages, *weþer* and its equivalents meant 'male sheep' in general; see Lockwood, 1969, 179.

8/6. Tamm (1890–1905, s. v. *bulle*) gives one meaning of *bulle* as 'drykeskärl utan fot, tumlare, mots. isl. *bolli*, m. drykesskål av kupig form'. See also Introduction, pp. xl–xli.

8/7. The *braiþyx* was the principal attribute of St Olaf. One of the oldest pictorial representations of him with an axe is from circa 1150 at Hängelösa in Västergötland; see *KL*, s. v. *Øks*, cols 667–673; *Olav den hellige*, cols 568–576 and references.

8/7–8. Some, including Fritzell (1972, 34–35) and Ochsner (1973, 27) have argued that the specific, Hamburg–Bremen form of Christianity fostered by St Olaf himself is referred to here, which would imply that an earlier teaching, possibly Celtic or Russian, but more probably English, had existed in Gotland previously. This interpretation is based partly on a precise definition of the meaning of *kennidombr* and partly on the lack of other written evidence for St Olaf having been the apostle of Gotland. Pernler (1977, 12) questions this interpretation, on the very reasonable grounds that *Guta saga* was written at least 200 years after the supposed event and it is hardly likely either that the exact relationship between Ormika and St Olaf would have been known, or that Ormika was, in fact, the first convert.

8/8. A *bynahus* was a private chapel for a family or community; see Introduction, pp. xli, xlv; *KL*, s. v. *Kapel*; *Oratorium*; *Privatkirke* and references.

8/9. Akergarn/S:t Olofsholm is 30 kilometres from Hejnum. Pernler (1977, 13) questions whether Ormika would have had his private chapel built at that distance from his home and Tiberg (1946, 22) dismisses the whole St Olaf episode as a later addition; cf. Smedberg, 1973, 163. It is possible, however, that the author included the passage, perhaps placed out of chronological sequence, because there was already a thriving cult on the island at the time he was writing. A letter to the clergy and laity of Gotland from Bishop Laurentius (Lars) of Linköping in August, 1246 (*DS* I, 315–316, no. 336) allocates the income from the altar of St Olaf's at Åckergarn to the nuns of the convent of Solberga in Visby. This allocation was confirmed in May, 1248 by a letter from the papal legate, Bishop Wilhelm of Sabina (*DS* I, 335, no. 362) in which the name is given as *Ackergarn*. The matter is raised again in April, 1277, in a letter from Bishop

Henrik of Linköping (*DS* I, 516, no. 625), which allocates half the income to the parish priest and parishioners of *Helghavi* and calls the place *Hakergarn*. Three years later, the bishop confirms the arrangement in relation to *Akirgarn* (*DS* I, 571–572, no. 702). Further letters concerning the nuns' rights in *Akergarnaholm* or *Akergarn* from Bishops Petrus and Nicholaus, in 1349 and 1360 respectively, are mentioned by Wallin (1747–1776, II, 119, 121). A map of Gotland from 1646, held in the General Landmäteri-kontoret, and other maps from the seventeenth century show a *S:t Oluf* church on the site of the present ruins and Schlyter points out that Akergarn and S:t Olofsholm are one and the same; cf. *CIG*, 314–315 and references. This does not imply that the building shown on the map was the one raised in the eleventh century; see Pernler, 1978; 1981, 103–109.

8/10. Jaroslav, sometimes called the Lawgiver or the Wise (*c.*978–1054), Prince of Kiev, was one of the legitimate sons of Prince Vladimir (†1015). From 1016 until 1019 he fought against his half-brother, Svyatopolk I, for his share of the principality, while ruling in Novgorod. When Mstislav, his other half-brother, died in 1036, Jaroslav took over the whole of the principality of Kiev, which covered the larger part of Russia at that time, and set up a bishopric in Novgorod, and his son Vladimir as ruler there. Kiev had been converted to Christianity under Vladimir I (called 'The Christianiser of Russia'), after his baptism in 989, and Jaroslav was responsible for authorising the first Russian law code. He established his seat of government in Novgorod and spent more time there than in Kiev; see below; Franklin and Shepard, 1996, 201–202. Jaroslav was a natural source of assistance in Olaf's exile as he was related by marriage to Olaf, being married to Olaf's sister-in-law. She was the daughter of Olaf Skötkonung, king of Sweden and founder of the first Swedish bishopric, at Skara. Ingegärd, Jaroslav's wife, was originally, according to Snorri Sturluson (*ÍF* XXVII, 117), pledged to St Olaf, but was married in 1019 to Jaroslav, leaving Olaf to marry her illegitimate half-sister. Contact was maintained, however, and Jaroslav brought up Olaf's illegitimate son, Magnús, later king of Norway. Ingegärd (referred to as Irina, Eirene in Russian sources) is buried in the St Sophia church in Novgorod. Jaroslav also sheltered another Norwegian royal refugee: Harald Sigurdsson harðráði, who was Olaf's half-brother. Harald stayed some four

years with Jaroslav on his way to Byzantium, where he led the
Varangian guard, and married Jaroslav's daughter; see *DMA*, s. v.
*Yaroslav the Wise*; *Chronicle of Novgorod*, 1914, viii, 1–3; *RPC*,
59–135; *Medieval Scandinavia*, 1993, s. v. *Haraldr harðráði.*
Holmgarðr was the Scandinavian name for Novgorod. It appears
that the name was transferred from one settlement to another at
some point in its history. Although there is no agreement on its
original site, Hulmgarþr has been identified with the Russian
*Gorodishche*, 'hill-fort, fortified settlement', which was widely
believed to have been founded around AD 800 on an island in
Lake Ilmen, and this would be consistent with the meaning of the
word *Holmgarðr*. Archaeological finds also point to a Scandinavian
connection; see Franklin and Shepard, 1996, 40, 105. Novgorod,
meaning 'new fortification', is thought to have been built in the
tenth century, not on the island, but two or three miles north of
the point where the River Volchov runs from Lake Ilmen towards
Lake Ladoga, perhaps uniting two smaller settlements on either
side of the river; see *DMA*, s. v. *Novgorod*; *RPC*, 233. There is no
evidence at the site of Novgorod of a settlement prior to that
time, but equally there are objections to identifying Gorodishche
as the 'old' town; see Thompson, 1967, 12. It seems that the
name *Novgorod* was used in some sources to denote the older
settlement (Gorodishche), this name being transferred to the
later settlement in the same way that Scandinavian sources retained the name *Holmgarðr*, although the meaning no longer
applied; see Franklin and Shepard, 1996, 130, note 36. Jaroslav
and the monarchy had moved from the island to the new settlement by the eleventh century; see Thompson, 1967, 10. Trade
between Sweden and Russia was important from the early ninth
century and was at that time largely conducted from Birka. As
Birka declined, the Gotlanders took over and in the eleventh century
the trade from Gotland was concentrated on Novgorod, which
lay on the major route between the Baltic and Constantinople.
*Guta saga* contains one of the classic descriptions of this route;
see Note to 4/6. Two fragments of a runestone (G 220) from
Hallfrede in Follingbo parish, south-east of Visby, carry the
inscription: . . . **tkaiʀ : aʀ : to i : hulmka** - . . . | . . . **iþi** - : . . .
which has been interpreted as '. . . (after) Uddgair. He died in
Hulmgarþr . . .'; cf. *GR* II, 244–246; *GV*, 437. In the first half of
the twelfth century the Gotlanders had a trading station in Novgorod

with a church dedicated to St Olaf. According to one interpretation (von Friesen, 1913, 70), this church is mentioned in a runic inscription (U 687) from Sjusta(d) in Skokloster parish in Uppland; see Jansson, 1987, 49–50; Montelius, 1914, 101. This is, however, not undisputed; cf. Brate and Bugge, 1887–1891, 334. If von Friesen's interpretation is taken as correct, the inscription tells of a Spjallbude (Spjalbode) of whom it is said, 'Hann var dauðr i Holmgarði i Olafs kirkiu': **an uar : tauþr : i hulmkarþi : i olafs kriki.** The Russians also had trading stations in Gotland. The details of trade with Russia are discussed by Hugo Yrwing; see *KL*, s. v. *Rysslandshandel*; *Östersjöhandel* and references.

## Chapter 3

8/11. This section in the manuscript has been marked in the margin: 'conuersio ad fidem christianam', that is 'conversion to the Christian faith'.

8/11–12. The word *\*kaupmannaskepr* is variously translated to refer to the goods, 'köpmansvaror' (Schlyter, *CIG*, 98; Wessén, *SL* IV, 293) or to the trading itself, 'kiöpenskap' or 'köpenskap', with 'voyages' understood (Hadorph, 1687, 50; Pipping, *GLGS*, *Ordbok*, 43). The latter interpretation would seem to be preferable since the suffix *-skap* is widely used to form abstract nouns denoting skills.

8/13. *kristnum landum.* These would presumably include England and Russia as well as Denmark, Norway and Germany, but not Finland or the Baltic countries, with whom the Gotlanders also traded.

8/14. Pernler (1977, 18) has suggested an Anglo-Saxon influence on the ecclesiastical law in *Guta lag* and, as there was considerable trade between Gotland and England from the twelfth century, it is possible that the priests referred to here were of English origin; cf. Chaucer, 1987, *The Canterbury tales: General Prologue*, line 408; *KL*, s.v. *Englandshandel*. This proposal is supported to some extent by the more frequent occurrence of the name *Båtel* ('Botulf') in personal and place-names in Gotland than in mainland Sweden and Norway, and the appearance of *Botulf* in *Gotländska runkalendern*, a fourteenth-century calendar written in runes (Lithberg and Wessén, 1939, 7, 59, 92). There his day is marked as one of relative importance; see Pernler, 1977, 18–19. A similar Anglo-Saxon missionary influence could equally have come through the medium of trade with Norway (which certainly came under English ecclesiastical influence) or with Denmark. If there was a partial conversion in the eighth or ninth centuries, the interpretation of the conversion of Ormika as being to St Olaf's *specific* form of Christian doctrine should not be dismissed without consideration, although there is no direct support for it; see Note to 8/7–8. Ochsner (1973, 22–24) suggests that the missionaries who came during this period were from Ireland. Internal events in Ireland at the time, however, seem to preclude Irish Celtic missionary activity in Gotland at the end of the eighth and start of the ninth century; see Pernler, 1977, 38–39. A more likely factor during the ninth and tenth centuries was the Hamburg–Bremen mission of Ansgar and his followers. As a result of trade along the Dvina, it would also have been possible for contacts to have been made with the Eastern Church, whose missionaries were active amongst the Slavs of that area in the ninth century. These former clashed with German missionaries in Moravia (now Slovakia) during that period, thus providing another Christian point of contact for Gotlandic merchants; cf. Pernler, 1977, 35–36; Ware, 1976, 82, 83. See also Introduction, pp. xxxvi–xxxvii, note 2.

8/15. The name *Botair* does not occur elsewhere before 1350, but there are several medieval instances of the name *Botair* from Gotland, including a priest, *Botherus*, from the parish of Tofta, on the west coast of Gotland. Names in *Bot-* were generally common in Gotland; cf. *Sveriges medeltida personnamn*, 1974– , s. v. *Boter*.

The first element of the name *Akubekkr*, as in the case of Akrgarn, could refer to a field (*akr*), but Olsson (1984, 43) thinks that it is related to the word *aka* in an oblique form *aku*, meaning 'lort i fårull' amongst other things. The second element is likely to be related to *bekkr*, 'stream'. Olsson's explanation would suggest a meaning 'Skitbäcken', or something similar, which is a possible interpretation when related to the topography of the area near the present church. A farm called *Bäcks* lies just to the north of the parish church.

8/16. The implicit explanation in *Guta saga* for the place-name *Kulastepar* is that it was the site on which Botair's first church was burned, and it has been surmised that the name has some such meaning as 'place with burnt coals'; see Introduction, pp. xliii–xliv. The identification of Kulstäde with *Kulastepar* would place

the supposed first church in Gotland at the meeting point of four
assembly districts (Dede, Hejde, Bande and Stenkumla) and
also at the meeting point of four parishes (Akebäck, Roma,
Björke and Vall), but isolated from the surrounding farms by
woodland and marsh; see Fritzell, 1974, 7–9. An alternative,
more likely, explanation of the place-name to that offered by the
author of *Guta saga* is that *Kol* is a common male name and the
suffix -*städe* often attached to personal names. Both the medial
-*a*- and the -*ar* ending are, however, difficult to explain linguistically. Olsson (1984, 36) suggests a personal name *Kuli* as a
possible origin, but also that the -*a*- could be an intrusive
vowel. Of the -*ar* ending, Pipping (*GLGS, Ordbok*, 45) remarks
that the name was originally a genitive singular form. Olsson
(1984, 35–38) notes several similar place-names with alternative
forms, but he offers no suggestion concerning this version of the
place-name element -*städe*. It is possible that the ending is a
parallel to the nominative ending of *Þieluar*. On the meaning of
the element -*städe* itself, different interpretations have been
suggested, namely 'slåttervall' ('hayfield') or 'ställe' ('place');
cf. Hellberg, 1958, 15, 29; Olsson, 1964, 49.

8/17. The Icelanders attempted, but failed, to burn the first church
built in Iceland; see *Kristnisaga*, 1905, ch. 3.

8/18. As Gun Westholm (1985, 293) points out, there seems to be
no doubt in the mind of the author of *Guta saga* that by *Vi* was
meant Visby, or at least a settlement near enough to the site of
Visby to be thought of as its predecessor. It is worth considering,
however, whether Visby was really intended, or some more general holy place. Carlén (1862, 88) maintains that *Vi* does actually
designate what is now Visby and that the latter name derives
from *Vi* and not from *Vikingaby*, *Viksby* or *Vinetasby*, as has been
suggested by other scholars. This last would refer to the Slav
town Vineta, on the island of Wolin, adjacent to the island of
Ysedom (Usedom) in the mouth of the Oder in Pomerania. The
town was destroyed, and its inhabitants were thought to have fled
to Visby. Vineta was at one time the richest trading town on the
Baltic. It fell before the start of the thirteenth century, either in
814 under Charlemagne, in 840 as a result of civil war, or in 1182
under Waldemar I. There is a story that it sank and that its walls
can still be seen. Traditions seem to agree, however, that the
inhabitants fled to the already famous Visby and exerted an

influence upon it. Carlén concedes that the present town of Visby was apparently not an important trading site before AD 1000. There is no record of Visby's *Gotlandic* inhabitants or officials before the final quarter of the thirteenth century and several sources point to Visby having been a German town, in which case it is unlikely that it was the natural successor to *Vi*. The first mention of there being two communities in Visby is, according to Björkander (1898, 30), Magnus Ladulås's letter, dated 23rd May, 1276, confirming the Gotlanders' privileges in Sweden; cf. *STFM* I, 273–274, no. 126. Excavations in 1932 at S:t Pers Plats failed to find any evidence of a settlement in the vicinity that could have been *Vi*; cf. Knudsen, 1933, 34. On the other hand, there is archaeological evidence for a Viking-Age trading settlement along the shoreline at Visby and there is a rich burial site at Kopparsvik, about 600 metres to the south of the city wall; cf. Westholm, 1985, 296. The predominance of males in that community would indicate that it was not originally a permanent settlement, although it became so towards the end of the Viking Age. The question of the relationship between the name *Vi* and the current name Visby is also one which has been much discussed; see Introduction, pp. xlii–xliii. The name of Visby is first recorded, as *Wysbu*, in an entry for 1203, by Henry of Livonia (Lettland) in the seventh chapter of his chronicle; see *Heinrici Chronicon Livoniae*, 1959, 26, 27, note 1. Since the Chronicle was not completed until around 1226, it might be pre-dated by a reference to *Wisby* in 1225, in a letter of consecration for the church of St Maria from Bishop Bengt of Linköping; see *DS* I, 241, no. 231; Yrwing, 1940, 217–220, 225–226; Knudsen, 1933, 33. Against the traditional interpretation of *Visby* as coming from *Vi-s-by*, Knudsen (1933, 33–34) reasons, first, that most, though not all, Scandinavian place-names ending in -*by* have a natural feature as their first element and do not carry the genitive -*s*-, secondly, that most Swedish and Danish *Viby* place-names are related to *vik* or *vig* respectively ('inlet', 'creek') and thirdly, that it is more likely that the name *Visby* is related to *vis* or *ves* (<\**wis*) meaning 'bending or fast-moving water course' or 'low-lying land'. This latter interpretation has also been put forward by Herbert Gustavson (1938, 35) and is both topographically relevant to Visby and philologically consistent. It might also be preferable to what Knudsen (1933, 32) calls 'Iveren for at forklare et Stednavn . . . saa interessant som muligt, og navnlig saa gammelt som muligt'. On the other hand, Olsson (1984, 20) considers that the -*s*-, which he refers to as 'det besvärande -*s*-', can be satisfactorily explained by theories put forward by Lars Hellberg (1960, 143), as an explanatory, 'epexegetisk', genitive, added when the -*by* was appended. Cf. also Olsson, 1996, 23–25.

8/22. Likkair's nickname, *snielli*, is open to several interpretations. The word could mean 'wise', 'clever' but alternatively 'brave', 'strong', perhaps even 'rash' or 'hasty'; see Hellquist, 1980, s. v. *snille*; *snäll*. If the *e* in the manuscript is taken to replace the *i*, *snelli* could be an example of a doublet for the form *snielli* which exhibits vowel-breaking; see textual note to 8/22; Noreen, 1904, 74. See also Introduction, pp. xliii–xlv.

8/23. The name *Stainkirkia* suggests that the place was the site of a stone church at a time when these were not very common. The author of *Guta saga*, however, states later (10/3–4) that Likkair's church was *þar nu kallar Stainkirkiu*, and does not necessarily imply by this that the church Likkair built was of stone. Since the church was on Likkair's farm, it seems most probable that it was initially a private chapel. As Wessén (*SL* IV, 312) suggests, the farm must have had another name originally. The present church at Stenkyrka dates from the latter half of the thirteenth century, but there are remains of an earlier building under the nave; cf. Lagerlöf and Svahnström, 1991, 231–233. See also Introduction, pp. xliv–xlv.

8/24–25. *Herþin ai brenna*. The form *herþin* is taken as the second person plural imperative by Pipping (*GLGS, Ordbok*, 37) and others, giving the meaning 'Do not burn' or similar. On the other hand, Hadorph (1687, 50) translates the phrase as 'Söken wij at upbränna', that is as the first person plural subjunctive (although the expected form would appear to be *herþum*), giving the meaning 'Let us seek to burn'. This interpretation clearly misreads the negative *ai*, but includes Likkair himself in the decision, and seems to make some sense, especially in view of the argument that Likkair presents for sparing the church and its builder; see Note to 8/25. If one substitutes 'ej' for 'at' in Hadorph's translation, the interpretation could be 'Let us not seek to burn', with the infinitive mark understood. Noreen (1904, 470, 476) gives -*um* or -*om* as the usual endings for the first person plural in both indicative and subjunctive, but notes that in two runic inscriptions from Gotland -*im* appears for the first person plural subjunctive with an imperative function. Assuming this ending to be the one intended in *Guta saga* at this point would involve only a small change to the text and would certainly make good sense. The verb *herþa* means 'harden', but also 'stubbornly persist', which is evidently the meaning here; see Wadstein, 1894–1895, 6.

8/25. Wessén (*SL* IV, 293) and others translate *þy et* as 'ty' ('since'). Lindqvist (1960–1962, 113) argues that this does not make sense if *vi* was a cult site and it seems, perhaps, unlikely that the fact that the church had been built at such a place would be put forward as a reason for *not* burning it. Lindqvist suggests that *vi* did not only denote a cult site, but also a secular place of refuge, such as a market, or where the assembly was held. A sacrifice is, however, specifically mentioned. Even so, there is no need to link the site of the church with the actual place of sacrifice, and there could have been both a cult and a secular site in the area, which lies at the meeting-point of several thing-districts; cf. Pernler, 1977, 21; Introduction, pp. xlii–xliii. Fritzell (1972, 44) suggests an alternative, that the phrase means 'fastän', but *þy et* consistently means 'because, since' in *Guta saga*. An alternative is that it is a misreading by the scribe of *þau et*, 'although'; cf. 8/11. Likkair's argument could also be explained, without significantly changing the meanings of the words involved, in two ways. The first would be that the holy place should not be desecrated by the shedding of blood, even the blood of a non-believer. Such an interdict in a sanctified area seems to have been a common one in pre-Christian Scandinavian society; cf. *ÍF* I, 125–126; Snorri Sturluson, 1982, 46. The second explanation is that Likkair did not think it was a good enough reason to burn the church *simply* because of its siting. See also the preceding Note.

8/25–26. *firir niþan klintu*. This has been taken by Schlyter (*CIG*, 99) to be an explanatory phrase, not intended to be part of the direct speech, and there would certainly be no need for Likkair to add this explanation for his audience. Since *vi* is a common noun for a sacred place, however, the phrase was possibly added in order to distinguish this particular site. Arnfinn Brekke, in a study of Icelandic and Norwegian farm names (1918, 4, 19, 71), lists a number that consist of the preposition *undir* and equivalents (which would correspond to *firir niþan*), usually followed by a word meaning 'hill' or 'cliff'. As examples of place-names from Sweden, *Underlund* and *Underliden* may be mentioned, both of which are in Halland, although only the latter has a sense of a hill incorporated in the name; cf. Pamp, 1988, 11. There are several examples in England of place-names with distinguishing additions (for example, Newcastle-under-Lyme, Weston Underwood). On the other hand, the interpolation of phrases by the author into direct speech is not unknown in other Scandinavian texts; cf. 'er býr þar, *er nú heitir* at Stað í Skagafirði' in *Heiðarvíga saga*, ch. 37 (*ÍF* III, 1972, 319, note 2). There seems to be some doubt whether the form *klintu* is the dative singular of *klint* (i. e. feminine vowel-stem) or the dative or accusative of *klinta* (i. e. feminine *ōn*-stem). The dative was more commonly used after prepositions in Old Swedish than was the case later, although *firir niþan* seems usually to have taken the accusative. Cf. Söderberg, 1879, 14; Söderwall, 1884–1973, s. v. *klinter*; Noreen, 1904, 301, 307, 336; *GLGS, Ordbok*, 44.

8/27. *aldra helguna namni*. Archaeologists have excavated for a number of years in search of a possible site for this church. Eric Swanström (1982, 79–80) considers that the orientation of graves found in the vicinity of S:t Hans's and S:t Pers church in Visby indicates that there was an earlier church than the latter on the same site. Gustavson (1982) describes an inscription found there and suggests that it was associated with a heathen burial site. It is interesting to note that the day of dedication of S:t Pers church would be June 29th and that of S:t Hans's church June 24th, the nearest major saint's day. This assumes S:t Hans to be St John the Baptist, rather than St John the Evangelist; cf. Lagerlöf and Svahnström, 1991, 61.

8/28. *Petrs kirkia*. The remains of this church, now called S:t Pers, consisting of a stretch of wall only, form a part of the southwestern corner of the ruins of S:t Hans's church in Visby. A possible chronology for the development of this archaeological site is proposed by Eric Swanström (1985; 1986). This suggests that what he calls 'Allhelgonakyrka' was a limestone Romanesque church (remains of which have been found within the perimeter of S:t Hans's church), rather than the wooden building which was probably intended by the author of *Guta saga*. Swanström dates the oldest remains ('Allhelgonakyrka') to the end of the eleventh century on the basis of a picture-stone, re-carved to form a gravestone. He suggests that during the twelfth century the population of the area grew, and S:t Pers was built, 16 metres

to the south of the original church. The German-speaking population then took over 'Allhelgonakyrkan' towards the end of the
century. When that church proved inadequate, a new church,
dedicated to S:t Hans, was started between the two older churches
around the turn of the century, with a result that, by 1300, S:t
Hans's had expanded to cover 'Allhelgonakyrka' and the latter
had to all intents and purposes disappeared; see Swanström,
1985, 122; 1986, 46, 50. It is a possibility that the author of *Guta
saga* knew of the subsumed 'Allhelgonakyrka' and used its name
as that of Botair's church. There is, however, no evidence of the
remains of a *wooden* church on the site of S:t Hans's church and,
although it seems probable that its construction had commenced
when *Guta saga* was written, the author makes no mention of S:t
Hans's; cf. Lagerlöf and Svahnström, 1991, 61.

8/28–29. The statement that *Aldra helguna* was the first church that
was allowed to stand in Gotland would seem to contradict the
episode concerning Ormika's chapel, if the erection of the latter
were presumed to have occurred earlier. The relative chronology
of these two accounts of church-building is a matter for speculation. Spegel (1901, 66) dates the introduction of Christianity to
Gotland to around 800 and Ochsner (1973, 25) links the conversion to an Irish mission of the period, based on the dating of the
remains of wooden churches. Fritzell (1972, 42) also subscribes
to an early dating for the original Allhelgonakyrka. There is,
according to Pernler (1977, 22), nothing to support this view, and
the dating of buildings purely on the basis of accounts in *Guta
saga* seems to have little justification. If Spegel's supposition
were correct, it would mean that *Guta saga* was preserving a
tradition more than 400 years old. Certainly, as Pernler argues,
the granting of permission for Botair's church to stand does not
imply a wider decision by the general assembly to accept Christianity
on behalf of the island, according to the narrative of *Guta saga*
as it is preserved. It is specifically stated that Christianity was
accepted later, when there had been further exposure to it both at
home and abroad. In terms of probability this gradual acceptance
seems far more likely than a sudden conversion on the basis of
Likkair's oratory. On the other hand, if the conversion of the
majority of the islanders were dated to some time later than
Botair's church-building activity, this would still, perhaps, place
the latter in the ninth or early tenth century, and certainly before

St Olaf's visit; cf. Söderberg, 1922, 242–243, 246; Smedberg, 1973, 163–166; Introduction, pp. xxxvi–xxxvii, note 2.

10/3. The Swedish dialect word *häskap*, 'hushåll, matlag' (so Hellquist) and the Old Swedish *häskaper*, 'familj' appear to be related to the Old Icelandic *hýski* with a similar meaning; see *ÍO*, s. v. *hyski*. Hellquist compares these forms to the southern Swedish dialect word *höske*; see Hellquist, 1980, s. v. *hjon* and references.

10/4. In the manuscript, a sixteenth-century hand has added in the margin: 'consecratum A.° 1', that is 'consecration number one'.

10/7. *sielfs vilia*: 'free-will' in the sense of their own volition. A similar expression was used in relation to the forging of links with Sweden; see Note to 6/16. The concept of a free acceptance of Christianity contradicts the legend recorded by Strelow (1633, 131) and seems more likely; see Note to 8/1–10.

10/10. According to Olsson (1984, 29) the first element of the place-name *Atlingabo* contains the personal name *Atle* and the whole is to be interpreted as 'Atles ättlingars område' ('Atle's family's area'). He cites as additional evidence the existence of a farm in the parish called *Lilla Atlings*. The name-element *-ings* is thought to indicate the inhabitants of a certain area, or descendants from a certain family, but not all names with this element have such a derivation; cf. Olsson, 1984, 27–28.

10/11. *Farþaim*. The element *-haim* corresponds to *-hem* in place-names on the mainland. Olsson (1984, 25) proposes the meaning 'bygd', 'bebyggd trakt', 'gård', 'by' and states that in 'genuin dialekt' the pronunciation of this element is /aim/, /um/ or /ume/, which might account for the lack of an *h* following the *þ*. Söderberg (1879, 36) notes that *h* is frequently dropped at the beginning of the second element of composite words. Olsson assumes that the first element contains *\*fardh*, 'ställe där man kan färdas fram', related to the verb *fara* in the sense of 'färdas' ('travel forth') and suggests that a natural gravel ridge in the area could have provided a suitable causeway. It seems likely that a natural feature lies behind this place-name and Gustavson (1938, 11) dismisses the suggestion, put forward by Pipping (1919, 19), that the first element could be related to a personal name with the form *Fardhe*.

10/12. The verb *briskas* is probably related to a word meaning 'broad'. Compare Swedish *bred*, Norwegian *brei(d)ska*, 'spread out', Riksmål *briske sig* (Nynorsk *briska seg*), 'puff oneself up', and Swedish dialect *breska*, 'to spread out', particularly to spread out one's legs; cf. Falk and Torp, 1903–1906, s. v. *briske sig*; *Norsk riksmålsordbok*, 1937–1957, s. v. *briske*; *Norsk ordbok*, 1966– , s. v. *briska*.

10/13. *at mairu maki*. Cf. Swedish *mak* in *i sakta mak*, 'without hurrying', and *maka* in *maka åt sig*, 'move something nearer'. In Norwegian Riksmål, *make seg* means 'take it easy', in Danish dialect *mag* means 'comfortable', and in Icelandic *makindi* means 'rest, ease'; cf. *SAOB*, s. v. *mak*; *maka*; *Norsk riksmålsordbok*, 1937–1957, s. v. *mak; make*; C–V, s. v. *makindi*; Note to 10/18–19.

10/14. In the manuscript, a sixteenth-century hand has added in the margin 'LEX et conditio Episcopo Lincopensj Visitaturo designata', that is 'The law and agreement concerning the bishop of Linköping's visits drawn up'. Most editions record the following section as chapter 5.

10/16. The natural route eastwards from Scandinavia would have been down through Russia, as the text says. To stop in Gotland on the way would have been convenient and, once Gotland had been converted, the itinerant bishops would no doubt have wished to encourage church-building; cf. Note to 8/10; Introduction, p. xlvi.

10/16–17. *Þan tima war vegr oystra um Ryzaland ok Grikland fara*. The concept of a well-used eastern route (via the Dvina and the Dnieper) existed also in Old Icelandic and passed through Russia, the Baltic countries and parts of Eastern Europe; cf. C–V, s. v. *austrvegr*. During the twelfth century, this easterly route was dropped in favour of a more westerly route, along the Vistula to the Dniester and the Black Sea, and Gotland's importance as a staging post might have declined. The author appears to indicate that *vegr oystra* was no longer by that route; cf. Pernler, 1977, 60 note 3; Foote and Wilson, 1979, 227–228.

10/18–19. The first churches were certainly privately-sponsored by land-owners, principally as baptismal and burial churches. A private church (called a *hœgendiskirkja* in Norway) is referred to in the laws. Such churches were usually built on the estates of the men who paid for them and the word *hœgendi* is related to words meaning 'convenience' and 'comfort'; cf. Note to 10/13. As late as the twelfth century, churches were being built and financed privately, but by the end of the following century, churches were self-financing; cf. Hildebrand, 1879–1953, III, 80–81; *KL*, s. v. *Fabrica*; *Patronatsrätt*; *Privatkyrka*; Introduction, p. xlv.

10/21. *hoygsta*: 'highest'. This word possibly reflects what would have been written in the salutation of a letter, and Pernler (1977, 62) suggests that the Gotlanders had sent to the bishop for assistance in a time of famine. One of the courtesy adjectives for bishops as late as the nineteenth century was *högvördig*, an attributive employed in much the same way as the word 'Lord' is used in addressing English bishops, and *Herra* in Iceland; see Rask, 1843, 56. The adjective might be in the superlative because there is evidence that the see of Linköping, founded in 1120, was ranked only next below the archbishopric of Uppsala, preceding Skara; cf. Schück, 1959, 400–401; Hellström, 1996, 112. Certainly, Linköping was regarded as important enough, during the twelfth century, to be the venue for a meeting in 1152 or 1153 led by the papal legate and future pope, Nicholas Breakspear, and was being considered for the primacy; cf. Schück, 1959, 49–50; Pernler, 1977, 57. The term 'highest' would not have been used in this sense after 1164 when the archbishopric of Uppsala was founded and Lindqvist notes that it was not because the bishop of Linköping was the 'highest' that he was approached, but because he was the 'nearest'. Alternatively, 'highest' could be distinguishing the permanent bishop in Linköping from a number of itinerant bishops, in which case the phrase about his being the 'nearest' was an explanation inserted by the author; see Lindqvist, 1960–1962, 115.

*Leonkopungr* is one of several forms of the name *Linköping*. Others, include *Lingköpunger, Liongköpunger, Lynköpunger*, and *Liungaköpunger*; see Hellquist, 1980, s. v. *Linköping*. Läffler (1877, 77) interprets the form of the place-name in *Guta saga* as an attempt by a Gotlander to render the Swedish pronunciation. See also Noreen, 1904, 119 note 2. The *laghþing* of Östergötland was called the *Liongaþing* and its meetings were held at a cross-roads near Linköping; cf. *KL*, s. v. *Liongaþing*; *Ting*; Palmqvist, 1961, 40–47. The see of Linköping was the third to be instituted in Sweden, after Skara and Sigtuna, probably at about the same time as those of Strängnäs and Västerås, that is around 1100, and before Uppsala in the 1130s; see Introduction, pp. xlvii–xlviii; Tunberg, 1913, 16, 21; Gallén, 1958, 6.

10/22. *þaim nestr*. During the Middle Ages the bishopric of Linköping covered Östergötland, north and west Småland (i. e. excluding Värend, south-east Småland, which transferred to the see of

Växjö in 1163), Kalmar, Öland and Gotland; see Hildebrand, 1879–1953, III, 85; *KL*, s. v. *Småland.* As suggested in Note to 10/21 the bishop might have been solicited for help and the inclusion of Gotland in the see of Linköping may have been a consequence of that request.

Pernler (1977, 67) thinks it probable that the phrase *steddum ret* implies that the *Gutnalþing* had made the arrangements now recorded with the bishop. The details are not only given here, but in a number of ecclesiastical diplomas and are set out by Bishop Bengt and his predecessor, Karl (†1220), and confirmed by the papal legate, Wilhelm; see *DS* I, 690–691, 693, nos. 832, 837; *DS* II, 219, no. 1174; *SL* IV, 313–318; Introduction, pp. xlvii–xlviii. The archbishop, Andreas Suneson, was also called upon to support the Gotlanders in their claim for special status. Pernler and Wessén both draw attention to the several correspondences between the texts of *Guta saga* and *DS* I, 690–691, no. 832 (the letter from Archbishop Andreas Suneson of Lund and Bishops Karl and Bengt of Linköping) as well as differences in their perspective; see, for translation, *SL* IV, 313–314.

10/23. *reþskep giera*: 'lend [his] support'. From the Gotlanders' perspective the bishop was serving their pastoral needs rather than exercising a right.

10/24. The text of the Latin letter adds *non nisi*, 'only' and that the island was divided into thirds, *in tribus terræ trientibus*; see *DS* I, 690; *SL* IV, 314.

10/25. *miþ tolf mannum sinum.* Pernler (1977, 71) notes that there is a discrepancy here between *Guta saga* and the primary sources, in that the latter specify that the farmers should supply twelve horses, which would be one short if the bishop had not brought his own. In Östgötalagen the expression is specifically 'mæþ mannum tolf ok sialuær han þrattande'; cf. *CIO*, *Kristnu balkær*, 12; *SL* I, 12, 26–27.

10/26. *miþ bonda hestum.* The bishop could not easily have brought horses across to Gotland and would therefore have had to borrow horses for himself and his entourage. A similar arrangement is mentioned in the Gulaþing area, which is broken by fjords; see Pernler, 1977, 73. Paragraph 33 of the church law section of *Gulaþingslǫg*, *Um reiðskiota biscopi* (*NGL* I, 20), states that 18 horses are to be provided.

10/29. *þry borþ ok ai maira.* Nothing is mentioned of these arrangements in *Guta lag* and there are no exactly parallel descriptions of the number of meals to be provided at visitations in other Swedish secular laws; see Pernler, 1977, 74. There is evidence that the number of days which the bishop of Linköping's visits could last was reduced to two in 1248 and in 1279 the amount of food to be provided was specified, but not the number of meals; cf. *SL* I, 26–27; Pernler, 1977, 77; *KL*, s. v. *Gengärd* and references.

10/30–31. *att borþ, miþ tolf oyrum.* Each öre was 1/8 mark. The details about payments relating to the consecration of altars and churches do not occur in the letter from Archbishop Andreas and Bishops Karl and Bengt and could be a later addition; cf. *DS* I, 690, no. 832; Pernler, 1977, 80. It is probable that it was the lay people who 'caused the churches to be built' that paid for these consecrations; see Note to 10/18–19.

12/2–3. *Af presti andrum huerium*: 'From every second priest'. It is clear from *DS* I, 690, no. 832, which refers to 'half the churches', that this phrase must be parallel to the earlier *þriþia huert ar*, which certainly means 'every third year'. The phrase thus means 'every second priest (on the island)', or half the priests on the island, and not 'every other priest', referring to all priests who have not had any consecration performed, as assumed by Schlyter (*CIG*, 101). As indicated in the Note to 10/30–31, it is probable that it was not, in fact, the priests who paid for the consecrations.

12/3. *um tilquemda siþ*: 'as a visitation tax'. Schlyter's reading is *um tilqwemd sina*, meaning 'at his visit'; see *CIG*, 101. This involves two changes to the text. Hjelmqvist (1903, 169–173) suggests a single change, to *um tilquemda tiþ*, 'at the time of arrival'. Pipping (*GLGS*, 67 note 5) simply interprets the word *siþ* as 'tax', that is, equivalent to a Latin *pro visitationis consuetudine.* It seems preferable not to alter the text where a reasonable meaning can be obtained from the manuscript as it stands, but cf. *SL* IV, 318.

12/4. *Af andrum huerium presti*: 'From every other priest'. Hjelmqvist (1903, 162–169), appears to be correct when he takes this phrase to refer to the remainder of the priests in this instance, that is, those who do not pay a tax *in kind* that year (but cf. Note to 12/2–3), and the Latin text supports this view. The stipulation is open to misinterpretation as first stated and the author expands on it (*sum ai gierþi gingerþ a þy ari*) to remove the ambiguity; cf. *SL* IV, 314–315.

12/5. The word *lausn* was often used to convey the sense of a payment made to free one from an obligation. Here it seems to be used to contrast payment made in money with that made in kind, on every alternate visit.

12/6. The expression *til skurapar* originally meant 'notched' into a wooden tally, and is another instance of the difference between *Guta saga* and Archbishop Suneson's letter (*DS* I, 690, no. 832). The letter refers in this connection to a more formal written agreement which is not implied in the wording in *Guta saga*; cf. Läffler, 1908–1909, Part 1, 165–167; *SL* IV, 315–316, 318; Introduction, p. xlvii. There is a possible indication in this passage that there was some opposition to the money being collected, and a reminder that the payment was one supported by custom and regulation. The letter states that the payment must be made *humiliter*. Details of the visitation taxes paid are recorded in a number of sources; see *SRS* III, 290–293; *SL* IV, 316.

12/11. *i sama þiþiungi.* The question of disputes is not covered by *DS* I, 690–691, no. 832, although the division of Gotland into thirds is referred to. Disputes would, however, have been resolved during the bishop's visitation. *Guta lag* and *Guta saga* are the only sources giving details of the thirds as *administrative* areas, as opposed to ecclesiastical divisions, in Gotland. Since other sources refer only to *siettungs-* and *landsþing*, it is possible that the stress laid upon the thirds was the result of clerical influence in the writing of both *Guta lag* and *Guta saga*; cf. Steffen, 1945, 247–248; Note to 2/19. Laws similar to that described here applied in Iceland in relation to the Quarter Courts. Disputes could not be referred from one Quarter Court to another, but had to be referred to the fifth Court for appeal.

12/13. *til aldra manna samtalan.* This would involve the referral of the case to the *Gutnalþing*. Although the concept of courts at various levels, to which disputed cases were referred, seems to have existed, and is mentioned in Gutnish law, the nature of the actual mechanism involved is not clear; cf. *GLGS*, 46; *KL*, s. v. *Ting på Gotland.* The genitive -*ar* ending was sometimes dropped in nouns after the preposition *til*, as in this case; see Noreen, 1904, 300–301.

12/14. The phrase *hetningar eþa dailu mal* could simply be an example of parallelism, or it could be that the scribe intended to replace the single word by the following phrase, and omitted to delete *hetningar eþa*; cf. Wadstein, 1894–1895, 7; Bugge, 1877–1878, 263–264.

12/17. A detailed discussion of the history and function of the office of *proastr* is given by Pernler (1977, 151–216). The only inference that can be made from the cryptic reference here to offences too great for the *proastr* to absolve is that the *proastr* was the equivalent of the rural dean (*praepositus ruralis*). Whether at the time there were three (one for each third) or more, and whether any particular dean is being referred to here, it is not possible to say; cf. Pernler, 1977, 161, 162. The first dean for whom any record remains is Nicolaus of Dalhem, the parish east of Roma. His monument is incorporated in the porch of the church at Dalhem and is dated to the end of the twelfth century. The first mention of *proastr* in a datable written source is from 1213, in a letter from Pope Innocent III; cf. *DS* I, 178, no. 152; Pernler, 1977, 153. It is worth noting that in Gotland the local priests had the right to elect their dean. This privilege was specifically confirmed by Pope Innocent IV in September, 1253, probably because it had been questioned by the bishop of Linköping, along with the division of the tithe and the selection of parish priests; cf. *DS* I, 366, nos. 411, 412; Pernler, 1977, 155. The arrangement was further confirmed by Pope Boniface VIII in a letter dated August, 1296, where it was also implied that Pope Gregory X had issued a similar edict, although this latter is not preserved; cf. *DS* II, 217, no. 1171.

12/18. *millan Valborga messur ok helguna messur.* This period covers the late spring to early autumn months (1st May to 1st November). The stipulation is obviously in part a practical measure: the crossing would have been uncomfortable and dangerous outside these dates. Walburga (†779) was an English nun who, according to tradition, took part in the conversion of the Germans and was canonised after the appearance of a miraculous healing oil on her tombstone. Her four festivals are often associated in medieval Sweden with events in the fiscal year, rather like Lady Day (March 25th). For example, *Valborgsmässoskat* was a spring-time tax, which was connected with the *ledung*; see *KL*, s. v. *Valborg*.

12/20. The low level of fines to be paid by Gotlanders to the bishop was the subject of much disputing and dissatisfaction on the part of Bishop Bengt, as witnessed by his letters. The fact that no part of the tithe was due to the bishop, but that it was divided between the priest, the church and the poor had also been confirmed by Popes Gregory IX and Innocent III, despite the objections at various times of the bishops of Linköping; cf. *DS* I, nos. 256, 270, 271, 411; *Bullarium Danicum*, 1931–1932, I, 190, 191, 223; Skov, 1946, 114; Pernler, 1977, 133–138.

## Chapter 4

12/21. In the manuscript, a sixteenth-century hand has added in the margin: 'Bellica expeditio qva conditione suscepta olim fuerit', that is 'Under what conditions war expeditions were undertaken at that time'.

12/23. The word *snekkia* or *sneckia* is one of several used in Scandinavia to describe ships used in the levy (longships), although it could also apparently be used to designate a nonmilitary ship; cf. *KL*, s. v. *Skibstyper*. In the context of war, *snekkia* appears to have been applied to a long and narrow craft, and especially to the Swedish levy ships; see Foote and Wilson, 1979, 236. It seems probable that *snekkia* designated the smallest type of warship; see Falk, 1912, 99. The standard capacity of the levy ship was 20 benches and thus seven standard rowing crews would have amounted to 280 men, at two men per bench; see Foote and Wilson, 1979, 235. Evidence shows, however, that the carrying capacity of the ships was much larger than that, perhaps 80 warriors or more and, since it is particularly stated that the vessels should sail to the levy, the forces expected to be provided along with the ships might have been in the region of 560 men; cf. Falk, 1912, 100, 102. The other type of warship was a 60-oared 'dragon' or *skeið*, which was a deeper-draughted vessel, unsuitable for coastal waters; cf. Christiansen, 1997, 15–16. The fact that seven ships were stipulated has led to discussion about the administrative arrangements in Gotland at the time. The three thirds were each divided into two giving six *siettungar* and each of these would obviously be expected to supply one vessel. It is suggested by Björkander (1898, 48–50) that the seventh vessel was to be provided by Visby, which by that time had begun to distance itself administratively from Gotland at large, and this seems to be a reasonable assumption, although he argues that it was specifically the German community that had the commitment. In a letter dated 1353 from the *rådmän* of Visby to their counterparts ('consules') in Lübeck, in which it is implied that Visby only has an obligation to support the king of Sweden's conflicts with the heathens, there is specific mention of a ship ('navis dicte snicke') with the implication that it is to be provided by the Visby community as a whole; cf. *DS* VI, 453–454, no. 4958; Yrwing, 1978, 21, 22. There are a number of placenames on the coast of Gotland containing the element *snäck-*. Of these, *Snäckviken*, just north of Visby, is one that has a suitable harbour for the *ledung* to assemble in. The name could in this case be related to *snekkia*, although other such names would not necessarily have had that connection; cf. Olsson, 1984, 132–135.

From the middle of the twelfth century until the beginning of the thirteenth there was a campaign against the heathens of the Baltic countries instigated by the papacy and supported by the Scandinavian monarchy. In 1199, as a result of an appeal from Pope Innocent III, Bishop Albert visited Gotland to recruit for his crusade in defence of the Christian Livonians (inhabitants of northern Latvia and southern Estonia) against their heathen countrymen; see *STFM* I, 113–114, no. 55. The Gotlanders were reluctant to take part in this crusade, since the objects of the attack were their own trading partners, although they had apparently taken part in an earlier mission to Estonia; cf. Pernler, 1977, 62, 108; Björkander, 1898, 28; Yrwing, 1991, 164. In 1226, the Gotlanders (and the Danes on Gotland) actually refused to take part in a similar crusade against the islanders of Ösel when urged by the Papal Legate, although the Germans agreed to do so; see *Heinrici Chronicon Livoniae*, 1959, 328; Yrwing, 1963, 94; *KL*, s. v. *Korståg*; Christiansen, 1997, 100.

12/24–25. The *ledung* was the name given to the arrangements made for seaborne warfare in Scandinavia in the early Middle Ages. The landowning farmers were obliged to supply both men and equipment for the fleet as a levy. Gradually, this obligation was discharged by the payment of a land tax in kind. In mainland Sweden, the *hundari* was the unit used to determine the level of support to be given to the levy, but in *Guta saga* there is no mention of the *hundari* and the *siettungr* seems to have been the administrative division behind the number of ships specified, with the addition of an extra ship for Visby; cf. Note to 12/23. The levy is considered to be at least as old as the Vendel time and possibly as old as the Migration period, while the *hundari* division is considered by some scholars to be not much older than the eleventh century. Hyenstrand, however, thinks that this was the original division; cf. Introduction, p. xxv. By the time of Magnus Eriksson, the *ledungslami* had replaced the actual provision of ships, and armies of mounted knights had replaced the seaborne forces; cf. *KL*, s. v. *Leidang*.

12/26. *firir missumar.* Any summons for a levy after midsummer would be unreasonably close to the harvest, since the muster would extend beyond the middle of August. The summons had therefore to be made before 25th May.

12/27–14/1. The Gotlanders probably exercised the option of not taking part in certain of the musters for the reason given earlier; cf. Note to 12/23.

14/1. *atta vikna vist.* This indicates the maximum expected duration of the muster. The men would have to have returned by mid-August for the harvest. The change in time unit used from *manaþr* to *vika* might have been motivated to some extent by desire for alliteration with *vist* in the original statute.

14/2–3. The option of making payment *instead* of providing men and vessels was probably current at the time of writing. In 1285 a standard tax was imposed whether the levy was called out or not, and if this tax had already been brought in, it is reasonable to suppose that it would have been mentioned; cf. Introduction, pp. xlviii, l, li–lii. Four marks in coin was equivalent to one mark in silver, so the amount of the tax would correspond to 10 marks in silver; see *SL* IV, 259, 263.

14/5. The word *laiþingslami* means literally 'levy-hindrance' or 'levy-incapacity'. The evidence seems to point to a tax being enforced as an alternative to the provision of warships in Denmark, Sweden and Åland, while the conversion of the levy to a fixed annual tax occurred in Norway from middle of the twelfth century; see Wadstein, 1894–1895, 7; *KL*, s. v. *Leidang*, cols 438–442, 446–450, 455–458.

14/6. The method of summoning people to some meeting or action by the passing around of a specially marked token was used widely in Scandinavia in the Middle Ages. The token was sometimes an iron arrow, sometimes a wooden stick with a burned end and sometimes a cross (if the summons were to church services). In Sweden, the form of the baton seems to have also varied with its use, and according to whether it was intended to be used once only or repeatedly as an official symbol; see *KL*, s. v. *Budstikke*. Ihre (1769, s. v. *Budkafle*) describes it thus: 'baculus nuntiatorius

. . . Utebantur hoc nuntii genere veteres scripturae & literarum ignari, ut certis in vulgus cognitis figuris indicarent, quid rerum ageretur. In primis vero notabile est, quod ab altera parte ustulati essent, ab altera fune trajecti.' This description refers to a missile-like baton with a scorched end, used to pass messages before reading and writing were widespread. It seems more likely, however, that a marked baton, passed from area to area to act as a call to arms, was intended here; cf. Rietz, 1862–1955, s. v. *Bu(d)-kavel.*

14/8. *halfan manaþ til ferþar boas.* The information here enables a typical timetable to be constructed, assuming that the levy day was just before midsummer:

| | |
|---|---|
| 25th May: | summons issued and baton passed around (St Urban's day) |
| 1st June: | men gather and prepare their ships, arms and provisions |
| 15th June: | men wait in readiness for a favourable wind |
| 22nd June: | levy day, four weeks after the summons |
| 25th June: | midsummer |
| 29th June: | last day for sailing (St Peter's day) |
| 24th August: | last day for return |

The summons could have been issued earlier, but time had to be allowed for sowing to be completed; cf. *SL* IV, 321.

14/9. The word *\*garlakr* is related to Swedish *gar*, used of the copper-refining process, and the Old Icelandic *gǫrr*, 'complete'. The more recent dialect forms found in Gotland, *garlak* and *garlaker*, are translated as 'waken, tilreds, färdig'; cf. Hellquist, 1980, s. v. *gar*; *GO*, s. v. *garlak.*

14/10. The expression *byriar biþa* occurs in mainland Swedish, Norwegian and Icelandic sources and was obviously an accepted concept; cf. for example *Upplandslagen, SL* I, 95; *Fornsvenska texter*, 1959, 22; *Konungs skuggsjá*, 1920, 89; *Flóamanna saga*, ch. 21 (*ÍF* XIII, 278). The Swedish dialect *bör*, sometimes *byr*, retains the meaning 'medvind'; see Hellquist, 1980, s. v. *bör*; Rietz, 1862–1955, s. v. *Byr*; Kalkar, 1881–1918, s. v. *Bør*; *Børfast*; Söderwall, 1884–1973, s. v. *byr* and references.

14/13. *at saklausu.* This was a very commonly occurring legal phrase to indicate 'without blame'; cf. *CIS* XIII, s. v. *saklös.*

14/13–14. The ships would have been able to hold many more men under sail than under oar, and the work would have been less physically demanding.

14/18. Here *byr* is being used to mean 'wind' in general rather than specifically 'favourable wind', which is the more common usage; cf. Note to 14/10.

14/19–21. St Peter's and St Paul's day is June 29th, so this assembly would be the summer or early autumn one, that is the first one after the final sailing day for the levy. This date is consistent with the chronology suggested in the Note to 14/8.

14/20. In Norwegian the word *nefndarmenn* is used to designate men who have been chosen to perform a particular duty, particularly in relation to the *leidang*. It is clear that the men referred to here are fulfilling a similar function and the number 12 might point to a *hundari* division of the island; cf. Hyenstrand, 1989, 122; *KL*, s. v. *Nefndarmenn*, col. 282; *Nämnd*, col. 446; *Edgärdsman*.

14/22–23. *kunungs aiþr*. That is, the oath just described concerning the inability to satisfy the levy obligation. The stipulation that no other commissioned oath must be given on the island, except this particular one, is puzzling. It might refer to a specific incident when oaths were taken illegally; or perhaps be an indirect reference to the civil war, and the building of the wall around Visby, in 1288, in which case *Guta saga* must be dated later than generally assumed; cf. *STFM* I, 300–303, no. 144.

14/24 *bort rekinn af sinu riki*. It has been suggested that this passage refers to a specific incident; see Introduction, pp. xlviii, xlix–l.

14/25. *haldi hanum um þry ar*. The implication is that until the situation had been stable in Sweden for three years, the Gotlanders should not release their money, but that when the new regime was established, all outstanding tax should be paid.

14/26. *liggia lata*. It is possible that it was intended that the money should be invested in the interim.

14/29. *Lykt bref*. The implication here is that any negotiations between the Gotlanders and the king were to be confidential.

The oldest Swedish royal seal belonged to kings Karl Sverkersson (1161–1167) and Knut Eriksson (1167–*c*.1196) who reigned after St Erik (†1160). A portion of the seal of Erik X Knutsson (1208–1216) is preserved, showing two crowned leopards facing each other; cf. Hildebrand, 1884–1885, 9. The seal would act not only to preserve privacy, but also as an identification of the letter and a guarantee of its being genuine. The immediate recipient of the letter might be illiterate, or not be privy to its contents.

# GLOSSARY

All words are listed in the form found in the text, but only under the head-word if they are in an oblique case or conjugated form and would otherwise occur within two lines of the head-word. Translations refer principally to the words as used in the text of *Guta saga*, although alternatives are given if they provide additional support for the interpretation.

References are to page and line numbers of the text. All instances are cited except for the nominative of personal pronouns and common adverbs and conjunctions. References to words and forms that are the subject of editorial emendations are placed in square brackets [ ]. Head-words that do not occur in that form in the text of *Guta saga* are marked by asterisks.

## Abbreviations

\* form not found in the text of *Guta saga*
*acc.* accusative
    *a[s] [a[s]m, a[s]f, a[s]n]* accusative [singular] [masculine, feminine, neuter]
    *ap [apm, apf, apn]* accusative plural [masculine, etc.]
*adj.* adjective
*adv.* adverb(ial)
*comp.* comparative
*conj.* conjunction
*dat.* dative
    *d[s] [d[s]m, d[s]f, d[s]n]* dative [singular] [masculine, etc.]
    *dp [dpm, dpf, dpn]* dative plural [masculine, etc.]
*def. art.* definite article
*dem.* demonstrative
*f.* feminine noun
*gen.* genitive
    *g[s] [g[s]m, g[s]f, g[s]n]* genitive [singular] [masculine, etc.]
    *gp [gpm, gpf, gpn]* genitive plural [masculine, etc.]
*i[p]* infinitive [passive]
*imp.* imperative
*m.* masculine noun
*md.* middle voice
*n.* neuter noun
*nom.* nominative
    *n[s] [n[s]m, n[s]f, n[s]n]* nominative [singular] [masculine, etc.]
    *np [npm, npf, npn]* nominative plural [masculine, etc.]
*num.* numeral
*pers.* personal
*pl.* plural
*poss.* possessive
*pret.* preterite
*pron.* pronoun
*prp.* preposition

*ptc.* participle (present or past)
*refl.* reflexive
*rel.* relative
*sing.* singular
*subj.* subjunctive
*sup.* supine
*superl.* superlative
*v.* verb
   *2s* 2nd person singular present indicative
   *3s[p]* 3rd person singular present indicative [passive]
   *1p* 1st person plural present indicative
   *2p* 2nd person plural present indicative
   *3p* 3rd person plural present indicative
   *subj. 1s* 1st person singular present subjunctive
   *subj. 3s* 3rd person singular present subjunctive
   *subj. 3p* 3rd person plural present subjunctive
   *pret. 2s* 2rd person singular past indicative
   *pret. 3s[p]* 3rd person singular past indicative [passive]
   *pret. 3p[p]* 3rd person plural past indicative [passive]
   *pret. subj. 3s* 3rd person singular past subjunctive
   *pret. subj. 3p* 3rd person plural past subjunctive

**a**¹ *prp. with dat.* in; at. 2/6. 10/4. 10/10. 10/11. 12/5. 14/19. *with acc.* into; to; in; against; (on) top of. 2/3. 4/17. 4/18. 4/18. 6/1. 6/11. 6/21. 8/19. 12/23.

**a**² see **aiga**.

**af** *prp. with dat.* from, away from, out of; of, about, concerning. 2/21. 2/23. 4/8. 4/15. 4/16. 6/4. 6/13. 8/1. 8/3. 8/15. 10/12. 10/24. 12/2. 12/4. 12/5. 12/11. 12/14. 14/24. *as adv.* 6/10.

**agin** *adv.* in return, back. 8/6.

**ai** *adv.* not, no. 2/23. 2/27. 4/2. 4/5. 4/9. 4/15. 8/16. 8/24. 10/26. 10/29. 12/4. 12/4. 12/6. 12/12. 12/13. 12/16. 12/17. 12/18. 12/20. 12/23. 12/26. 12/27. 14/2. 14/2. 14/4. 14/10. 14/12. 14/13. 14/15. 14/17. 14/24. 14/30. Cf. **e**.

**aiga** *v.* own, have (possession); claim, have right (to do something); have duty (to do something); shall (*auxiliary use*). *i* 2/14. 2/16. 2/24. *3s* **a** 10/28. 12/3. 12/10. 12/15. 12/24. 14/15. *3p* **aigu** 6/18. 6/23. 6/25. 12/8. 14/12. 14/18. 14/24. 14/26. *pret. 3p* **attu** 2/25.

**aina** see **\*ann**.

**\*ainsambr** *adj.* alone. *nsn* **ainsamt** 10/31.

**aiþr** *m.* oath. *ns* 14/22. 14/23. *as* **aiþ** 14/20.

**al** see **\*skulu**.

**\*aldr** *pron.* and *adj.* whole, everything; each; all. *nsn* **alt** 2/12.

4/20. *dsm* **allum** 14/29. *asm* **allan** 10/3. *asn* **alt** 2/24. 10/26. *npm*
**allir** 4/23. *gp* **aldra** 8/27. 12/13. *dp* **allum** 2/15. *apm* **alla** 2/23.
6/23. *apf* **allar** 6/18. *apn* **all** 8/12.

**aldri** *adv.* never (again). 2/4.

**allar**[1] *adv.* everywhere. 10/12.

**allar**[2], **allir, allum** see *aldr.

**almennilika** *adv.* generally. 10/7. 10/9.

**alt** see *aldr.

**alteri** *n.* altar. *ns* 10/31. 12/1. *gs* **alteris** 10/30.

*ann **num.** one. Also used as the indef. art. (4/2. 4/4. 4/9. 8/7). *asm*
**ann** 2/5. 4/9. *asf* **aina** 4/2. 4/4. 8/7. 14/6. *asn* **att** 6/8. 10/30. See
also *ainsambr.

**annar** *num.* and *adj.* second; other; following. *nsm* 2/17. *nsf* **annur**
10/10. *dsm* **andrum** 12/2. 12/4. *dsn* **andru** 14/3. *asm* **annan**
12/14. *asf* **aþra** 8/18. *asn* **annat** 6/9. *dp* **andrum** 8/5. *apn* **annur**
6/19.

*annar huer *num.* and *adj.* every second; every other. *dsm* **andrum**
**huerium** 12/2. 12/4. Cf. *þriþi huer.

*annsuara *v.* answer. *pret.* *3p* **annsuaraþu** [4/11].

**annur** see **annar**.

*ar *n.* year; (good) harvest. *ds* **ari** 12/5. 12/8. 14/4. 14/4. *as* **ar**
6/12. 10/24. 14/26. *np* **ar** [14/27]. *ap* **ar** 14/25.

**at**[1] *prp.* *with dat.* for; in; by, at, with; in respect of, concerning. 4/5.
10/13. 10/29. 10/30. 12/7. 12/8. 14/3. 14/4. 14/13. 14/15. 14/18.
14/29. *as adv.* at (bieras) 14/23.

**at**[2] *infinitive mark* to. 6/6. 6/20. 12/15. 12/22. 12/27.

**at bieras** *v. md.* happen. See *biera.

**atr** *adv.* back. 8/6. 12/8.

**att** see *ann.

**atta** *num.* eight. 14/1.

**attu** see **aiga**.

*auka *v.* increase. *pret.* *3sp* **aukaþis** 2/22.

**aþra** see **annar**.

*baiþas *v. md.* ask permission, request. *pret.* *3p* **baddus** 4/7.

*band *n.* prohibition. See *kornband.

*barmbr *m.* womb; lap; bosom, breast, esp. of a woman. *ds* **barmi**
2/9. 2/9.

*barn *n.* child. *ap* **barn** 10/2.

*baugr *m.* ring. *dp* **baugum** 2/12.

baþu see *biþia.

*beþi (. . . ok) *conj.* both (. . . and). baþi 8/12. Cf. *beþir.

*beþir *pron.* both. *nn* baþi 10/31. 12/1.

biauþa *v. with dat.* summon. *i* 12/24. *ptc. nsn* buþit 12/27. 14/4.

*biera *v.* give birth to; *md.* happen, occur. *i* (at) bieras 14/23. *ptc. dsm* burnum 6/9.

*binda *v.* bind. *ptc. nsn* bundit 2/12.

biskupr *m.* bishop. *ns* 10/24. 10/28. 12/3. 12/5. 12/7. 12/10. *gs* biskups 10/21. 12/16. 12/19. *ds* biskupi 10/14. 12/15. *as* biskup 12/21. *np* biskupar 10/15.

biþa *v.* await; *with gen.* wait for. *i* 12/15. 14/10. 14/11.

*biþia *v.* beg, request. *pret. 3p* (til) baþu 6/6.

*blota *v. with dat.* sacrifice. *pret. 3p* blotaþu 4/18.

blotan *f.* sacrifice. *ns* 8/18. *as* blotan 4/21. 4/22.

bo *n.* property. See boland, *Atlingabo.

boa *v.* live; *md.* arm oneself. *i* boas 14/8. *3p* boa 12/12. *ptc. nsm* boandi 8/22.

boland *n.* inhabited land. *ns* 2/13.

*bondi *m.* husband; farmer. *ds* bonda 2/10. *gp* bonda 10/26.

*borg *f.* fortification. *as* burg 4/4. See also *Þorsborg.

bort *adv.* away; on (one's) way. 2/23. 2/25. 2/26. 2/28. 4/1. 4/10. 14/24.

*borþ *n.* meal (time). *as* borþ 10/30. *ap* borþ 10/29. 12/2. 12/4.

*bragþ *n.* time, point in time. *ds* bragþi 12/7. 12/9.

*braiþyx *f.* battle-axe. *as* braiþyxi 8/7.

bref *n.* letter. *ns* 14/29.

brenna *v.* burn. *i* 8/19. 8/20. 8/20. 8/25. *pret. 3p* brendu 8/17. *ptc. nsf* (o)brend 8/26.

*briskas *v. md.* spread, spread out. *pret. 3p* briskaþus 10/12.

*bulli *m.* round drinking vessel. *ap* bulla 8/6.

bundit see *binda.

burg see *borg.

burnum see *biera.

*buþ *n.* command, summons, bidding. *ds* buþi 10/6. *np* buþ 14/14. 14/17. See also *forbuþ.

buþit see biauþa.

buþkafli *m.* summoning baton, message staff. *ns* 14/6.

byggia *v.* live; settle (down), establish oneself. *i* 4/14. 4/16. *i md.* (þar) byggias (firir) 4/8. *pret. 3p* bygþu 2/6. *pret. 3p md.* bygþus (þar firir) 2/27. 4/1. 4/3. 4/15.

*byn *f.* request. *ds* byn 10/18.

**\*bynahus** *n.* oratory. *as* **bynahus** 8/8.
**byr** *m.* favourable wind; wind. *ns* 14/11. 14/12. 14/18. *gs* **byriar** 14/10.

**dagr** *m.* day; specified day. *ns* 12/26. *as* **dag** 12/25. 14/12. *dp*
  **dagum** 2/2.
**daila** *f.* dispute, conflict. *ns* 12/12. *np* **dailur** 12/10.
**\*dailumal** *n.* matter of conflict. *np* **dailumal** 12/14.
**\*dombr** *m.* domain. See **\*kristindombr.**
**\*dotir** *f.* daughter. *as* **dotur** 8/22. *dp* **dytrum** 4/19.
**draumbr** *m.* dream. *ns* 2/8. *as* **draum** 2/10. 2/11.
**\*droyma** *v. impersonal with dat.* dream. *pret. 3s* **droymdi** 2/7.
**\*drytning** *f.* empress, queen. *as* **drytningina** 4/12.
**dyma** *v.* judge. *i* 12/10.
**dytrum** see **\*dotir.**

**e** *adv.* always, (for) ever; continuously. 4/11. 4/11. 4/14. 4/14. 6/2.
  14/26. Cf. **ai.**
**\*efla** *v.* be able to. *3p* **efla** 14/2. *pret. 3s* **elpti** 2/23.
**\*eldr** *m.* fire. *ds* **eldi** 2/3.
**ella** *conj.* or. 8/25. Cf. **ellar**[1], **eþa.**
**ellar**[1] *conj.* or. 6/19. Cf. **ella, eþa.**
**ellar**[2] *adv.* otherwise. 4/21. 12/27.
**elpti** see **\*efla.**
**elzti** see **\*gamal.**
**\*eluitskr** *adj.* bewitched. *nsn* **eluist** 2/2.
**en**[1] *conj.* if. 6/7. 6/20. 10/31. 14/1.
**en**[2] *conj.* but, however; and. 2/3. 2/5. 2/21. 4/11. 4/22. 6/3. 6/14.
  12/8. 12/18. 14/2. 14/8. 14/26.
**en**[3] *adv.* as part of the conjunctions **fyr en, siþan en, þa en** 6/6.
  6/15. 10/9. 10/14. 10/20. 10/31. 14/2. 14/7. 14/10. 14/12.
**engin** *pron.* and *adj.* none, no one; no. *pron. nsm* 6/3. 10/8.
  *adj. nsm* 14/22.
**enn** *adv.* still, moreover. 4/4. 4/15. 4/16. 8/17. 14/11.
**eptir** *prp. with acc.* after. 8/1. 8/17. 12/25. 14/11. 14/19. *with dat.*
  in accordance with, according to. 4/20. 8/7. *as adv.* after, afterwards, after that. 4/17. 10/1. 12/19.
**et** *conj.* that. 2/2. 2/19. 2/23. 2/24. 4/7. 4/9. 4/11. 6/8. 6/12. 10/8.
  10/22. 10/23. 12/17. 12/24. 14/7. 14/10. 14/17. 14/17. 14/21.
  14/23. See also **miþ þy et, þy**[2].
**eþa** *conj.* or. 12/14. 14/17. Cf. **ella, ellar**[1].

**\*fa** *v.* get; achieve; be allowed. *1p* **faum** 2/14. *pret. 3s* **fikk** 6/4. 8/26. 8/29.

**\*faigr** *adj.* doomed. *superl. asm* **\*faigastr** most doomed. **faigastan** 6/7.

**\*faldr** *adj.* ill-fated, condemned to failure. *superl.* **\*fallastr** most ill-fated. *asm* **fallastan** 6/7.

**fara** *v.* go (home); travel, leave, cross, pass; move. *i* 2/26. 6/6. 10/17. 10/28. 12/16. 12/17. 12/27. 14/6. 14/13. [14/15]. *subj. 1s* **fari** 6/8. *pret. 3s* **for** 8/3. 8/9. 8/19. *pret. 3p* **foru** 2/26. 4/1. 4/2. 4/5. 4/7. 10/16. *pret. subj. 3s* **fori** 6/15. *sup.* **farit** 14/14.

**faum** see **\*fa**.

**\*ferþ** *f.* voyage, journey. *gs* **ferþar** 14/8. *as* **(her)ferþ** 12/23.

**fiauratigi** *num.* forty. 6/13. 14/2.

**fielkunnugr** *adj.* skilled in many things, versatile. *nsm* [6/10].

**fierri** *adv.* a distance, far away. 4/6.

**fikk** see **\*fa**.

**\*fileþi** *n.* cattle, beast. *ds* **fileþi** 4/19. 4/22.

**firir** *prp. with acc.* before (in time), prior to; to the notice of; in compensation for. 4/12. 4/17. 12/1. 12/25. 12/26. 14/3. 14/9. *with dat.* for. 2/10. *as adv.* **þar firir** in that place, see **byggia**.

**firir niþan** *prp. with dat.* or *acc.* below. 8/25.

**firir utan** *prp. with acc.* without. 6/18.

**flairi, flairum** see **\*margr**.

**\*flya** *v.* flee. *ptc. nsm* **flyandi** 8/1.

**for** see **fara**.

**\*forbuþ** *n.* prohibition. *ap* **forbuþ** 6/19.

**\*forfall** *n. pl.* reasons, (legal) causes. *dat.* **forfallum** 14/21.

**fori** see **fara**.

**\*forskiel** *n. pl.* conditions, reasons. *dat.* **forskielum** 10/23.

**foru** see **fara**.

**\*frels** *adj.* unhindered, free. *npm* **frelsir** 6/17.

**\*frest** *f.* or *n.* period, specified time; respite. *ds* **frest** 14/12. *as* **frest** 12/25. *dp* **frestum** 14/15. 14/18.

**\*frir** *adj.* free. *npm* **frir** 6/17.

**\*friþr** *m.* peace; freedom. *as* **friþ** 6/4. 6/5. 6/23.

**\*froyia** *f.* wife. See **\*husfroyia**.

**fulk** *n.* population; (*collective noun*) humans; people. *ns* 2/22. *ds* **fulki** 4/21.

**\*fulkumin** *adj.* (*ptc.*) complete. *dsm* **fulkumnum** 12/21. See also **kuma**.

**fydum** see **fyþa**.

**fylgia** *v. with dat.* follow, go (along) with, accompany, take part. *i* 10/26. 12/22. 14/2.

**fyr** *adv. comp.* before, previously. *superl.* **fyrsti** first. 2/1. 2/3. 2/6. 6/5. 8/15. 10/18. **fyr en** *conj.* before 6/15. 10/14. **fyr þan** *conj.* before. 6/4.

***fyra** *v.* bring. *pret. 3p* **fyrþu** 8/14.

***fyrri** *adj. comp.* previous, former. *dsn* **fyrra** 12/8. *superl.* ***fyrstr** first. *nsf* **fyrsti** 8/28. 10/4. 10/10. *asf* **fyrstu** 2/7.

**fyrsti**[1] see **fyr**.

**fyrsti**[2], **fyrstu** see ***fyrri**.

**fyrþu** see ***fyra**.

**fyþa** *v.* give birth to; support. *i* 2/23. *ptc. dp* **(o)fydum** 2/15.

**gaf** see **giefa**.

***gamal** *adj.* old. *superl.* **elzti** eldest. *nsm* 2/20.

**ganga** *v.* go (with a purpose); pass, circulate; enter. *i* 14/8. *3p* **ganga** 6/11. *pret. 3s* **gikk** 6/11. *pret. 3p* **gingu undir** submitted to. 6/16. *ptc. dsm* **gangnum** 4/10. *npn* **gangin** 14/27.

**gar** see **giera**.

***garlakr** *adj.* prepared, ready. *npm* **garlakir** 14/9.

**gart** see **giera**.

***garþr** *m.* fence, enclosure; farm, estate; (church-, grave-)yard. *ds* **garþi** 10/3. **(Hulm)garþi** 8/10. *ap* **(kirkiu)garþa** 10/18. **(staf)garþa** 4/18.

**gatu** see ***gieta**.

**gialdin** see ***gielda**.

***gief** *f.* gift. *dp* **giefum** 8/4.

**giefa** *v.* give, grant; hand out, release. *i* **(ut) giefa** 14/25. 14/27. *3sp* **gief‹s›** 14/22. *pret. 3s* **gaf** 2/15. 8/5. 8/6. *imp. 2p* **giefin** 6/7.

**giefum** see ***gief**.

***gielda** *v.* pay a fine, pay out. *subj. 3p* **gialdin** 14/2.

**giera** *v.* do; collect; make, build; lend; pay. *i* 10/18. 10/23. 12/7. 14/26. *pret. 3s* **gierþi** 6/5. 6/15. 8/8. 8/15. 8/18. 10/3. 12/5. *pret. 3sp* **gierþis** 10/9. *pret. 3p* **gierþu** 4/4. 4/20. 10/13. 12/6. 12/9. *ptc. nsf* **gar** 10/11. *asn* **gart** 6/4.

***gieta** *v.* be able to, have strength to. *pret. 3p* **gatu** 4/2. 4/5. 14/13.

**gikk** see **ganga**.

***gingerþ** *f.* payment in kind; a sort of tax, paid in the form of provisions. *as* **gingerþ** 12/3. 12/5. 12/6. 12/7. 12/9. *gp* **gingerþa** 10/29.

**gingu** see **ganga**.

**ginum** *prp. with acc.* through. 4/6.

**\*gutnalþing** *n.* General assembly (**alþing**) of the Gotlanders. *as* **gutnalþing** 6/22.

**\*guþ** *n.* idol, (heathen) god. *ap* **guþ** 4/18.

**\*haf** *n.* sea. *as* **haf** 6/23. 14/14.

**hafa** *v.* have (*also as an auxiliary verb*); take; hold, retain, keep. *i* 2/25. *3p* **hafa** 4/16. 12/27. *subj. 3s* ‹**hafi**› 6/13. **hafi** 6/14. *pret. 3s* **hafþi** 2/5. 4/20. 4/21. 8/22. *pret. 3p* **hafþu** 4/22.

**\*hailigr** *adj.* holy, saint. *nsm* **helgi** 8/1. 8/3. 8/6. 8/9. *gsm* **helga** 8/8. *gsn* **helga** 10/15.

**haim** *adv.* home(wards). 10/16. 14/13.

**haima** *adv.* at home. 14/15. 14/21.

**haiman** *adv.* from home. 6/15.

**haita** *v.* be called, be named. *i* 2/17. *3s* **haitir** 4/3. 4/6. 8/16. 14/4. *3p* **haita** 4/23. *pret. 3s* **hit** 2/1. 2/5. 2/6. 8/15. 8/22.

**\*haiþin** *adj.* heathen. *nsn* **ha‹i›þit** 6/1. *npm* **hainir** 8/11. *apn* **haiþin** 4/18. 8/12. 12/23.

**\*halda** *v. with dat.* or *acc.* hold, retain, keep; support, protect. *subj. 3p* **haldi** 14/25. *pret. 3p* **hieldu** 6/2. *ptc. asn* (**sik uppi**) **haldit** 4/2. (**sik**) **haldit** 4/5.

**\*halfr** *adj.* half. *asm* **halfan** 14/8.

**halp** see **\*hielpa**.

**\*hamn** *f.* harbour. *as* **hamn** 8/2.

**hann** *m.*, **han** *f. pers. pron.* he, she. *nm* 16 times. *nf* 8 times. *gm* **hans** 8/4. 8/25. 10/1. *gf* **hennar** 2/9. 2/10. *dm* **hanum** 8/5. 8/6. 10/25. 14/25. *df* **henni** 2/7. 2/9. *am* **hann** 6/6. *af* **hana** 8/17.

**\*haugr** *m.* grave howe. *ap* **hauga** 4/18.

**\*haur** *adj.* high. *comp.* **\*hoygri** higher. *nsf* **hoygri** [12/20]. *superl.* **\*hoygstr** highest; also courtesy title, equivalent to 'Lord'. *gsm* **hoygsta** 10/21. *asf* **hoystu** 4/21.

**\*hegnan** *f.* protection, defence. *as* **hegnan** 6/19.

**helga, helgi** see **\*hailigr**.

**\*helgun** *n.* saint; *pl.* All Saints. *gp* **helguna** 8/27. 12/18. See also **\*messa**.

**hennar, henni** see **hann**.

**\*her** *m.* armed force. See **\*herferþ**.

**\*herferþ** *f.* military expedition. *as* **herferþ** 12/23. See also **\*ferþ**.

**herra** *m.* lord. *ns* 4/13.

**\*herþa** *v.* persist in; *in negative imp.* = desist from, let (*or* leave) alone. *imp. 2p* **herþin** 8/24.

*hestr *m.* horse. *dp* **hestum** 10/26.

hetningar *f. pl.* hostilities. *np* 12/14.

hieldu see *halda.

*hielp *f.* assistance, help, support. *as* **hielp** 6/19.

*hielpa *v.* support, help, assist. *pret. 3s* **halp** 8/24.

hier *adv.* here. 12/15.

*hindra *v.* hinder. *pret. subj. 3s* **hindraþi** 14/18.

hinget *adv.* here, hither, i. e. to Gotland. 6/25.

*hinn *pron., def. art.* the other, the one (that, who). *npm* **hinir** 12/8.

*hiskepr *m.* household. *as* **hiskep** 10/3.

hit see **haita**.

*hitta *v.* discover, find. *pret. 3s* **hitti** 2/1.

*hoygri, hoygsta see *haur.

*hoyra *v.* belong. *3s* **(til) hoyrir** 6/24. *3p* **(til) hoyra** 12/15.

hoystu see *haur.

huer *pron.* and *adj.* each one; every, each. *nsm* 4/21. *dsm* **huerium** 6/17. 12/3. 12/4. 12/5. *dsf* **huerri** 10/30. *asf* **hueria** 14/3. *asn* **huert** 2/24. 6/12. 10/24. 14/26.

huer þriþi see þriþi huer.

hugþi see *hyggia

*hult *n.* grove. *ap* **hult** 4/17.

*hus *n.* house. See *bynahus.

*husfroyia *f.* (house)wife. *as* **husf‹r›oyu** 10/2.

*hyggia *v.* think. *pret. 3s* **hugþi** 4/9.


i *prp.* in, into; on; to; of, within, during. *with dat.* 2/8. 2/22. 6/17. 8/10. 8/13. 8/18. 8/25. 8/28. 10/3. 10/4. 10/10. 10/10. 10/11. 10/11. 10/12. 10/21. 12/11. 12/19. 14/6. 14/11. 14/12. 14/14. 14/22. *with acc.* 2/19. 4/1. 4/2. 8/2. 8/8. 8/15. 12/14. 12/23.

iek *pers. pron.* I. *ns* 6/8. *ds* **mir** 6/7. 6/8. *as* **mik** 6/7. 8/21.

iemlika *adv.* constantly. 6/2.

ier see **vara**.

ierl *m.* jarl, earl. *ns* 6/14. 6/21.

illa *adv.* unfortunately, badly. 14/23.

*-in *suffixed def. art. asm* **(veg)in** 6/24. *asf* **(Faroy)na** 4/1. **(drytning)ina** 4/13.

innan *prp. with acc.* in, to, into. 2/26. 6/8. 8/12. 8/27.

insigli *n.* authority, seal. *ds* 14/29.

*iorþ *f.* ground. *gs* **(ufan) iorþar** 2/25.

**ir**[1] *pers. pron. pl.* you. *nom.* 6/7. 6/8. 8/20. 8/20.

**ir**[2], **iru** see **vara**.

**kafli** *m.* baton. See **buþkafli**.

*****kalla** *v.* call, name; request, call for. *3s* **kallar** 8/2. 8/17. 8/23. 8/28. 10/4. *pret. subj. 3p* **kallaþin** 6/21.

**kann** see *****kunna**.

*****kaupmannaskepr** *m.* trading (voyages). *ds* **kaupmannaskap** 8/11.

*****kaupmaþr** *m.* merchant. *np* **kaupmenn** 8/13.

*****kenna** *f.* teaching. *ds* **kennu** 10/6.

*****kennidombr** *m.* teaching. *ds* **kennidomi** 8/8.

**kirkia** *f.* church. *ns* 8/9. 8/26. 8/28. 10/4. 10/10. 12/1. *gs* **kirkiu** (**vigsla**) 10/28. **kirkiu** (**vigsl**) 10/29. *ds* **kirkiu** 8/21. *as* **kirkiu** 8/15. 8/18. 8/19. 8/20. 8/25. 10/3. (**Petrs**) **kirkiu** 8/28. (**Stain**)**kirkiu** 8/23. 10/4. *np* **kirkiur** 10/12. 12/6. *ap* **kirkiur** 10/13. 10/18. 10/19.

**kirkiugarþa** see *****garþr**.

*****kirkiugarþr** *m.* graveyard, churchyard. See *****garþr**.

**kirkiur** see **kirkia**.

*****klenat** *n.* valuable. *dp* **klenatum** 8/5.

*****klint** or *****klinta** *f.* cliff. *ds* or *as* **klintu** 8/26.

*****kornband** *n.* prohibition against trade in corn. *as* **kornband** 6/19.

*****kristin** *adj.* Christian. *npm* **kristnir** 10/9. *gpm* **kristna** 10/5. *dpn* **kristnum** 8/13. *apn* **kristna** 8/13. *apn* **kristin** 8/12. 12/24.

*****kristindombr** *m.* Christianity. *as* **kristindom** 10/20. *ds* **kristindomi** 8/7. 10/7. 12/22.

*****kristna**[1] *f.* Christianity. *gs* **kristnur** 10/8.

**kristna**[2] see **kristin**.

**kristna**[3] *v.* baptise, christen. *i* 8/14. 10/2.

**kristnir**, **kristnum** see **kristin**.

**kristnur** see **kristna**[1].

*****kruna** *v.* crown. *ptc. nsm* **krunaþr** 14/23.

**kuma** *v.* come; *with dat.* bring. *i* 10/24. *3s* **kumbr** 12/8. 14/10. 14/12. *3p* **kuma** 14/14. *pret. 3s* **quam** 2/3. 4/12. 8/1. *pret. 3p* **quamu** 4/7. 10/15. *pret. subj. 3s* **quami** 10/22. *pret. subj. 3p* **quamin** 14/17. *ptc. dsm* (**ful**)**kumnum** 12/21.

**kuna** *f.* wife. *ns* 2/6. *ds* **kunu** 6/9.

*****kunna** *v.* may, should. *3s* **kann** 14/10. 14/23. *3p* **kunnu** 12/10. 12/14.

*****kunnugr** *adj.* skilled. See **fielkunnugr**.

**kunu** see **kuna**.

**kunungr** *m.* king; (Byzantine) emperor. *ns* 4/8. 4/13. 6/13. 6/20. 6/21. 8/1. 8/6. 12/24. 14/17. 14/23. *gs* **kunungs** 14/18. 14/20. 14/22. 14/29. 14/29. *ds* **kunungi** 4/8. 6/24. 12/22. *as* **kunung** 6/5. 6/11. 6/16. *np* **kunungar** 6/1.

**la** see **liggia**.

**laglika** *adv.* lawfully, legally. 12/27. (o)**laglika** 14/17.

***laglikr** *adj.* lawful, legal. *dp* **laglikum** 14/21.

**laiþingr** *m.* levy, (sea-borne war) expedition, muster. *ns* 14/7. *gs* **laiþings(lami)** 14/5. **laiþings (menn)** 14/9. **laiþings (buþ)** 14/14. *as* **laiþing** 12/24.

**laiþingslami** *m.* tax which was paid on failure to take part in a sea-borne war expedition, 'levy-hindrance (tax)'. *ns* 14/5.

**land** *n.* land; country, island, realm; people of the island, islanders, population; 'authorities'. *ns* 2/23. 2/27. 4/20. 8/16. 8/19. (**bo)land** 2/13. *gs* **lanz** 6/15. 10/15. *ds* **landi** 2/24. 10/4. 10/10. 10/11. *as* **land** 2/3. 10/26. *dp* **landum** 8/13. *ap* **land** 8/12. 12/23. See also ***Aistland, *Grikland, Gutland, *Ryzaland**.

***langr** *adj.* long. *asm* **langan** 2/22.

**lata** *v.* leave, allow, permit; cause, arrange (for). *i* 6/22. 14/26. *pret. 3s* **lit** 10/1. *pret. 3p* **litu** 8/13. 10/19.

***laus** *adj.* free from. See ***saklaus**.

***lausn** *f.* fee, fine. *as* **lausn** 12/5.

**laut** see ***liauta**.

***leggia** *v.* lay. *pret. 3s refl.* **legþis** 8/2.

***lenda** *v.* resolve (a dispute). *ip* **lendas** 12/11. *ptc. nsf* **lent** 12/13.

**lengi** *adv.* for a long time. 4/17. 8/3.

***lerþr** *adj.* learned. ***lerþr maþr** = priest. *gpm* **lerþra** 10/6.

***liauta** *v.* inherit. *pret. 3s* **laut** 2/20. 2/21.

**liggia** *v.* lie. *i* 14/26. *pret. 3s* **la** 8/3.

**lit, litu** see **lata**.

***liþ** *n.* group of men. See ***liþstemna**.

***liþstemna** *f.* mobilisation, muster of forces. *gs* **liþstemnu** 12/25. 12/26. 14/12. *as* **liþstemnu** 14/9.

**loysa** *v.* pay fee or fine; give absolution. *i* 12/8. 12/17.

***lufa** *v.* I. promise. II. grant, allow. *pret. 2s* **lufaþi** 4/13. *pret. 3s* **lufaþi** 4/9. *ptc. asn* **lufat** 4/12.

***luta** *v.* cast lots. *pret. 3p* **lutaþu** 2/23.

**lydu** see ***lyþa**.

**\*lykia** *v.* seal down, close. *ptc. nsn* **lykt** 14/29.

**lysa** *v.* proclaim. *i* 6/23.

**\*lyþa** *v.* obey. *pret. 3p* **lydu** 10/6.

**\*maga** *v.* be able to. *2s* **matt** 4/14. *3s* **ma** 12/17. *pret. subj. 3p* **mattin** 6/17.

**\*magr** *m.* (son-)in-law. *ds* **magi** 8/24.

**maira, mairu** see **\*mikil.**

**\*mak** *n.* convenience. *ds* **maki** 10/13.

**\*mal** *n.* language; matter, case before the law. *ds* **mali** 4/16. *np* **(dailu)mal** 12/14.

**manaþr** *m.* month. *ns* 4/9. *gs* **manaþar** 12/25. 14/15. *ds* **manaþi** 4/10. 14/6. *as* **manaþ** 14/8.

**\*mangr** *adj.* many (a), a large number of. *npm* **mangir** 6/1. *dp* **mangum** 10/26. *apm* **manga** 6/3. Cf. **\*margr.**

**mann, manna, mannum, manz** see **maþr.**

**\*margr** *adj.* many (a). *comp.* **flairi** several (other), more. *npm* 8/4. *dp* **flairum** 10/27. Cf. **\*mangr.**

**\*mark** *f.* mark (amongst other meanings in weight of gold or silver, or in coin). *np* **markr** 12/20. *gp* **marka** 6/12. 14/3. *dp* **markum** 10/30. *ap* **markr** 6/13. 6/14. 12/2.

**\*matr** *m.* food. *ds* **mati** 4/19. 4/22.

**matt, mattin** see **\*maga.**

**maþr** *m.* man, person. *ns* 2/1. 2/3. *gs* **manz** 8/22. *as* **mann** 8/25. *np* **menn** 4/17. 8/4. 10/9. 10/13. 12/11. 14/9. **(kaup)menn** 8/13. **(sendi)menn** 14/18. 14/20. *gp* **manna** 10/5. 10/6. 12/13. **(nemda)manna** 14/20. **(kaup)manna(skap)** 8/11. *dp* **mannum** 10/25. 14/7. *ap* **(sendi)men** [6/3]. 6/21.

**men** *conj.* but (instead). 2/26.

**menn** see **maþr.**

**\*messa** *f.* mass, (ecclesiastical) feast. *gs* **(helguna) messur** 12/18. **(Valborga) messur** 12/18. 12/19. *as* **(Petrs) messu** 14/20.

**mest**[1] see **mikil.**

**mest**[2] *adv.* most. 12/11.

**mik** see **iek.**

**\*mikil** *adj.* great, much, large. *nsf* **mikil** 12/17. *nsn* **mikit** 2/22. *comp.* **\*mairi** greater, more, larger. *dsn* **maira** [4/9]. 14/2. **mairu** 10/13. *asn* **maira** 10/29. 12/4. *superl.* **\*mestr** most, largest, greatest. *asn* **mest** 8/23.

**millan** *prp. with gen.* between. 12/18.

**minn** *poss. pron.* or *poss. adj.* mine; my. *nsm* 4/13. *dsm* **minum** 6/9.

***minni** *adj. comp.* shorter, lesser. *asf* **mindri** 4/22. *dp* **minnum** 14/14.

**mir** see **iek.**

**missumar** see ***miþsumar.**

**miþ** *prp. with dat.* with, together with; in accordance with, according to; by; on; of. 25 times. **miþ þy** as a result, therefore (literally, 'with this'). **miþ þy et** *as conj.* because, since; in order that. 14/13. See also **þy²**.

**miþal(-)þriþiungr** *m.* middle third; the middle of Gotland's three divisions or ridings. See **þriþiungr.**

**miþan** *conj.* while. 6/1.

***miþsumar** *m.* midsummer. *as* **missumar** 12/26.

***mungat** *n.* ale, beer, feast. *ds* **mungati** 4/20. 4/23.

***namn** *n.* name. *ds* **namni** 8/27. *as* **namn** 2/15.

***nat** *f.* night, 24 hours. *as* **nat** 2/7. *dp* **natum** 2/2. See also ***siau netr.**

***nauþugr** *adj.* forced. *npm* **nauþugir** 2/26.

**nekrum** see ***nequar.**

**nemda aiþr** *m.* oath of a commissioner or chosen man. *ns* 14/22.

***nemdamaþr** *m.* commissioner, chosen man. *gp* **nemdamanna** 14/20.

**nemna** *v.* announce; select; decree, lay down. *i* 14/21. *ip* **nemnas** 14/7.

***nequar** *indefinite pron.* some, any. *dsm* **nekrum** 10/14. *dsn* **nequaru** 14/24. *asm* **nequan** 10/1.

***ner¹** *adj.* close, near(by). *superl.* **nestr** closest, nearest. *nsm* 10/22. *nsn* **nest** 14/19.

***ner²** *prp. with dat.* and *adv.* near. *superl.* **nest** nearest to 12/12.

**nest¹,²** see ***ner¹,².**

**nestr** see ***ner¹.**

***netr** *f. pl.* nights. See ***siau netr.**

***niþ** *f.* waning (of the moon). *np* **niþar** 4/11. *ap* **niþar** 4/8. 4/14.

**niþan** see **firir niþan.**

***norþastr** *adj. superl.* northern(most). *dsm* **norþasta** 10/5. *asm* **norþasta** 2/20.

**nu** *adv.* now. 6/7. 8/9. 8/16. 8/28. 10/3.

**ny** *n.* waxing moon, new moon. *ns* 4/11. *as* **ny** 4/8. 4/14.

**o-** *negation* see **brenna, fyþa, laglika, *vigia.**

**obrend** see **brenna.**

**ok** *conj. adv.* and, also, as well. 86 times.

**ofydum** see **fyþa.**

olaglika see laglika.
*ormbr *m.* snake. *np* ormar 2/8.
orþu see varþa.
ovigþ see *vigia.
*oy *f.* island. *as* oy 4/2. See also *Faroy.
*oyri *m.* öre; coin. *dp* oyrum 10/31.
oystra *adv.* eastwards. 10/16.

*penningr *m.* coin. 1/8 mark or *ertaug*; *pl.* coin; money. *gp* penninga 12/2. 14/3.
*pilagrimbr *m.* pilgrim. *np* pilagrimar 10/15.
*prestr *m.* priest. *ds* presti 12/2. 12/4. *ap* presti 8/14. 12/21.
proastr *m.* rural dean. *ns* 12/17.

quam, quami, quamin, quamu see kuma.
*quemd *f.* arrival. *gs* quemdar 12/16. See also *tilquemd.
*queþa *v.* say. *pret. 3p* quaþu 4/11.

raku see *reka.
*raþ *n.* advice. *ds* raþi 6/15.
*raþa *v.* carry authority; *with dat.* rule; *with acc.* interpret. *3s* raþr 14/28. *pret. 3s* reþ [2/11]. 8/23.
*reka *v.* drive, force, direct. *subj. 3s* reki 12/16. *pret. 3p* raku 2/27. *ptc. nsm* rekinn 14/24.
ret see *retr¹.
*retr¹ *m.* right(s), statute, law; treaty. *ds* ret 6/2. 10/22. 14/30. *as* ret 6/11.
*retr² *adj.* proper, right, lawful. *dp* retum 14/18.
retta *v.* judge. *i* 12/15.
retum see *retr².
reþ see *raþa.
*reþskepr *m.* support. *as* reþskep 10/23.
*riki *n.* kingdom, realm. *gs* (Suia)rikis 6/3. 6/13. *ds* riki 14/24. (Suia)riki 14/28. *as* (Suia)riki 6/17.
rikr *adj.* influential, powerful, mighty. *nsm* 8/21. *npm* rikir 8/4. *superl.* *rikastr richest. *gsm* rikasta [8/21].
*roa *v.* row. *ptc. npm* roandi 14/13.

*saga *f.* tale, account. *np* sagur 6/10.
sagu see *sia.

**sak** *f.* fine, obligation. *ns* 12/19.

**\*saklaus** *adj.* free from charges. *dsn* **(at) saklausu** with impunity. 14/13. 14/16.

**saman** *adv.* together. 2/7. 2/8. 4/24. 12/1. 14/26.

**\*sami** *adj.* and *pron.* same, the same. *dsm* **sama** 12/11. *dsn* **sama** 14/4. *asm* **sama** 8/8. *asf* **samu** 8/18.

**\*samtalan** *f.* consideration. *gs* **samtalan** 12/13.

**samulaiþ** *adv.* likewise, similarly. 6/21.

**sank** see **\*sinqua**.

**\*sanktus** *Latin adj.* saint(ed). *gsm* **sankti** 14/19.

**\*sannund** *f.* truth. *dp* **sannundum** 12/12.

**satin** see **sitia**.

**\*segia** *v.* say; **\*segia firir** relate (to). *pret. 3s* **segþi** 2/10. 4/13. 8/20. 8/24.

**sei** see **vara**.

**\*semia** *v. impersonal with dat.* be agreed. *3s* **sembr** 14/7.

**senda** *v.* send. *i* 6/22. *ip* **sendas** 14/30. *pret. 3p* **sentu** 6/3. 10/20.

**\*sendibuþi** *m.* messenger; message. *np* **sendibuþar** 6/22. *ap* **sendibuþa** 10/21.

**\*sendimaþr** *m.* messenger. See **maþr**.

**sendimen(n)** see **maþr**.

**\*senn** *poss. pron. refl.* (his, her, its, their) own. *dsm* **sinum** 2/10. 6/2. 8/24. 10/3. 10/7. *dsf* **sinni** 4/20. *dsn* **sinu** 14/24. *asm* **sin** 6/22. 10/3. *asf* **sina** 10/2. *gp* **sinna** 10/29. *dp* **sinum** 4/19. 8/4. 10/25. 14/1. *apn* **sin** 10/2.

**sentu** see **senda**.

**\*setia** *v.* establish, set (out), lay down. *ptc. nsf* **sett** 8/27.

**\*sia** *v.* see. *pret. 3p* **sagu** 8/13. 10/5.

**siau** *num.* seven. 12/23.

**\*siau netr** *f. pl.* a week. *ap* **siau netr** 14/9. 14/11.

**\*siauþa** *v.* cook, boil. *pret. 3p* **suþu** 4/23.

**sielfr** *pron.* self. *nsm* 8/19. 8/21. *gsm* **sielfs (viliandi)** 6/16. **sielfs (vilia)** 10/7. *dsm* **sielfum** 6/9.

**\*sielfs vili** *m.* free will. See **sielfr**, **\*vili**.

**\*sielfs viliandi** *adj.* of (one's) free-will, voluntary. See **sielfr**, **\*vilia**[2].

**sielfum** see **sielfr**.

**siextigi** *num.* sixty. 6/14. 6/12.

**\*sigla** *v.* sail. *pret. 3p* **silgdu** 8/11. *ptc. npm* **siglandi** 14/14.

**\*sigr** *m.* victory. *ds* **sigri** [6/2].

**sik** see ***sina**<sup>2</sup>.

***silfr** n.* silver. *gs* **silfs** 6/12. 6/13. 6/14.

**silgdu** see ***sigla**.

**sin, sina**<sup>1</sup> see ***senn**.

***sina**<sup>2</sup> *pers. pron. refl. gen.* himself, herself, itself, themselves; on (his, her, its, their) own (account). *dat* **sir** 2/25. 4/12. 4/21. 4/22. 8/8. 10/13. 12/21. *acc.* **sik** 4/2. 4/5. 8/14. 10/2.

**sinn, sinna, sinni** see ***senn**.

***sinqua** v.* sink. *pret. 3s* **sank** 2/2. 2/4.

**sinu(m)** see ***senn**.

**sir** see ***sina**<sup>2</sup>.

**sitia** *v.* remain, stay. *i* 14/15. *pret. subj. 3p* **satin** 14/21.

**siþ** see ***siþr**.

**siþan**<sup>1</sup> *adv.* then, afterwards, later, subsequently; after, further. 14 times.

**siþan**<sup>2</sup> *conj.* since, after. 10/5. 12/21.

**siþan en** *conj.* after, since. 10/9. 10/20.

**siþar** *adj.* later. 12/26.

**siþir** see **um siþir**.

***siþr** *m.* custom; tax, customary payment. *as* **siþ** 12/3. *ap* **siþi** 8/13. 10/5.

**skal** see ***skulu**.

**skap** see ***kaupmannaskepr**

**skattr** *m.* tax. *ns* 6/12. *as* **skatt** 6/22. 14/19. 14/25. 14/26.

***skepr** *m.* quality, characteristic; manner. See ***hiskepr**, ***kaupmannaskepr**, ***reþskepr**.

***skiauta** *v.* refer. *ip* **skiautas** 12/13.

***skip** *n.* ship. *dp* **skipum** 8/2.

***skipta** *v. with dat.* divide. *pret. 3p* **skiptu** 2/19.

***skriþa** *v.* crawl, creep. *pret. subj. 3p* **skriþin** 2/9.

***skulu** *v.* will; should, ought to; be obliged to, have to; be. *3s* **al** 2/13. 2/16. 2/17. 6/21. **skal** 10/31. 12/13. 12/17. 12/26. 14/6. 14/7. 14/8. 14/29. *2p* **skulin** 8/20. *3p* **skulu** 12/1. 12/7. 12/10. 14/9. 14/11. *pret. 3s* **skuldi** 6/20. *pret. 3p* **skuldu** 2/24. *pret. subj. 3p* **skuldin** 10/25.

***slikr** *adj* such, so great (a). *asm* **slikan** 6/8.

***slingua** *v.* coil, plait, entwine. *ptc. npm* **slungnir** 2/8.

***smar** *adj.* small. *comp.* ***smeri** smaller. *npn* **smeri** 4/22.

***snekkia** *f.* longship; warship. *as* **snekkiu** [14/3]. *dp* **snekkium** [12/23]. [14/1].

**snieldr** *adj.* wise, clever; (weak form as personal nickname). *nsm* [6/10]. **snielli, sn⟨i⟩elli** [8/22]. 10/2.

**so** *adv.* so, thus, just so, as follows, the case; such, just; in such a way (that), in this way; on the understanding, to the effect (that); similarly. 24 times.

**\*sokn** *f.* parish. *ds* **sokn** 6/4.

**\*stafgarþr** *m.* ancient site. See Note to 4/18 and **\*garþr.**

**stafgarþa** see **\*garþr.**

**staggaþan** see **\*staþga¹.**

**standa** *v.* stand. *i* 8/26. 8/29. *3s* **standr** 8/9. 8/25.

**staþ** see **\*steþr.**

**\*staþga¹** *v.* bind, establish, confirm. *ptc. asm* **staggaþan** 6/11.

**staþga²** see **\*staþgi.**

**\*staþgi** *m* statute. *as* **staþga** [6/14].

**steddum** see **\*steþia.**

**\*stemna** *f.* meeting. See **\*liþstemna.**

**steþi** see **\*steþr.**

**\*steþia** *v.* confirm. *ptc. dsm* **steddum** 10/22.

**steþilika** *adv.* permanently, lasting. 10/14.

**\*steþr** *m.* location, place; (every)where. *ds* (**i huerium**) **staþ** 6/17. *as* **staþ** 8/9. 8/16. 8/28. *ap* **steþi** 6/23. See also **Kulasteþar.**

**\*strida** *v.* fight, battle. *pret. 3p* **stridu** 6/1.

**suafu** see **\*sufa.**

**\*suara** *v.* answer. *pret. 3s* **suaraþi** 6/6. Cf. **\*annsuara.**

**suer** *m.* father-in-law. *ns* 10/1.

**\*sufa** *v.* sleep. *pret. 3p* **suafu** 2/7.

**sum** *rel. pron.* which, who, that; *conj.* as, as if. 35 times. **so sum** 2/8. 6/10. 12/6.

**\*sumar** *m.* summer. See **\*miþsumar.**

**\*sumbr** *pron.* some (of). *asn* **sumt** [4/16]. *npm* **sumir** 8/14.

**\*sun** *m.* son. *ds* **syni** 6/9. *as* **sun** 2/5. *dp* **synum** 4/19. *ap* **syni** 2/14.

**\*sunnarstr** *adj. superl.* southern(most). *dsm* **sunnarsta** [10/12]. *asm* **sunnarsta** 2/21.

**\*suþnautr** *m.* a person with whom one boils meat; comrade-in-sacrifice; 'boiling-companion'. *np* **suþnautar** 4/23.

**suþu** see **\*siauþa.**

**sykia** *v.* visit; travel. *i* 6/17. 6/18. 6/25. (**til**) **sykia** 6/23.

**\*synas** *v. md.* be seen, be visible. *3s* **synis** 4/4.

**synd** *f.* sin. *ns* 12/17.

**syni, synum** see **\*sun.**

**synis** see **\*synas.**

**taka** *v. with dat.* take; collect, receive, embrace. *i* 4/15. 6/22. 10/29. 12/3. 14/20. *3p* **taka** 14/19. *subj. 3s* **taki** 12/5. **taka viþr** receive, accept; undertake, take upon one; ally oneself to. *pret. 3s* **tok (viþr)** 8/7. *pret. 3p* **toku (viþr)** 10/6. 12/21 (verb understood). 12/22. *pret. subj. 3s* **toki (viþr)** 10/14. **taka sir** *with acc.* accept. *pret. 3p* **toku (sir)** 12/21.

**til**¹ *prp.* to; until; for. *with gen.* 4/7. 6/3. 8/4. 8/10. 8/14. 10/8. 10/15. 10/21. 10/23. 10/24. 10/28. 12/19. 14/8. *with undeclined head-word* 10/15. 10/17. 12/13.

**til**² *adv.* thereto. 12/16.

**\*til biþia** *v.* beg (for something). See **\*biþia**.

**\*til hoyra** *v. with dat.* belong to. See **\*hoyra**.

**\*tilquemd** *f.* visitation, visit; arrival. *gs* **tilquemda (siþ)** 12/3. See Note.

**\*til skura** *v.* lay down, define. *ptc. npf* **til skuraþar** 12/6.

**til sykia** *v.* visit. See **sykia**.

**\*timi** *m.* (period of) time. *as* **tima** 2/22. 4/17. 8/18. 8/23. 10/1. 10/16. **(vintr)tima** 12/19.

**tiugu** *num.* twenty. 6/14.

**tok, toki, toku** see **taka**.

**\*tolf** *num.* twelve. *dm* **tolf** 10/25. 10/31. *am* **tolf** 8/5. 14/20.

**\*tro** *f.* belief. See **\*vantro**.

**troa** *v.* believe. *i* 14/17. *pret. 3p* **troþu** 4/17.

**\*tuair** *num.* two. *nn* **tu** 2/6. *am* **tua** 8/6.

**\*tuldr** *m.* toll, excise duty. *as* **tull** 6/18.

**ufan** *prp. with acc.* on, against. 12/24. *with gen.* above. 2/25.

**ufan a** *prp. with acc.* on, against. 12/23.

**um** *prp. with acc.* through; around, over; in respect of. 2/22. 4/8. 4/14. 6/12. 8/23. 10/1. 10/17. 10/26. 10/28. 12/19. 14/25. as. 12/3, see Note. *adv.* of, around. 12/27. 14/6.

**um siþir** *adv.* at last. 4/13.

**undir** *prp. with acc.* under. 6/16.

**\*ungr** *adj.* young. *superl.* **yngsti** youngest. *nsm* 2/21.

**upp** *adv.* up; forward. 4/5. 4/6. 8/19.

**uppi** *adv.* up, raised up. 2/3. 10/4. See also **\*halda**.

**ut** *adv.* out; over. 14/7. 14/25. 14/27. 14/27. See also **\*utgift**.

**utan**¹ *prp. with acc.* without; exempt from. 6/17. 6/19. 10/7.

**utan**² *conj.* but; without, unless, apart from. 2/27. 4/2. 4/5. 8/17. 12/16. 14/14. 14/15. 14/22. 14/25.

**\*utgift** *f.* charge, expense. *ap* **utgiftir** 6/18.

**vaita** *v.* give. *i* 6/20.

**\*vald** *n.* force, power; choice. *ds* **valdi** 14/24. *as* **val** 12/27.

**\*vantro** *f.* ignorance of the true faith; mistaken belief. *ds* **vantro** 4/20.

**\*var**¹ *poss. pron.* our. *dsn* **varu** 4/16.

**var**², **vari, varin, varu**¹ see **vara**.

**vara** *v.* be, continue; mean. *i* 4/12. 12/26. 14/10. *3s* **ir** 2/12. 4/14. 6/12. 12/20. 12/27. 14/17. 14/19. *3p* **iru** 10/31. 12/6. 14/27. *subj. 3s* **sei** 12/17. *pret. 3s* **var** 2/2. 2/3. 6/1. 6/10. 8/18. 8/21. 8/27. 8/28. 10/4. 10/10. 10/16. 10/22. 14/4. *pret. 3p* **varu** 8/11. *pret. subj. 3s* **vari** 4/10. 4/11. *pret. subj. 3p* **varin** 2/8.

**varu**² see **\*var**¹.

**varþa** *v.* become, be; happen, arise, occur. *i* 2/13. 12/10. 12/15. 14/10. *3s* **varþr** 12/12. 14/23. *pret. 3s* **varþ** 10/11. *pret. 3p* **orþu** 10/9.

**\*vatn** *n.* watercourse. *ds* **vatni** 4/5.

**\*vaþi** *m.* peril, danger. *as* **vaþa** 6/8.

**vegr** *m.* route, way; side. *ns* 10/16. *as* **vegin** 6/25. See also **\*Norvegr.**

**\*venia** *v.* accustom. *pret. 3pp* **vendus** 10/20.

**\*vereldi** *n.* wergild. *ap* **vereldi** 6/8.

**\*veþur** *m.* (yearling) ram. *ap* **veþru** 8/5.

**\*vi** *n.* holy place. *ap* **vi** 4/18.

**\*vigia** *v.* consecrate, dedicate. *ip* **vigias** 10/31. 12/1. *pret. 3p* **vigþu** 10/17. *ptc. npn* **(o)vigþ** 12/1.

**\*vigsl** *f.* consecration, dedication. *ds* (**alteris**) **vigsl** 10/30. (**kirkiu**) **vigsl** 10/29. *gp* (**kirkiu**) **vigsla** 10/28.

**\*vika** *f.* week. *ds* **viku** 14/11. *as* **viku** 14/6. *gp* **vikna** 14/1.

**vil, vildi, vildu** see **\*vilia**².

**\*vili** *m.* will. *ds* (**sielfs**) **vilia** 10/7.

**vilia**¹ see **\*vili.**

**\*vilia**² *v.* wish to, want to; be willing to, be prepared to. *3s* **vil** 14/17. *2p* **vilin** 6/8. 8/20. *3p* **vilia** 14/1. 14/21. *pret. 3s* **vildi** 2/27. 4/10. 8/16. 8/19. *pret. 3p* **vildu** 2/25. *pret. subj. 3s* **vildi** 10/24. *ptc. npm* (**sielfs**) **viliandi** 6/16.

**viliandi, vilin** see **\*vilia**².

**\*vintrtimi** *m.* winter(time). *as* **vintrtima** 12/19.

**visa** *v. with dat.* send, command. *i* 4/10.

**\*vist** *f.* food, provisions. *ds* **vist** 14/1.

**\*vita** *v.* know. *2p* **vitin** 6/7. *3p* **vita** 12/11.

**\*vittr** *m.* winter; year. *as* **vittr** 12/25. Cf. **\*vintrtimi.**
**viþr** *prp. with acc.* off; with; to, towards. 4/2. 6/5. 6/11. 10/20.
**viþratta** *f.* dispute, conflict. *ns* 4/12.
**\*viþr taka** *v. with dat.* or *with* **at** *and infinitive* receive, take over; take upon oneself, assume. See **taka.**
**\*viþr þorfa** *v.* need (something), be in need. See **\*þorfa.**

**yfir** *prp. with acc.* over. 6/23. 14/14. *adv.* over. 12/16. 12/17.
**yngsti** see **\*ungr.**
**\*ypin** *adj.* open. *nsn* **ypit** [14/30].
**yr** *prp. with dat.* out of. 2/9.
**\*yx** *f.* axe. *see* **\*braiþyx.**

**þa**[1] *adv.* then, at that time; now; (as an introduction to a resultant clause) so. 39 times.
**þa**[2] see **þann**[1].
**þa en** *conj.* when; (but) if. 6/6. 10/31. 14/2. 14/7. 14/10. 14/12. 14/27.
**þaar, þaim, þair, þaira, þairi, þan**[1] see **þann**[1].
**þan**[2] *conj.* than. [4/9]. 6/4. 12/20. 14/15.
**þann**[1] *pers.* (*n.* and *pl.*), *dem.* or *rel. pron.* it; they; that, that one, such; the following; which. *nsm* 2/1. 2/3. 4/9. 8/5. 8/15. *nsf* **þaun** 8/26. 12/12. *nsn* **þet** 2/2. 2/4. 4/14. 6/12. 14/4. *dsm* **þaim** 14/6. 14/27. *dsf* **þairi** 14/11. 14/12. *dsn* **þy** 4/6. 8/26. 12/5. 12/7. 14/4. 14/19. *asm* **þan** 4/17. 6/24. 8/16. 8/18. 8/23. 8/27. 10/16. 10/23. *asf* **þa** 8/2. 8/18. 8/20. *asn* **þet** 4/20. 8/1. 8/16. *npm* **þair** 2/9. 2/19. 2/23. 2/24. 2/25. 2/26. 4/1. 4/2. 4/5. 4/7. 4/7. 4/7. 4/11. 4/15. 4/16. 4/19. 4/20. 4/23. 6/16. 6/20. 6/22. 6/24. 8/11. 10/6. 10/17. 10/20. 12/6. 12/7. 12/11. 12/22. 14/1. 14/11. 14/13. 14/13. 14/21. 14/26. *npf* **þaar** 12/10. *npn* **þaun** 2/6. 2/7. *gp* **þaira** 4/12. 6/4. 10/18. *dp* **þaim** 2/15. 4/9. 4/10. 4/14. 4/15. 6/13. 10/12. 10/22. 10/23. *apm* **þaim** 2/23. 2/27. 2/28. 10/8.
**þann**[2] *dem. adj.* the. *nsm* 2/20. 2/21.
**þar** *adv.* and *conj.* there, (in) the place (that), at the place (where); then, subsequently. 2/27. 4/1. 4/1. 4/3. 4/5. 4/7. 4/15. 6/22. 8/3. 8/14. 8/17. 8/18. 8/23. 8/27. 10/3. 12/12. 12/12. 12/18. **þar firir** see **byggia.**
**þau** *adv.* however, nevertheless, still; furthermore, besides. 6/2. 8/11. 12/25. 14/3. 14/25.
**þau et** *conj.* although. 8/11. 12/24.

þaun see þann[1].

þegar (sum) *conj.* as soon as. 12/7.

þet see þann[1].

þeþan *adv.* from there, thence. 2/28. 8/9. 10/16.

*þiauþ *n.* person, *pl.* people. *as* þiauþ 2/24.

þing *n.* assembly, thing. *ns* 14/7. *ds* þingi 14/19. *as* (gutnal)þing 6/22. *np* þing 4/22.

þissi *dem. pron.* and *adj.* this (same). *nsm* 2/5. *nsf* þissun 4/12. *nsn* þitta 2/13. *dsf* þissi 8/21. *asm* þinna 2/10. 2/11. 6/14. *dp* þissum 2/21.

*þorfa *v.* have to. *þorfa viþr need (something), be in need. *pret. subj. 3p* (viþr) þorftin 6/20.

þrir *num.* three. *nm* 2/8. *nf* þriar 12/20. *nn* þry 14/27. *dat.* þrim 2/22. 10/30. *am* þria 2/14. 2/19. *af* þriar 12/2. *an* þry 6/8. 10/29. 12/2. 12/3. 14/25.

þriþi *num.* third. *nsm* 2/18. *nsf* þriþi 10/11. *dsn* þriþia 12/8. *asn* þriþia 6/9.

*þriþi huer *num.* every third. *asn* þriþia huert 10/24. huert þriþia 2/24. Cf. *annar huer.

þriþiungr *m.* third, riding; *treding.* *ns* 4/21. *ds* þriþiungi 10/5. 10/12. 12/11. 12/14. (miþal)þriþiungi 10/11. *as* þriþiung 2/20. (miþal) þriþiung 2/20. *ap* þriþiunga 2/19. See Note.

þry see þrir.

þu *pers. pron. sing.* you. *nom.* 4/13. 4/15.

þuang[1] *n.* necessity, duress. *ns* 12/16. *as* þuang 10/8.

þuang[2] see *þuinga.

*þuinga *v.* force. *pret. 3s* þuang 10/8.

þula *v.* tolerate, endure. *i* 2/27. 8/16.

þy[1] see þann[1].

þy[2] *adv.* for that reason, because. 8/17. þy et *as conj.* because, since; in order that. 4/23. 6/9. 6/16. 8/25. 10/13. 10/21. ‹þy› et 12/11. See also miþ.

*þykkia *v.* *impersonal with dat.* seem. *pret. 3s* þytti 2/9.

# INDEX OF PROPER NAMES

Further details of the places and persons in this glossary are discussed, where appropriate, in the notes. In the text a single variant of personal and place names has been selected from those that occur in the manuscript. In particular, the form *Olaf(r)* has been selected for the king of Norway. In the translation, the nominative of each personal name has been used. Nicknames have not been translated but are explained or discussed in this Index. Place-names have been given in modern Swedish form where appropriate or in English or local form.

**\*Aistland** *n.* Estonia. *as* **Aistland** 4/3.

**\*Akrgarn** *n.* or *f.* Akergarn or Åkergarn, now called S:t Olofsholm. A port on the east coast of Gotland, in the parish of Hellvi, in the northern third of the island. *as* **Akrgarn** 8/3. *gs in compound* **Akrgarna (kirkia)** 8/9.

**\*Akubekkr** *m.* Akebäck, a parish in the northern third of Gotland, north of Vall and Roma parishes and to the east of the main road between Visby and Roma. *ds* **Akubek** 8/15.

**\*Alfa** *f.* Alva, a parish in the southern third of Gotland, between the parishes of Hemse and Havdhem. *gs in compound* **Alfa (sokn)** 6/4.

**\*Atlingabo** *n.* Atlingbo, a parish in the middle third of Gotland. *ds* **Atlingabo** 10/10.

**Avair** *m. personal name.* A farmer from Alva, sent to negotiate with the Swedish king. *ns* 6/4.

**bain** *n.* leg, bone; *adj.* straight. See **Strabain.**

**\*bekkr** *m.* beck, stream. See **\*Akubekkr.**

**Botair** *m. personal name.* A farmer from Akebäck, who built the first church on Gotland. *ns* 8/15. *ds* **Botairi** 8/24.

**Dagaiþi** *f.* or *n.* Dagö, now belonging to Estonia, the fourth largest island in the Baltic. *ns* 4/3.

**Dyna** *f.* river, the Western Dvina (German *Düna*, Latvian *Daugava*), which flows westwards to the Gulf of Riga. *ns* 4/6.

**\*Faroy** *f.* Fårö, an island off the north-eastern coast of Gotland, separated from it by a narrow sound. *as* **Faroyna** 4/1.

**\*Farþaim** *n.* Fardhem, a parish in the southern third of Gotland. *ds* **Farþaim** 10/11. See also **\*haim.**

**\*garn** *n.* or *f.* I. yarn. II. gut. In place-names possibly meaning 'something stretched out'. See **\*Akrgarn.**

**Graipr** *m. personal name.* The second (or eldest) son of Hafþi, *q. v. ns* 2/17. 2/19.

***Grikland** *n.* Byzantine empire. *gs* **Griklanz** 4/7. *as* **Grikland** 10/17.

***grikr** *m.* Byzantine (person). *gp* **grika** 4/8.

**Gunfiaun** *m. personal name.* The youngest son of Hafþi, *q. v. ns* 2/18. 2/21.

**Guti**[1] *m. personal name.* The eldest (or second) son of Hafþi, *q. v. ns* 2/16. 2/20.

***guti**[2] *m.* Gotlander. *np* **gutar** 6/2. 6/3. 6/6. 6/16. 8/11. 10/5. 10/20. 12/21. 12/27. 14/2. 14/25. *gp* **guta** 6/12. *dp* **gutum** 6/20. 6/23. 12/24.

**Gutland** *n.* Gotland. *ns* 2/1. 10/14. *gs* **Gutlanz** 8/14. 10/15. 10/23. 10/25. *ds* **Gutlandi** 2/6. 2/19. 2/22. 8/29. 10/13. 12/20. 14/22. *as* **Gutland** 2/2. 2/16. 6/1. 6/18. 10/28.

***Guþ** *m.* God. *gs* **guz** 10/6.

**Hafþi** *m. personal name.* The first settler on Gotland. *ns* 2/5. *gs* **Hafþa** 2/5. *ds* **Hafþa** [2/10].

***haim** *n.* home; in place-names, settlement. See ***Farþaim**, ***Hainaim**.

***Hainaim** *n.* Hejnum, a parish in the northern third of Gotland. *ds* 8/4.

**Huitastierna** *f. personal name.* 'White Star', the wife of Hafþi, *q. v. ns* 2/6.

***Hulmgarþr** *m.* Novgorod in Russia; Holmgård. *ds* **Hulmgarþi** 8/10.

***Ierusalem** *n.* Jerusalem. *gs* **Ierusalem** 10/16. 10/17.

***Ierslafr** *m. personal name.* Jaroslav, Russian ruler in Kiev. *gs* **Ierslafs** 8/10, see Note.

***kaupungr** *m.* town, particularly a trading or market town. *ds* (**Leon**)**kopungi** 10/21. 10/24.

**Kulasteþar** *m.* (originally *gs*) Kulstäde, today a farm in Vall parish, about three kilometres south of Akebäck church, in the middle third of Gotland. *ns* 8/16. *as* **Kulasteþar** 8/17.

**Likkair** *m. personal name.* Landowner on Gotland, Botair's father-in-law, *q. v. ns* 8/22. 10/1.

***Linkaupungr** *m.* Linköping, cathedral town in Östergötland. *ds* **Leonkopungi** 10/21. 10/24.

**\*Norvegr** *m.* Norway. *ds* **Norvegi** 8/2.

**Olafr** *m. personal name.* St Olaf Haraldsson, king of Norway. *ns* 8/1. 8/3. 8/6. 8/10. *gs* **Olafs** 8/8.

**Ormika** *m. personal name.* Farmer from Hejnum parish. *ns* 8/3. 8/5. 8/7.

**\*oy** *f.* island. See **\*Faroy**.

**\*Petr** *m. personal name.* St Peter. *gs* **Petrs** 8/28. 14/19.

**\*Petrs messa** *f.* St Peter's mass, 29th June. See **\*messa** in Glossary.

**\*Ryzaland** *n.* Russia. *as* **Ryzaland** 4/6 (here probably refers to the principality of Kiev). 10/17.

**snielli** *weak m. adj. as personal nickname.* clever, wise. *ns* [8/22]. **sn⟨i⟩elli** 10/2. See **\*snieldr** in Glossary.

**\*Stainkirkia** *f.* Stenkyrka, parish in the northern third of Gotland. *as* **Stenkirkiu** 8/23. 10/4. See also **kirkia** in Glossary.

**stierna** *f.* star. See **Huitastierna**.

**Strabain** *m. personal nickname.* Possibly 'straw legs' or 'straw-straight'. *ns* 6/4. See also **Avair**.

**suiar** *m. pl.* Swedes. *np* 6/18. *gp* **suia (kunung)** 6/5. 6/11. 6/16. **suia (kunungi)** 12/22. **suia(riki)** 6/17. **suia(riki)** 14/28. **suia(rikis)** 6/3. 6/13.

**\*Upsalir** *m. pl.* Gamla Uppsala, about five kilometres north of modern Uppsala, the seat of the king of the Swedes (Svear). *gp* **Upsala** 6/24.

**\*Vi** *n.* the ancient holy place where Visby now stands. *ds* **Vi** 8/18. 8/25.

**\*Valborg** *f. personal name.* St Walburga. *gs in* **\*Valborga messa** Walburga's day, 1st May. 12/18. 12/19. See **\*messa** in Glossary.

**Þieluar** *m. personal name.* The legendary discoverer of Gotland. *ns* 2/1. 2/5.

**\*Þorsborg** *f.* A fortification, now called Torsburgen, in the parish of Kräklingbo on its border with Ardre and Gammelgarn, in the middle third of Gotland. *as* **Þorsborg** 2/26.

# BIBLIOGRAPHY AND ABBREVIATIONS

## Manuscripts

Biblioteca Medicea Laurenziana, Florence. Codex Laur. Ashburnham, 1554. *c*.1120. The so-called 'Florensdokumentet'; a list of church provinces, bishoprics, etc.

Royal Library, Copenhagen. Gammel kongelig samling 2414 4to. Niels Pedersen. Early 17th century. *De Cimbris et Gothis Libri II.* Includes a Danish translation of *Guta saga.*

Royal Library, Copenhagen. Gammel kongelig samling 2415 4to. Niels Pedersen. Early 17th century. *Danmarcks første begyndilse oc herkomst*... Condensed translation by Niels Michelsen of the so-called *Gullandskrønike.*

Royal Library, Copenhagen. Ny kongelig samling 408 8vo. Early 16th century. Danish translation of *Guta saga.*

Royal Library, Stockholm B64. 14th century. *Gottlandz landzlagh.*

Royal Library, Stockholm B65. 1401. *Gottlands landslag på Plattyska.*

Royal Library, Stockholm D2. Codex Holmiensis. 1470–1480. Contains 54 lines of a medieval Swedish translation of *Guta saga.*

Royal Library, Stockholm F.m. 57:10. C. F. Hilfeling. 1801. *1801 års resa på Gottland af Herr Conducteur Hilfeling.* Included in Hilfeling, 1994–1995.

Säve 1862 = *Kungliga Vitterhets-, historie- och antikvitetsakademien,* Stockholm. Riksantikvarieämbetet och Statens historiska museer ämbetsarkivet 2. *Serie E IV Antikvitetsintendenternas ämbetsberättelser.* Per Arvid Säve. *Berättelse för 1862 rörande Östergötland och Västergötland.* Vol. 3.

University Library, Copenhagen. AM 54 4to. 1587. *Guta lag.* Copy by David Bilefeld of a lost manuscript from 1470.

## Printed books

Adam of Bremen. 1961. *Gesta Hammaburgensis ecclesiae pontificum.* Ed. W. Trillmich and R. Buchner.

AL = Noreen, A. G. 1892–1894. *Altschwedisches Lesebuch mit Anmerkungen und Glossar.*

Birkeland, H. 1954. *Nordens historie i middelalderen etter arabiske kilder.*

Björkander, A. 1898. *Till Visby stads äldsta historia. Ett kritiskt bidrag.*

BoG = *Boken om Gotland.* 1945. Ed. M. Stenberger and R. Steffen. 2 vols.

Brate, E. and Bugge, S. 1887–1891. 'Runverser: Undersökning af Sveriges metriska runinskrifter', *Kungliga Vitterhets-, historie- och antikvitetsakademien, Antiqvarisk tidskrift för Sverige* 10, 1–442.

Brekke, A. 1918. *Om præpositionsbruken ved islandske og norske gaardnavne.*

Bugge, S. 1877–1878. 'Sproglige Oplysninger om Ord i gamle nordiske Love. I. Svenske Ord', *Nordisk Tidskrift for Filologi* 3 (Ny række), 258–275.

Bugge, S. 1907. 'Om nordiske folkenavne hos Jordanes', *Fornvännen* 2, 98–101.

*Bullarium Danicum. Pavelige aktstykker vedrørende Danmark. 1198–1316.* 1931–1932. Ed. A. Krarup. 2 vols.

C–V = R. Cleasby and G. Vigfusson. 1957. *An Icelandic–English dictionary.*

Carlén, O. 1862. *Gotland och dess fornminnen. Anteckningar rörande öns historia.*

Chaucer, Geoffrey. 1987. *The Riverside Chaucer.* Ed. L. D. Benson.

Child, F. J., ed., 1882–1898. *The English and Scottish Popular Ballads.* 5 vols.

Christiansen, E. 1997. *The northern crusades.*

*Chronicle of Novgorod 1016–1471, The.* 1914. Tr. R. Michell and N. Forbes, ed. C. R. Beazley and A. A. Shakhmatov.

*CIG = Codex iuris Gotlandici, cum notis criticis, variis lectionibus, nova versione suecana, glossariis et indicibus nominum propriorum. Gotlands-lagen.* 1852. Ed. C. J. Schlyter. (*CIS* VII)

*CIO = Codex iuris Ostragotici. Östgötalagen.* 1830. Ed. H. S. Collin and C. J. Schlyter. (*CIS* II)

*CIS = Corpus iuris Sueo-gotorum antiqui . . . Samling af Sweriges gamla lagar.* 1827–1877. Ed. H. S. Collin and C. J. Schlyter. 13 vols.

*Codex iuris Vestrogotici. Västgötalagen.* 1827. Ed. H. S. Collin and C. J. Schlyter. (*CIS* I)

Constantine Porphyrogenitus. 1962–1967. *De administrando imperio.* Ed. G. Moravcsik and R. J. H. Jenkins, tr. R. J. H. Jenkins. 2 vols.

Debes, L. 1673. *Færoæ & Færoa Reservata. Det er: Færøernis oc Færøeske Indbyggeris Beskrifvelse.* [Facsimile edition with introduction and notes, ed. J. Rischel. 1963. 2 vols]

Delisle, M. L. 1886. *Notice sur des manuscrits du fonds libri conservés à la Laurentienne, à Florence.*

*DMA* = *Dictionary of the Middle Ages.* 1982–1989. Ed. J. R. Strayer. 13 vols.

Dolley, M. 1978. 'En ny penny från Olaf den helige i Gotlands fornsal', *Meddelande från Klinte hembygdsförening.*

*DS* = *Diplomatarium Suecanum.* 1829–1995. Ed. J. G. Liljegren et al. 8 vols and 2 appendices.

Dudo of St Quentin. 1865. *De moribus et actis primorum Normanniae ducum auctore Dudone Sancti Quintini decano.* Ed. J. Lair.

*Encyclopaedia of religion and ethics.* 1908–1926. Ed. J. Hastings. 13 vols.

Engström, J. 1979. 'Torsburgen—en gåta inför sin lösning', in *Arkeologi på Gotland.* Ed. W. Falk et al., 121–132.

Engström, J. 1984. *Torsburgen. Tolkning av en gotländsk fornborg.*

Envall, P. 1950. 'Svenska stift och landskap i början av 1100-talet', *Namn och bygd* 38, 81–99.

Envall, P. 1956. 'Liunga, Kaupinga och Arosa', *Historisk tidskrift* 76, 372–392.

*Erikskrönikan enligt Cod. Holm. D2.* 1963. Ed. R. Pipping.

Falk, H. 1912. 'Altnordisches Seewesen', *Wörter und Sachen* IV, 1–122.

Falk, H. and Torp, A. 1903–1906. *Etymologisk Ordbog over det norske og det danske Sprog.* 2 vols.

Faulkes, A. 1978–1979. 'Descent from the gods', *Mediaeval Scandinavia* 11, 92–125.

Feilberg, H. F. 1886–1914. *Bidrag til en Ordbog over jyske Almuesmål.* 4 vols.

Fenger, O. 1979. Review of Sjöholm, 1976. *Historisk tidsskrift udgivet af Den danske historiske forening* 79, 112–124.

Finnur Jónsson. 1924. 'Kong Olaf den helliges ophold på Gotland', *Festschrift Eugen Mogk zum 70. Geburtstag 19. juli 1924*, 81–83.

*FL* = Noreen, E. 1932. *Fornsvensk läsebok på grundval av A. Noreens Altschwedisches Lesebuch.*

Foote, P. G. and Wilson, D. M. 1979. *The Viking achievement.*

*Fornsvenska texter med förklaringar och ordlista.* 1959. Ed. E. Wessén.

Franklin, S. and Shepard, J. 1996. *The emergence of Rus 750–1200.*

Friesen, O. von. 1913. *Upplands runstenar: en allmänfattlig ofversikt.*

Friesen, O. von. 1941. 'Runbrynet från Timans i Roma. Ett minne från Gotlands storhandel', *GArk* 13, 7–14.

Fritzell, G. 1971. *Visby i världshandelns centrum. Stadens tillblivelse och utveckling till forna dagars handelscentrum.*

Fritzell, G. 1972. 'Tankar kring Gutasaga', *Gotländska studier* 1, 11–46.

Fritzell, G. 1974. 'Kulstäde, platsen för Gotlands första kyrka', *Gotländska studier* 3, 5–16.

*Från stenåldersjägare till masmästare. Kulturmiljöer i Örebro län.* 1986–1987. Ed. P. Kåks.

G 216, G 220 = Inscriptions 216 and 220 in *GR*.

*G-L* = *Guta-Lagh das ist: Der Insel Gothland altes Rechtsbuch.* 1818. Ed. K. Schildener.

Gallén, J. 1958. 'Kring det sk. *Florensdocumentet* från omkring år 1120', *Historisk tidskrift för Finland* 43, 1–31.

*GArk* = *Gotländskt arkiv. Meddelanden från föreningen Gotlands fornvänner.* 1929– (in progress).

Geete, R. 1903. *Fornsvensk bibliografi: förteckning öfver Sveriges medeltida bokskatt på modersmålet samt därtill hörande litterära hjälpmedel.*

*GGD* = *Guterlov og Gutersaga paa dansk.* 1910. Ed. L. Jacobsen.

Gigas, E. 1903–1915. *Katalog over Det store kongelige Bibliotheks Haandskrifter vedrørende Norden, særlig Danmark.* 3 vols.

Gimbutas, M. 1963. *The Balts.*

Giraldus Cambrensis. 1867. *Topographia Hibernica. Expugnatio Hibernica.* Ed. J. F. Dimock.

*GLGS* = *Guta lag och Guta saga jämte ordbok.* 1905–1907. Ed. H. Pipping. [*Ordbok* has separate pagination]

*GO* = *Gotländsk ordbok på grundval av C. och P. A. Säves samlingar.* 1918–1945. Ed. G. Danell, A. Schagerström and H. Gustavson.

Goffart, W. 1988. *The narrators of barbarian history (AD 550–800). Jordanes, Gregory of Tours, Bede and Paul the Deacon.*

Gordon, E. V. 1962 (2nd edn, rev. A. R. Taylor). *An introduction to Old Norse.*

*Gotländska sägner upptecknade av P. A. Säve.* 1959–1961. I *Folktrosägner.* II *Historiska sägner.* Ed. H. Gustavson och Å. Nyman. (*Svenska sagor och sägner* 12)

*GR* = *Gotlands runinskrifter.* 1962–1978. Ed. S. B. F. Jansson, E. Wessén and E. Svärdström. 2 vols. (*Sveriges runinskrifter* 11–12)

*Grágás.* 1852. Ed. V. Finsen. Parts a and b.

Green, M. 1992. *Animals in Celtic life and myth.*

*GU* = Säve, C. 1859. *Gutniska urkunder: Guta lag, Guta saga och Gotlands runinskrifter språkligt behandlade. Academisk afhandling.*

Gustavson, Helmer. 1982. 'Hailgairs häll i S:t Hans', *GArk* 54, 85–90.

Gustavson, Herbert. 1938. 'Gotlands ortnamn. En översikt', *Ortnamnssällskapets i Uppsala årsskrift* 3, 3–58.

Gustavson, Herbert. 1940–1948. *Gutamålet: en historisk-deskriptiv översikt.* 2 vols.

Gustavson, Herbert. 1977. *Gutamålet—inledning till studium.*

*GV* = *Gutar och vikingar.* 1983. Ed. I. Jansson.

Hadorph, J., ed., 1687. *Gothlandz-Laghen på gammal Göthiska.*

Hallberg, G. 1985. *Ortnamn på Öland.*

*Heinrici Chronicon Livoniae.* 1959. Ed. L. Arbusow and A. Bauer, tr. into German by A. Bauer.

Hellberg, L. 1958. 'De gotländska ortnamnen på -*städe* och -*städar*', *Namn och bygd* 46, 1–114.

Hellberg, L. 1960. *Plural form i äldre nordiskt ortnamnsskick.*

Hellquist, E. 1918. *De svenska ortnamnen på '-by': en öfversikt.*

Hellquist, E. 1929–1932. *Det svenska ordförrådets ålder och ursprung: en översikt.*

Hellquist, E. 1980. *Svensk etymologisk ordbok.*

Hellström, J. A. 1996. *Vägar till Sveriges kristnande.*

*Herodotus.* 1926–1938. Tr. A. D. Godley. 4 vols.

Hildebrand, H. 1879–1953. *Sveriges medeltid: kulturhistorisk skildring.* 4 vols.

Hildebrand, H. 1884–1885. 'Heraldiska studier 1', *Kungliga Vitterhets-, historie- och antikvitetsakademien, Antiqvarisk tidskrift för Sverige* 7, 1–89.

Hilfeling, C. G. G. 1994–1995. *CGG Hilfelings gotländska resor 1797 och 1799; 1800 och 1801.* Ed. T. Gislestam. 2 vols. [Facsimile editions]

Hjelmqvist, T. 1903. 'Bidrag till tolkningen af Guta-saga', *Arkiv för nordisk filologi* 19, 162–173.

Hjärne, E. 1938. 'Bernstensriddare och Tacitus. Några anmärkningar om källor för Tacitus 44 och 45', *Handlingar angående professuren i historia vid Uppsala universitet*, 3–22.

Holmqvist, W. 1975. 'Was there a Christian mission to Sweden before Ansgar?' *Early medieval studies* 8, 33–55.

*Hungrvaka.* 1938. In *Byskupa sǫgur.* Ed. Jón Helgason.

Hyenstrand, Å. 1989. *Socknar och stenstugor: om det tidiga Gotland.*

*ÍF* = *Íslenzk fornrit.* 1933– (in progress).

Ihre, J. 1769. *Glossarium Suiogothicum.*

*ÍO* = Ásgeir Blöndal Magnússon. 1989. *Íslensk orðsifjabók.*

Jacobsen, L. 1911. 'Gamle danske Oversættelser af Gutasaga', *Arkiv för nordisk filologi* 27, 50–75.

Jansson, S. B. F. 1987. *Runes in Sweden.* Tr. Peter Foote.

Johansen, P. 1951. *Nordische Mission, Revals Gründung und die Schwedensiedlung in Estland.*

Johansson, G. 1968. *De norröna trosartiklarna. Lekmannafunderingar.*

Jordanes. 1997. *Getica. Om goternas ursprung och bedrifter.* Ed. and tr. into Swedish by A. Nordin.

Kalkar, O. 1881–1918. *Ordbog til det ældre danske sprog (1300–1700).* 5 vols.

Keil, M. 1931. *Altisländische Namenwahl.*

*KL = Kulturhistoriskt lexikon för nordisk medeltid.* 1956–1978. 22 vols.

Klintberg, M. 1909. *Några anteckningar om Gotland i verkligheten och Gotland i skrift.*

Knudsen, R. 1933. 'Visby. Bemærkninger om Navnet og Stedet', *GArk* 5, 26–36.

*Konung Alexander: en medeltids dikt från latinet vänd i svenska rim omkring år 1380.* 1855–1862. Ed. G. E. Klemming. 3 vols.

*Konungs skuggsjá. Speculum regale.* 1920. Ed. Finnur Jónsson.

Krause, W. 1953. 'En vikingafärd genom Djneprforsarna efter runinskriften på Pilgårdsstenen', *GArk* 24, 7–13.

*Kristnisaga.* 1905. In *Kristnisaga. Þáttr Þorvalds ens víðfǫrla. Þáttr Ísleifs biskups Gizurarsonar. Hungrvaka.* Ed. B. Kahle.

Kumlien, K. 1967. 'Biskop Karl av Västerås och Uppsala ärkesätes flyttning', *Historiskt arkiv* 14, 1–71.

Lagerlöf, E. and Svahnström, G . 1991. *Gotlands kyrkor: en vägledning.*

Landtman, G. 1919. *Folktro och trolldom: 1. Övernaturliga väsen.* (*Finlands svenska folkdiktning* 7)

Landtman, G. 1922. 'Hustomtens förvantskap och härstamning', *Folkloristiska och etnografiska studier* 3, 1–48.

Leach, H. G. 1946. *A pageant of old Scandinavia.*

Lemke, U. 1970. *Gotland. Ein geistesgeschichtlicher Quellort.*

Lemke, U. 1986. *Gotland. Insel der Götterschiffe.*

Lesch, B. 1916. 'Olof den helige, Gottlands apostel', *Historisk tidskrift för Finland* 1, 76–95.

*LG = Lex Gotlandiae svecice et germanice e codicibus B 64 et B 65 Bibl. Reg. Holm. Suecice et Britannice praefatus.* 1945. Ed. E. Wessén. (*Corpus codicum Suecicorum medii aevi*, V)

Lind, E. H. 1920–1921. *Norsk-isländska personbinamn från medeltiden.*

Lindquist, I. 1941. *Västgötalagens litterära bilagor: Medeltida svenska småberättelsekonst på poesi och prosa.*

Lindquist, S.-O. 1984. 'Sextio marker silver vart år . . .', *GArk* 56, 139–150.

Bibliography 91

Lindqvist, S. 1932. 'Forntida riksbyggare', *Arkeologiska studier tillägnade H. K. H. Kronprins Gustaf Adolf*, 70–78. Ed. N. Edén.

Lindqvist, S. 1933. 'Sveriges handel och samfärdsel under forntiden', in *Nordisk kultur* XVI:A, 49–67.

Lindqvist, S. 1941–1942. *Die Bildsteine Gotlands*. 2 vols.

Lindqvist, S. 1960–1962. 'Forngutniska altaren och därtill knutna studier', *Kungliga humanistiska vetenskaps-samfundet i Uppsala: Årsbok*, 85–120.

Lindqvist, S. 1967. 'Uppsala hednatempel och första katedral', *Nordisk tidskrift för vetenskap, konst och industri utgiven av Letterstedtska föreningen* 43, 236–242.

Lindroth, H. 1914a. 'Namnet Gottland', *Namn och bygd* 2, 75–83.

Lindroth, H. 1914b. 'En omdebatterad önamnsgrupp', *Fornvännen* 9, 125–202.

Lindroth, H. 1915. 'Gutnal þing och Gutnalia', *Från filologiska föreningen i Lund: Språkliga uppsatser* IV, 66–73.

Lindroth, H. 1941. 'Namnet Gotland', *Meijerbergs arkiv för svensk ordforskning* 3, 107–115.

Linschoten, Jan Huygen van. 1598. *Discours of voyages into y East & West Indies*. [Facsimile edition 1974]

Lithberg, N. and Wessén, E. 1939. *Den gotländska runkalendern 1328*.

Ljunggren, K. G. 1959. *En fornsvensk och några äldre danska översättningar av Gutasagan*.

Lockwood, W. B. 1969. *Indo-European philology*.

Lundmark, E. 1925. 'Bilefeld, Strelow och de gotländska kyrkornas kronologi', *Fornvännen* 20, 162–180.

Lundström, P. 1983. 'Gotlandshamnar', *GV*, 99–116.

Lyngby, K. J. 1858–1860. 'Anmeldelse af Svenske sprogværker. Skrifter om det svenske sproge og de svenske sprogarter', *Antiquarisk tidsskrift utgivet af Det Kongelige Nordiske Oldskriftselskab* 6, 234–271.

Läffler (here Leffler), L. F. 1877. *Om v-omljudet af ǐ, ī och ei i de nordiska språken*.

Läffler, L. F. 1908–1909. 'Till 700-årsminnet af slaget vid Lena (31 januari 1208). 3. Ett stadgande i Gutasaga, som ytterst föranledts af slaget vid Lena. En laghistorisk undersökning', parts 1 and 2. *Fornvännen* 3, 137–177 and 4, 120–125.

Magnusen, F. 1829. *Om de oldnordiske Gilders Oprindelse og Omdannelse. (Tidsskrift for nordisk Oldkyndighed—særskilt aftryckt)*

Magnusson, M. 1976. *Hammer of the North.*

Maillefer, J. M. 1985. 'Guta saga, histoire des Gotlandais: Introduction, traduction, commentaires', *Études Germaniques* 40,
131–140.

*Medieval Scandinavia. An Encyclopedia.* 1993. Ed. P. Pulsiano.

Mineur, W. H. 1984. *Callimachus. Hymn to Delos. Introduction
and commentary.*

Mitchell, S. A. 1984. 'On the composition and function of Guta
Saga', *Arkiv för nordisk filologi* 99, 151–174.

Mogk, E. 1909. 'Die Menschenopfer bei den Germanen', *Abhand-
lungen der philologisch-historischen Klasse Der königlichen
sächsischen Gesellschaft der Wissenschaften* 57, 601–644.

Montelius, O. 1914. 'Svenska runstenar om färder österut', *Fornvännen*
9, 81–124.

Måhl, K. G. 1990. 'Bildstenar och stavgardar—till frågan om de
gotländska bildstenernas placering', *GArk* 62, 13–28.

Nansen, F. 1911. *Nord i tåkeheimen. Utforskning av jordens nordlige
strøk i tidige tider.*

*National encyklopedin. Ett uppslags verk på vetenskaplig grund
utarbetat på initiativ av statens kulturråd.* 1989–1996. 20 vols.

Nerman, B. 1917–1924. 'Gravfynden på Gotland under tiden 550–
800 e. K.', *Kungliga Vitterhets-, historie- och antikvitetsakademien,
Antikvarisk tidskrift för Sverige* 22: 4, 1–102, I–XXX.

Nerman, B. 1923. *En utvandring från Gotland och öns införlivande
med sveaväldet.*

Nerman, B. 1932. 'The Grobin finds' evidence of the first incorporation of Gotland under the Svea kingdom', *Acta archaeologica*
3, 157–167.

Nerman, B. 1941a. 'En kristen mission på Gotland vid tiden omkring
år 800 e. kr.', *Fornvännen* 36, 30–40.

Nerman, B. 1941b. 'Forngutniska "kokkamrater"', *Fornvännen* 36,
238–242.

Nerman, B. 1958. '*Gutasagan:* Alt ir baugum bundit', *Saga och
sed*, 43–47.

Nerman, B. 1963. 'Den gotländska utvandringen och sveaväldets
expansion', *Historia kring Gotland*, ed. Å. G. Sjöberg, 15–26.

Nerman, B. 1969–1975. *Die Vendelzeit Gotlands.* 2 vols.

*NGL = Norges gamle love indtil 1387.* 1846–1895. Ed. R. Keyser
and P. A. Munch. 5 vols.

Nihlén, J. 1975. *Gotländska sagor.*

Bibliography    93

*NIYR* = *Norges innskrifter med de yngre runer.* 1941– (in progress). Ed. M. Olsen et al.

*NIÆR* = *Norges Indskrifter med de ældre Runer.* 1891–1924. Ed. S. Bugge and M. Olsen. 4 vols.

Nordin, F. 1881. 'Om Gotlands fornborgar', *Kungliga Vitterhets-, historie- och antikvitetsakademien, Månadsblad* 10, 97–147.

Noreen, A. 1879. *Fårömålets ljudlära.*

Noreen, A. 1904. *Altnordische Grammatik.* II. *Altschwedische Grammatik mit Einschluss des Altgutnischen.*

*Norsk ordbok. Ordbok over det norske folkemålet og det nynorske skriftmålet.* 1966– (in progress). Ed. A. Hellevik.

*Norsk riksmålsordbok.* 1937–1957. Ed. T. Knudsen and A. Sommerfelt. 2 vols.

Nylén, E. 1966. 'Gotländska fornminnen', *Svenska turistföreningens årsskrift,* 183–204.

Nylén, E. 1978. *Bildstenar i Gotlands Fornsal.*

Nylén, E. and Lamm, J. P. 1987. *Bildstenar.*

Ochsner, F. 1973. *Gotlands kristnande. Die Gotland-Saga: Die Christianisierung Gotlands.*

Olaus Magnus. 1909–1951. *Historia om de nordiska folken.* 5 vols.

Olrik, A. 1905. 'Tordenguden og hans dreng', *Danske studier* 2, 129–147.

Olrik, A. 1921. *Nogle grundsætninger for sagnforskning.* Ed. H. Ellekilde.

Olrik, A. and Ellekilde, H. 1926–1951. *Nordens gudeverden.* 2 vols.

Olsen, O. 1966. *Hørg, hov og kirke.*

Olsson, I. 1964. 'Om engelska ortnamn på -*stead* och gotländska på -*städe*', *Ortnamnssällskapets i Uppsala årsskrift* 29, 1–50.

Olsson, I. 1976. *Gotlands stavgardar—en ortnamnsstudie.*

Olsson, I. 1984. *Ortnamn på Gotland.*

Olsson, I. 1992. 'Stavgardsproblemet—ännu en gång', *Fornvännen* 87, 91–97.

Olsson, I. 1996. *Gotländska ortnamn.*

Olszewska, E. S. 1933. 'Illustrations of Norse formulas in English', *Leeds studies in English* 2, 76–84.

Olszewska, E. S. 1937–1945. 'Some English and Norse alliterative phrases', *Saga-Book* 12, 238–245.

*Ormulum, The.* 1852. Ed. R. M. White. 2 vols.

*Orosius* = *The Old English Orosius.* 1980. Ed. J. Bately.

Palmenfelt, U. 1979. *Gotländska folksägner.*

Palmqvist, A. 1961. *Kyrkans enhet och papalismen.*

Pamp, B. 1988. *Ortnamnen i Sverige.*

Paulus Diaconus. 1878. *Historia Langobardorum.* Ed. L. Bethmann and G. Waitz. Monumenta Germaniae historica. Scriptores rerum Langobardorum et Italicarum.

Peringskiöld, J. 1699. *Vita Theoderici Regis Ostrogothorum et Italiae.*

Perkins, R. M. 1974–1977. 'The dreams of *Flóamanna saga*', *Saga-Book* 19, 191–238.

Pernler, S.-E. 1977. *Gotlands medeltida kyrkoliv—biskop och prostar. En kyrkorättslig studie.*

Pernler, S.-E. 1978. 'S:t Olavs kapell i Akergarn', *De hundra kyrkornas ö* 56, 24–35.

Pernler, S.-E. 1981. 'Sankt Olav und Gotland', in *St. Olav, seine Zeit und sein Kult.* Ed. Gunnar Svahnström. *Acta Visbyensia. Visbysymposiet för historiska vetenskaper* VI, 101–114.

Pernler, S.-E. 1982. 'Kalvskinnshuset i Visby—namnet och funktionen', *GArk* 54, 103–108.

Pipping, H. 1904. 'Nya gotländska studier', *Göteborgs högskolas årsskrift* 10, 3–24.

Pipping, H. 1919. 'Till frågan om bosättningsförhållandena i östra Nyland', *Historisk tidskrift för Finland* 4, 1–30.

Pipping, R. 1943. 'Den fornsvenska litteraturen', *Nordisk kultur* VIII:A, 64–128.

*PRF = Privilegier, resolutioner och förordingar för Sveriges städer.* 1927–1985. 6 vols.

*Ragnars saga loðbrókar.* 1954. In *Fornaldar sögur Norðurlanda* I. Ed. Guðni Jónsson.

Rask, Erasmus. 1843. *A grammar of the Old Norse tongue translated from the Swedish.* Tr. G. W. Dasent.

Rietz, J. E. 1862–1955. *Svenskt dialekt-lexikon. Ordbok öfver svenska allmogespråket.* 2 vols.

*RPC = The Russian primary chronicle. Laurentian text.* 1953. Tr. and ed. S. H. Cross and O. P. Sherbowitz-Wetzor.

*SAOB = Ordbok öfver svenska språket, utg. Svenska Akademien.* 1898– (in progress).

Saxo Grammaticus. 1931–1957. *Gesta Danorum.* Ed. J. Olrik, H. Ræder and F. Blatt. 2 vols.

Schück, A. 1945. 'Gotlands politiske historia intill Brömsebrofreden', *BoG* I, 178–225.

Schück, H. 1959. *Ecclesia Lincopensis. Studier om Linköpings kyrka under medeltiden och Gustav Vasa.*

Schütte, G. 1907. *Oldsagn om Godtjod: Bidrag til etnisk Kildeforsknings Metode med særligt Henblik på Folke-stamsagn.*

Sjöholm, E. 1976. *Gesetze als Quellen mittelalterlicher Geschichte des Nordens.*

Skov, S. 1946. 'Anders Sunesøn og Guterloven', *Festskrift til Erik Arup den 22. november 1946.* Ed. A. Friis and A. Olsen, 107–117.

*SL = Svenska landskapslagar tolkade och förklarade för nutidens svenskar.* 1933–1946. Ed. Å Holmbäck and E. Wessén. 5 vols.

Smedberg, G. 1973. *Nordens första kyrkor. En kyrkorättslig studie.*

Snorri Sturluson. 1982. *Edda. Prologue and Gylfaginning.* Ed. A. Faulkes.

Spegel, Haquin. 1901. *Rudera gothlandica. Kort beskrivning om then øøn Gothland. Anno 1683.* Ed. O. v. Wennersten.

*SRS = Scriptores rerum svecicarum medii ævi.* 1818–1876. Ed. E. M. Fant, E. G. Geijer, J. H. Schröder and C. Annerstedt. 3 vols.

Steffen, R. 1945. 'Gotlands indelning och organisation', *BoG* I, 226–253.

Stenberger, M. 1945. 'Det forntida Gotland', *BoG* I, 44–107.

*STFM = Sveriges traktater med främmande magter jemte andra dit hörande handlingar.* 1877–1888. Ed. O. S. Rydberg. 4 vols.

Storm, G. 1895. 'Lofotens och Vesteraalens beskriffuelse 1591, af Erik Hansen Schönneböl', *Historisk-topografiske Skrifter om Norge og norske Landsdele forfattade i Norge i det 16de Aarhundrede*, 177–218.

Strelow, Hans Nielssøn. 1633. *Cronica Guthilandorum: Den guthilandiske Cronica.* [Facsimile edition 1978]

Ström, F. 1942. *On the sacral origin of the Germanic death penalties.* Tr. D. Burton.

Strömbäck, D. 1970. 'Att helga land', *Folklore och filologi. Valda uppsatser utgivna av Kungl. Gustav Adolfs Akademien 13.8.1970. Acta academiae regiae Gustavi Adolphi* 48, 135–165.

Suhm, P. F. 1792–1795. 'Om gammel Gwllandz Handell', in *Nye Samlinger til den danske Historie.* Ed. R. Nyerup, III, 133–138.

*Svenska medeltidens rim-kröniker III.* 1867–1868. *Nya krönikans fortsättningar eller Sturekrönikorna: fortgången af unionsstriderna under Karl Knutsson och Sturarne, 1452–1520.* Ed. G. E. Klemming.

Svensson, J. V. 1919. 'Ptolemæus' redogörelse för folken på ön Skandia', *Namn och bygd* 7, 1–16.

*Sveriges kyrkor: Got(t)land*. 1914–1975. Ed. S. Curman and J. Roosval. 8 vols.

*Sveriges medeltida personnamn*. 1974– (in progress).

*Sveriges runinskrifter*. 1900– (in progress).

Swanström, E. 1982. 'Ett bidrag till utforskandet av visbykyrkorna S:t Hans och S:t Pers historia', *GArk* 54, 77–84.

Swanström, E. 1985. 'Gutasagans "Allhelgonakyrka" återfunnen? Arkeologisk undersökning i S:t Hans ruin i Visby 1984–85', *GArk* 57, 117–126.

Swanström, E. 1986. 'Nya rön om "Allhelgonakyrkan", S:t Per och S:t Hans kyrkor i Visby', *GArk* 58, 45–52.

Syv, Peder. 1663. *Nogle Betenkninger om det Cimbriske Sprog*.

Säve, C. 1852. 'Om Gotlands äldsta fornlemningar', *Annaler for nordisk oldkyndighed og historie*, 130–170.

Säve, P. A. 1862. See above under Manuscripts.

Säve, P. A. 1873–1874. 'Några ord om konung Olof Haraldssons uppträdande på Gotland', *Svenska fornminnesföreningens tidskrift* 2, 247–255.

Säve, P. A. 1978–1983. *Gotlandsskrifter*. 5 vols. [Facsimile edition]

Söderberg, B. G. 1959. 'Gotland genom seklerna med bildkommentar av Sven E. Noreen', in *Gotland*, ed. S. E. Noreen et al., 27–154.

Söderberg, B. G. 1971. *Strövtåg i Gotlands historia*.

Söderberg, C. 1922. 'Om Gotlands kristnande. Uppsats i kyrkohistoriska seminariet i Uppsala', *Kyrkohistorisk årsskrift* 22, 213–246.

Söderberg, S. O. M. 1879. *Forngutnisk ljudlära*.

Söderwall, K. F. 1884–1973. *Ordbok öfver svenska medeltidsspråket*. 3 vols.

Tacitus, Cornelius. 1914. *De vita Iulii Agricolae, De origine et moribus Germanorum*. Ed. J. H. Sleeman.

Tamm, F. A. 1890–1905. *Etymologisk svensk ordbok*. 8 vols.

Thompson, M. W. 1967. *Novgorod the Great*.

Tiberg, N. 1946. 'Utvandringsberättelsen i Gutasagan', *GArk* 18, 16–47.

Troil, Uno von. 1777. *Bref rörande en resa till Island MDCCLXXII*.

Tunberg, S. 1911. *Studier rörande Skandinaviens äldsta politiska indelning*.

Tunberg, S. 1913. 'En romersk källa om Norden vid 1100-talets början', *Språkvetenskapliga sällskapets i Uppsala förhandlingar* in *Uppsala Universitets årsskrift* 1913: 1.

*Filosofi språkvetenskap och historiska vetenskaper*, 14–34; 96–98.

Tunberg, S. 1940. *Götarnas rike*.

U 614, U687 = Inscriptions 614 and 687 in *Upplands runinskrifter*. 1940–1958. Ed. E. Wessén and S. B. F. Jansson. (*Sveriges runinskrifter* 6–9). III.

*VABC = Vikingatidens ABC*. 1995. Ed. L. Thunmark-Nylén.

Vries, J. de. 1956–1957. *Altgermanische Religionsgeschichte*. 2 vols.

Wadstein, E. 1892. 'Alfer ock älvor. En språkligt-mytologisk undersökning', *Uppsalastudier tillegnade Sophus Bugge*, 152–179.

Wadstein, E. 1894–1895. 'Förklaringar och anmärkningar till fornnordiska lagar', *Nordisk Tidskrift for Filologi* 3 (Tredie Række), 1–16.

Wallin, J. 1747–1776. *Gothländska samlingar*. 2 vols.

Ware, T. 1976. *The Orthodox Church*.

Weibull, L. 1963. 'En forntida utvandring från Gotland', *Historia kring Gotland*, ed. Å. G. Sjöberg, 27–35.

Westholm, G. 1985. 'The settlement at Vi, at the foot of the cliff', in *Society and Trade in the Baltic during the Viking age*. Ed. Sven-Olof Lindquist and Birgitta Radhe. *Acta Visbyensia. Visbysymposiet för historiska vetenskaper VII*, 293–304.

William of Malmesbury. 1981. *The early history of Glastonbury: an edition, translation and study of William of Malmesbury's De antiquitate Glastonie Ecclesie*. Ed. and tr. J. Scott.

Wolfram, H. 1988. *History of the Goths*. Tr. T. J. Dunlop.

Yrwing, H. N. 1940. *Gotland under äldre medeltiden: Studier i baltisk-hanseatisk historia*.

Yrwing, H. N. 1963. 'Biskop Bengts brev för Mariakyrkan i Visby', *Historia kring Gotland*, ed. Å. G. Sjöberg, 71–99.

Yrwing, H. N. 1978. *Gotlands medeltid*.

Yrwing, H. N. 1991. 'Med anledning av en tysk doktorsavhandling', *GArk* 63, 155–176.

Ög 27, Ög 28 = Inscriptions 27 and 28 in *ÖR*.

Öhrman, Roger. 1994. *Vägen till Gotlands historia*. (*GArk* 66).

*ÖR = Östergötlands runinskrifter*. 1911. Ed. E. Brate. (*Sveriges runinskrifter* 2).

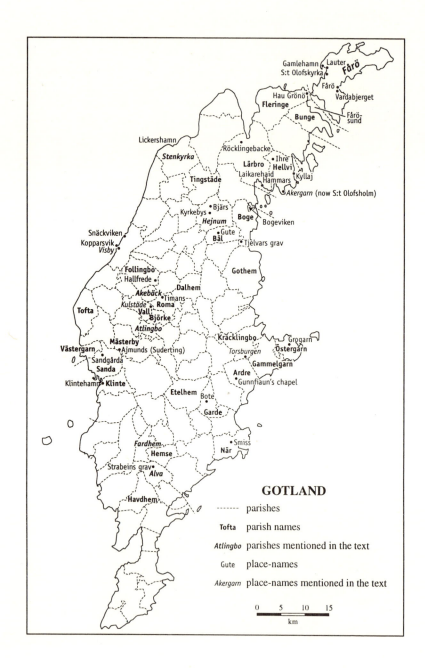

Gamlehamn — Lauter
S:t Olofskyrka — Fårö

Fårö
Vardabjerget

Hau Grönö
Fleringe
Bunge
Fårö-
sund

Lickershamn

Röcklingebacke

Stenkyrka

Lärbro — Ihre
Hellvi
Laikarehaid
Hammars — Kyllaj

Tingstäde

Akergarn (now S:t Olofsholm)

Kyrkebys — Bjärs
Hejnum — Boge — Bogeviken
Snäckviken — Gute
Kopparsvik — Bäl — Tjelvars grav
Visby

Follingbö — Gothem
Hallfrede
Dalhem
Akebäck — Timans
Kulstäde — Roma
Tofta — Vall
Björke
Atlingbo
Kräcklingbo — Grogarn
Mästerby — Östergarn
Västergarn — Ajmunds (Suderting)
Torsburgen — Gammelgarn
Sandgårda
Sanda — Ardre
Klintehamn — Klinte — Gunnfiaun's chapel
Etelhem — Bote
Garde

Fardhem — Smiss
Hemse — När
Strabeins grav
Alva

Havdhem

## GOTLAND

------- parishes

Tofta — parish names

Atlingbo — parishes mentioned in the text

Gute — place-names

Akergarn — place-names mentioned in the text

0    5    10    15
km

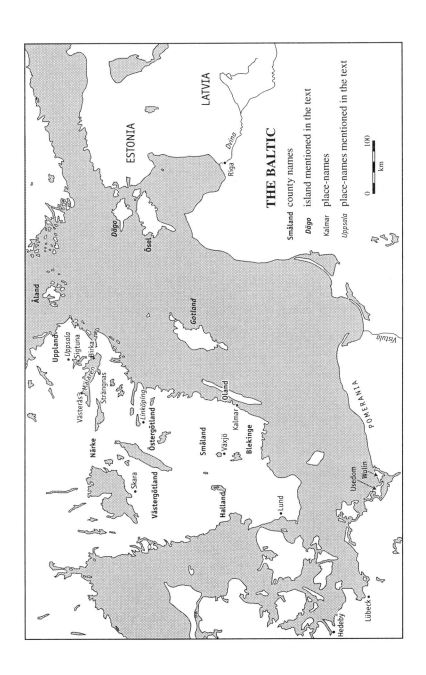

LATVIA

ESTONIA

*Dvina*

Riga

THE BALTIC

Småland  county names

*Dâgo*  island mentioned in the text

Kalmar  place-names

*Uppsala*  place-names mentioned in the text

0        100
         km

*Dâgo*

Ösel

Åland

*Gotland*

Uppland

*Uppsala*
Sigtuna
Birka
Mälaren
Strängnäs
Västerås

Närke

Östergötland

Skara

Västergötland

Linköping

Småland

*Öland*

Kalmar

Växjö

Blekinge

Halland

Lund

POMERANIA

*Vistula*

Usedom

Wolin

Lübeck

Hedeby

Härje-
dalen

Lake
Ladoga

*Volkhov*

Lake
Ilmen

Novgorod(*Holmgård*)

*Lovat*

*Volga*

*Dvina*

THE BALTIC

*Ryzaland*
Kiev

*Vistula*

*Dnieper*

MORAVIA

*Danube*

*Dniester*

Vienna

*Danube*

BLACK SEA

**SOUTHERN SCANDINAVIA AND
SOUTH-EASTERN EUROPE**

Place-names mentioned in the text are italicised

0        200
km